MANAGEMENT SOLUTIONS

Tough talking

How to handle awkward situations

■ ■ ■

DAVID MARTIN

the Institute
of Management

FOUNDATION

PITMAN
PUBLISHING

PITMAN PUBLISHING
128 Long Acre, London WC2E 9AN

A Division of Pearson Professional Limited

First published in this edition 1996

© David Martin 1994

British Library Cataloguing in Publication Data
A CIP catalogue record for this book can be obtained
from the British Library.

ISBN 0 273 62192 0

10 9 8 7 6 5 4 3 2 1

Typeset by Northern Phototypesetting Co Ltd, Bolton
Transferred to digital print on demand, 2002
Printed and bound by Antony Rowe Ltd, Eastbourne

*The Publishers' policy is to use paper manufactured
from sustainable forests.*

Tough talking

The Institute of Management (IM) is at the forefront of management development and best management practice. The Institute embraces all levels of management from students to chief executives. It provides a unique portfolio of services for all managers, enabling them to develop skills and achieve management excellence.

If you would like to hear more about the benefits of membership, please write to Department P, Institute of Management, Cottingham Road, Corby NN17 1TT.

This series is commissioned by the Institute of Management Foundation.

About the author

DAVID MARTIN FCIS, FIPD, is a well known author, with books including *Manipulating Meetings, Dealing With Demanding Customers* and *How To Be A Great Communicator*. He runs his own consultancy business, Buddenbrook, carrying out various projects including corporate communications, personnel documentation and management. A regular seminar speaker, he is a consultant editor of *Business Administration* and author/editor of *Employment Letters & Procedures* and *Employment Policies & Handbooks*.

Contents

■ ■ ■

ix

Introduction

■ ■ ■

When I was originally asked to write a title for this Institute of Management series the concept was for a book on 'internal communication'. After writing and re-writing the first few chapters four times and developing the book's theme, what emerged were comments aimed at helping readers achieve their aims in a variety of situations. Basically the book is all about identifying the tactics and strategies that will help us achieve our desired results at any time, but particularly when we are involved in a negotiation and confrontation.

In researching data and examples for the title it swiftly became obvious that very often people fail in their endeavours in such circumstances simply because they fail to determine and/or forget their desired result. Having failed to stick to their aims, it should come as no surprise if the discussion does not then go their way. There are two sides to every argument and if we allow ourselves to be carried away by the force of our views to the exclusion of all others then we are unlikely to achieve anything – other than a row. The secret of good negotiation (particularly if there is to be a repeat encounter) is to leave both sides feeling they have achieved something.

Since much of the success of *Tough Talking* has been its user-friendly presentation and in particular the use of real life case studies to demonstrate practical applications of theory, perhaps it is appropriate to use a case study to demonstrate the point just made.

The consumers had experienced what they thought was a very rough deal. Their reaction was to dash off a very sarcastic and irate letter to the supplier. The reaction from the supplier was similarly intemperate and a furious row ensued with correspondence lasting over a year. Who won?

Basically no-one, since the longer the dispute lasted the more entrenched became the respective attitudes of both parties. Facts became submerged under a torrent of rhetoric, anger and wounding phrases. Solutions seemed sublimated to the scoring of debating points and the protection of 'face'.

An alternative scenario:

The consumer determines their desired result. Surely that was to receive compensation for a rough deal?

Now how are we likely to achieve this? By making the other party angry and defensive? Hardly likely. By exaggerating the matter and incorporating unfair comments? Certainly not – all that does is to allow the other side to pick holes in the irrelevancies and avoid answering the main points.

Are we not more likely to achieve what we want by putting forward a case in a reasonable and logical format. If factual information is supplied in a low key manner, it becomes very difficult to challenge contentions.

Obviously in some instances, no matter how strong and reasonable is the case, you will not be assured of attaining the desited result, but you can improve your chances of success.

The theme is very simply: if you want to get someone to do as you wish, reasoned argument is likely to be more effectived than threats. Temper tends to generate an intemperate response and if that is the sort of response you have generated then you start with a considerable disadvantage – unless of course simply venting your spleen was your desired result! If we want to win in these instances we need to try and see things from the other person's point of view – how would we react to an intemperate accusation?

The other odd thing that the research indicated was that very often people make the same mistakes time and time again.

One would have thought that each failure would be a valuable learning exercise and applying the lessons would better equip them next time around. This is not always so. Obviously if we are on the receiving end of a blast from such a person, the dice are loaded in our favour. If we remain calm, we are in control. We can pick holes in the irrelevant and the intemperate and fail to answer the main thrust. We can win not by virtue but simply because the other side loses.

Basically having set out to write a book on communication, that is what was accomplished, since the essence of achieving our desired result is of course achieving good communication between the parties. The problem as highlighted in *Tough Talking* (and in its best-selling sequels *Manipulating Meetings*, *Dealing with Demanding Customers* and *How to be a Great Communicator*) is that very often we fail to understand what is meant by the word 'communication' – but to find out what I mean you'll have to read the book!

David M Martin, Buddenbrook
November 1995

1
■ ■ ■

Making tough talking easy

Key learning points

1 With a little forethought and planning (policies, rules and procedures) problem encounters can be, and are, best avoided.

2 Active and genuine two-way communication using simple, straightforward messages, will not only make people more receptive to what you have to say and understand it, but will also help you avoid problems arising in the first place, or if they do, mean that you can resolve them quickly.

3 Problems that do arise need to be solved swiftly if they are not to cause damage.

4 Solving problem encounters may depend as much on flexibility and an innovative approach as on a genuine desire for resolution.

In ancient times the Romans and Greeks used slaves, chained to their oars, to power their war galleys and triremes. The commanders of such galleys would galvanise the slaves to generate sufficient speed to ram and sink boats of the opposing navy by constantly using the whip. The commitment of those unfortunate slaves was total, as the alternative to high performance levels was a whipping or death, via the original early bath overboard. The slaves' comprehension of the message from their masters was, no doubt, total and unimpaired; it was simple, uncomplicated and unambiguous. In all communications, including dealing with problem encounters in the various instances covered later, these need to be our watchwords (having first ensured we are in full command of the facts):

- keep it simple
- make it clear
- avoid ambiguity

in order to generate comprehension, cohesion and commitment.

Keep it simple
■ ■ ■

The small plaques inserted into the grass lawns of parks and similar areas saying 'Please keep off the grass' may be irritating to visitors lured by the beautifully tended turf, but they convey their message with unchallengeable simplicity. Sadly this is not always the case.

Case study 1.1
NOT SO SIMPLE

At an Essex sports centre, visitors are greeted with a notice that reads, 'Please be advised that you are now entering an area where smoking is *not permitted, other than in the confines of the bar'*. Being charitable, it could be assumed that the printer was paid by the word and that business was a bit slack as *'No smoking - except in the bar'* is a far simpler, more easily understood message. By the same token, presumably *'Please keep off the grass'* would have appeared as *'Please be advised that this tended greensward is not to be used underfoot by visitors to this public recreational area'* at this particular sports centre!

> **Key technique**
> If the message is kept simple and brief, it will be understood easily and misunderstanding should be minimised.

Such notices are the simplest form of communication. The essence of the poster format is that its message is clear and simple, so if these rules are not followed, its aim will not be achieved. Similarly, in dealing with the communication errors that tend to be the root cause of many problem encounters, it is essential that such communication is kept simple, uncluttered and clear. Although this is essential and should be obvious, all too often, this aim is foiled by unclear and complicated messages that confuse rather than enlighten and aggravate rather than solve any problems.

3

Make it clear
■ ■ ■

The lack of message simplicity tends to be exacerbated by the seemingly ever-increasing number of layers between decision makers and those at the sharp end (though several UK companies have removed whole layers of management, which is a welcome move in this regard. Messages, as exemplified in the game of Chinese Whispers, tend to become confused the more times they are passed on - the classic example being the the General's message 'Send reinforcements we're going to advance' that was transformed by the time it reached the Headquarter's signal officer to 'Send three and fourpence we're going to a dance'. Equally, if only 10 per cent of a message is lost each time it is relayed by one person to another, over 50 per cent of its original import may be lost between the executive board's original request and its receipt by an employee on the shop floor if it has had to pass through the five layers of an average company.

Avoid ambiguity
■ ■ ■

In Case Study 8.4, part of the problem stemmed from the interpretation of several of the Journal's terms of business. One term referred to 'cancellation not more than six weeks before publication date'. The customer took this to mean the date when the Journal went on sale to the public, whereas the advertising agent for the Journal's owners understood it to mean the date that she had to pass copy to the typesetter. Ignoring the particular problems of this encounter, defining the ambiguous meaning of the term would have avoided the occurrence of these conflicting interpretations.

Ambiguity can lead to progress being sidetracked while the position is clarified and protects those who wish to avoid their responsibilities (they can use the ambiguity to defend their actions or inactions with such phrases as 'I didn't realise that was what it meant'). It also encourages action to be delayed.

Gaining ongoing commitment
■ ■ ■

In seeking to sell its products (in order to make a profit or achieve its aims) companies need to interface with people at all times, whether they be employees, customers, suppliers, owners, the media or the public. All these people need to be dealt with positively, virtually regardless of circumstances, in order to gain commitment to the aims of the organisation or to avoid damaging or interrupting the continued movement towards these aims. Often such dealings will take place during problem encounters and it is essential that they are conducted with care. This is is vital in a company's dealings with its employees' which will probably account for well over half such encounters. 'Our employees are our greatest asset' is often claimed by companies but little more than lipservice may be paid to the meaning and implications of the phrase. Employees are the greatest asset of any company, as without their effort and work nothing can be achieved. Good-quality, efficient, committed employees can improve the perception and performance of the organisation in all instances and, conversely, poor-quality and poorly motivated employees will damage it. Commitment to the organisation needs to be generated so that employees understand:

- what their employer is trying to do
- how their efforts and jobs contribute to the business.
- how and why decisions need to be made and why they are made in this way.

5

To generate commitment, the aims and aspirations of employees need to be moulded, even though they are likely to come from widely different backgrounds, with a range of skills and an array of perceptions and preferences, so that these meet the employers' requirements. This immediately poses two challenges. Firstly, the operating criteria of the company must be codified and promulgated. Secondly, the ways in which the employees' interests can be guided to satisfy those aims must be laid down. Essentially, this requires that employees be managed, motivated or led in certain, previously agreed, directions, by those who are responsible, for moving the company forward.

'He who communicates, leads'
■ ■ ■

Effective communication is not a science to be learned, but an art to be practised. The need to communicate is ingrained in human beings - from a baby's cry that tells its mother 'feed me' to the motives behind the buying of one car rather than another. At all stages of life and existence, we communicate in order to achieve our aims and needs. The human race is one of the most gregarious of earth's creatures, and, being, by nature, communicative has developed very sophisticated methods to achieve this end. Unfortunately, sometimes we can be so dazzled by the brilliance of the available technology that we can overlook the fact that the simplest, often the most effective, means of communication, is that of talking face to face with the other party and, more importantly, listening to each others' responses. Indeed, very often, the more sophisticated the means of communication, the less effective it may be in terms of getting the essential message across and obtaining a response. Effective communication is the key to progress and the key to the solution of *all* problem encounters - internal or external. Conversely, ineffective communication is a total bar to such progress.

Information and communication
■ ■ ■

The Confederation of British Industry (CBI) stated in the late 1980s that '... effective communication with employees will be one of the major issues facing management over the next decade'. The CBI did not mean here simply the dissemination of information, but true, two-way communication. If A tells B that the production target for this week is 1000 widgets, that is purely information and, although it is essential, in no way does it involve B or gain any commitment from him. However, if A sits down with B, asks what manpower is available, whether there are adequate supplies of raw material and power, whether there are any foreseeable problems with attaining the week's production target and actively listens (not passively 'hears' - see later) to the answers (which may include problems needing solutions), then A and B *jointly* decide a course of action, *that* is *communication*. Communication is a meeting of minds to attain consensus. It is a two-way dialogue involving understanding of the other party's viewpoint, concerns and priorities, that which can only be achieved when an *exchange* of information and feedback takes place (see Figure 1.1). It is a dynamic (not passive), process and helps avoid problem encounters occurring.

Sender	I	F	C
Data encoded	N	E	O
Transmitted	F	E	M
Received	O	D	M
Decoded	R	B	U
	M	A	N
	A	C	I
	T	K	C
Recipient	I		A
Received	O		T
Decoded	N		I
Comprehension			O
Clarification			N

Figure 1.1 Information does not equal communication
(from the author's 'How to control your costs and increase your profits')

Policies
■ ■ ■

Although most problem encounters can be successfully resolved, each will consume resources and the aim should be to avoid such loss of resources by minimising the incidence of the encounters. To this end, it is wise to develop, communicate and update policies for the various areas of the business where encounters occur. Such policies, with ancillary checklists and procedures, can convey how the company will inform/communicate in a number of areas, both to and with:

- employees
- customers
- shareholders/owners

7

- suppliers
- media, public and community.

The adoption of these policies (see Chapter 15), which will reflect the aims of the company can operate as an ongoing criteria against which performance can be measured, provides a framework for open and frank communication but also guidance for those needing to deal with problem encounters. Involvement in communication should be a constant requirement of all activity, for it is a really effective way in which to guide people's work. By communicating effectively, it is possible to:

- explain requirements
- agree action
- discuss performance
- guide progress and attainment
- consider problems, suggestions, complaints and so on
- agree solutions
- review results and implement new actions.

Formulating the policy is, of course, only the start of the process, since the keys to its success are its implementation and how well people follow it. There are several factors at work here and these are outlined below.

Relaying the policy

It is not just how *management* generates communication and deals with problems raised by its employees, suppliers, customers and so on, but how it involves the chain of command in the process. Thus the board needs to ensure that all those involved (those who will actually be working through problem encounters on its behalf) know about the commitment and know how they are expected to react in various circumstances (for example, avoiding discrimination, giving respect, reflecting the company's ethos and so on).

Reliability

Unless the process is reliable and ongoing, it will not be credible. It is better to have a little communication regularly than a great deal spasmodically as it then it becomes a habit and both parties come to rely on it. 'Praise me, scold me, but never ignore me' is a phrase that few may have heard, but many would subscribe to the sentiment, if only subconsciously. People want to be noticed, to be appreciated, to be treated as mature individuals - and to have their problems and complaints treated seriously and constructively. Failure to adopt such an approach alienates people and destroys progress.

Honesty

Similarly, unless the process is treated with complete trust and honesty by the company and those acting on its behalf, it can have no credibility. If the company states that it wishes to deal openly and positively with problems in order to ensure their solution (that is it adopts that ethos), then that commitment *must* be adhered to at all times, in all situations.

Suitability

The message must be designed to suit the requirements of its target audience. Before launching a new product, a producer will normally carry out market research. Using the results of such surveys, the producer will often adjust the product until it matches the target market's preferences. In communicating, a company may have a captive 'market' - employees, suppliers or customers - but this does not mean that they can be regarded as a homogeneous mass, generating one of a set number of responses. Individuals have a range of skills and expertise, preferences and prejudices, ignorance and experience. For example, research has indicated that 1 in 7 of the UK's adult population have difficulty reading, while numeracy skills are even poorer. It must therefore be accepted that the ability of the average target audience to receive and appreciate some information that is being given to them can be impaired, at least in part, no matter how otherwise effective the material may be.

Simplicity

The ability to respond in any discussion, but especially when there is a problem to be solved, depends very much on how well messages are accepted and understood. The material must be presented in such a way that the audience will be able to easily accept and understand it (without going so far along this path that it becomes patronising). 'Never underestimate intelligence and never overestimate knowledge' is a sound maxim, as most people are quite capable of understanding the most complicated information, provided that it is presented in a format they can relate to and understand. All communication should spurn jargon and instead use plain, straightforward language. Written information should be presented in a way that will attract the average reader and retain attention thereafter. If the aim is to make the reader receptive to the message, then the message itself must be constructed in a way that ensures the recipient can accept and understand it. If the message is presented in an unnecessarily complicated way, it will simply serve to irritate and become a barrier against the creation of rapport.

Perceptiveness

'The reason', goes the old saying, 'that we have one mouth and two ears,' is so we can listen twice as much as we talk'. Sadly the opposite tends to be more often the case. Further, the passive state of merely *hearing* the words spoken is all too often mistaken for active listening. Managers who proudly claim that they talk to their employees regularly may be more to be admired than those who do not, but talking to (or, more accurately, *at*) someone is *not* communicating with them. To foster *true* communication, thus resolving difficulties and achieving progress, *all* parties must be prepared to *listen*, which means not only taking in the words, but also receiving the underlying message of the other party - this becomes clear when there is an *ongoing dialogue*. It is easy to conceal your true feelings about something when a conversation consists of only two or three sentences, but far more difficult when the conversation is prolonged. Yet, it is this perception of the other's true point of view that is the key to the success of the resolution of problem encounters. Too often it is overlooked or ignored and so the desired result is unlikely to be achieved. Perception of the other party's viewpoint or motivation is often instinctive and some may have more of a talent for it than others. Nevertheless active listening to and questioning of the other party and analysing and checking their possible motivation can substitute for an instinctive 'feel' for their views.

11

LEEDS METROPOLITAN UNIVERSITY LIBRARY

Multiple response

This need for perception should not be underestimated. After all an individual responds to a particular situation in a number of ways but the other party in each situation will be aware of only one.

Case study 1.2
MULTIPLE RESPONSES

The boss was doing his rounds and met Joe, a Manager in the Production Planning Department. As he walked by, he called 'Hi Joe, everything OK?'

To a considerable extent Joe's response to this question is conditioned by the circumstances. Obviously in a hurry, his boss has given him the impression that he does not wish to dally to discuss problems. Joe felt that his boss expected to hear a positive response. Accordingly, Joe answered 'Yes sir, everything's fine'.

Five minutes later, Joe's response to the same question from another enquirer was different. When the Sales Manager asked if everything was OK, Joe replied 'No it's not, that's the fifth time this week you've let me down - I need those orders *now*'.

Joe later met one of his supervisors who asked him the same question 'No, this is a right mess again - we're not going to get those orders from those lazy so-and-sos in Sales until tomorrow, so start work on XYZ instead'.

On returning home, his answer when his wife asked if everything was OK, was 'If I have another day like today, I'm jacking it in'.

That is four different responses, to which we can add a fifth - in his own mind, Joe might have still another view - and who knows what that might be!

The boss, assured by Joe that everything was fine, was somewhat disconcerted to find Joe's resignation letter the following week. Joe did have 'another day like today' and found it too much.

Committing time to communication

Joe's boss was surprised, but Joe's decision is, at least in part, his own responsibility as he was hearing but not listening to Joe. 'Walking the job' is an essential part of the active communication process, but it requires far more than a swift trot round the works. Active listening (not passive hearing) is an essential part of the process and this cannot be achieved in the three-second - 'everything OK, Joe?','Yes sir' exchange. This said, if even this brief exchange is repeated often enough (so that the two come to understand each other better) tone alone may be sufficient to give the enquirer more insight into the true feelings of the employee. Normally, however, the longer the conversation and the more incisive the questions, the more likely is the astute listener to discern the true views of the other party.

In any problem encounter, unless true views are discovered, listened to, and reconciled, there is little likelihood that a lasting solution will be found. Active listening requires an investment in time or matters will never be improved as any decisions made will be based on an imperfect assessment and knowledge of the views and problems - there will be a lack of perception of the other party's viewpoint and aims. To gain this added dimension may be very time-consuming, but the benefits, in terms of greater awareness of aims and priorities, productivity and commitment, solution of problems and so on, can be considerable.

Feedback

In every conversation, we provide and accept feedback, virtually subconsciously, and, as a result the conversation may take a different course to that which was anticipated. Assessing the reactions of the other party and changing previously conceived ideas on how to conduct the session to suit the circumstances will not only achieve communication, understanding and rapport, but will also enable positive progress to be achieved. This should hold good whether the encounter concerns employee discipline, a sales promotion discussion, a customer complaint or is simply an updating chat. Failure to approach the session with an open mind and sticking rigidly to the preconceived plan will almost certainly result in the failure of the conversation and thus the absence of progress tc a 'solution' to the problem. The person who insists on maintaining opinions, pre- or misconceptions, or their version of the facts, some or all of which are shown to be incorrect during the discussion, will fail to achieve any consensus, and is likely to worsen the situation. Feedback and dealing with it - in other words flexibility of approach - is the key to dealing with problem encounters, particularly when there are wide differences of opinion.

13

Attempting the impossible

Flexibility of approach and response can help achieve a consensus, but sometimes all steps to this are hampered despite your best efforts. The person responsible may have prepared adequately, have been perceptive about the other party's needs, views and so on, be fully informed about the facts, argue logically and sensibly and still fail to achieve a consensus. Recent research in the United States disclosed that 94 per cent of the average population 'want to get along' and will normally respond positively to logical explanations and arguments. However, that leaves 6 per cent who will provide real problems and it must be realised that, despite all explanations, genuine investment of time and so on, it may prove impossible to achieve consensus with them. These are the real problem people who may defeat the most ardent communicator. With such awkward customers the only solution may be to agree to differ and to move on. However, even these people can sometimes be disarmed by a well-constructed and tactfully communicated case, so it is worth at least trying.

14

2

■ ■ ■

Key techniques for every encounter

Key learning points

1 Principles of negotiation need to be adopted, (finding facts, anticipating reactions and the other party's aims, progressing the encounter logically, listening and being perceptive and so on) then used to solve problem encounters.

2 The effects of change must be accepted, analysed and catered for before being implemented.

3 The response of the other party and that party's desired result needs to be anticipated in order to progress the encounter to an acceptable solution.

4 Letting the other party feel that they have affected the outcome of the negotiation can facilitate accomplishment of the aim.

Those required to deal with problem encounters will be required to negotiate and so will be referred to as 'negotiators' hereafter. Negotiation should depend on a wish to bring about a desired result, a degree of change or a movement forward. Often this will entail a degree of compromise, which should not imply weakness, merely a recognition that there will be, in most cases, a requirement for an ongoing relationship, which an unresolved dispute will inevitably threaten.

Managing change
■ ■ ■

16

In dealing with problem encounters, the negotiator's prime responsibility is to manage or bring about change from the status quo, because the reason for the encounter is that there is a degree of disharmony. Human beings are essentially creatures of habit, and so change can be extraordinarily difficult to bring about. There is an instinctive resistance to change that can be exacerbated by pride. Being prepared to acknowledge that you are wrong is exceedingly difficult for many people and impossible for some. This reminds me of the heartfelt plea of Oliver Cromwell when addressing the General Assembly of the Church of Scotland, 'I beseech you, in the bowels of Christ, think it possible you might be mistaken', which might be a suitable slogan for all negotiators.

Dealing with closed minds calls for all the negotiator's powers of persuasion, even though it seems as if the situation is impossible. After all, there can only be one reason for attempting to deal with a problem encounter - to bring about an end aim. Before beginning the encounter, therefore, the negotiator needs to establish what this end or desired result is. Achieving the desired result may seem a simple task but, surprisingly, even this may be confusing and, if it is, concluding things successfully will be difficult. For example, very often the disciplinary procedure in industrial relations is used (stick-like) as a means of applying sanctions, of discovering evidence and as a precursor to dismissal. This essentially negative use may be necessary in some cases, and will certainly enable facts about the transgression to be recorded in case of any tribunal action, but does it achieve the desired result? With the tiny minority of real problem employees, perhaps dismissal is the only and therefore the desired effect so swift progress to this state may be required. With most employees, however, the positive approach and use of the procedure is far more beneficial. In this case, the procedure can be used (carrot-like) to show the employee the 'way we do things around here' and, therefore, the way the employer would prefer the employee to act (or refrain from acting). Thus the employee is nudged into line and the investment in them (which can be considerable and yet is often underestimated) is not lost.

17

Anticipating responses
■ ■ ■

Negotiators are faced with the problem of calculating and anticipating another person's or group's response. In this the onus lies with negotiators as their initial actions and attitudes are key to such responses. Negotiators must realise that their own attitudes are key to the development of the encounter. Although their tone may become conditioned by the responses, initially they must set the tone for the encounter. If their attitude is negative and critical, then, almost inevitably, the instinctive response of the other party will be defensive and resentful, with no rapport being created - the negative *approach* creating a *negative* response. Conversely, if the interview starts on a positive note - seeking rapport and understanding of the other party's views and problems, a positive response is far more likely and the attainment of the desired result is more feasible.

If we live with criticism, we learn to condemn
If we live with hostility, we learn to fight
If we live with fear, we learn to be apprehensive

but

If we live with encouragement, we learn to be confident
If we live with praise, we learn to be appreciative
If we live with acceptance, we learn to respond. (Anon.)

Lee Iacocca, the man who saved the Chrysler Corporation from liquidation, once said 'It is important to talk to people in their own language. If you do it well, they'll say "God, he said exactly what I was thinking". The reason they're following you is that you are following them - that's what Bob Hope is doing when he sends an advance man to scout out his audience so he can make jokes that are special to them and their situation'. The negotiator needs the equivalent of Bob Hope's scout to assemble facts, to consider alternatives, to anticipate responses and to form these into a preferred route towards the desired result.

18

The desired result
■ ■ ■

In every problem encounter, the negotiator needs to take and to retain the initiative to ensure that there is continual movement towards a result. This is so even if the other party has requested the meeting. Of course it may be that there is more than one way to reach the desired result and so it is essential that the negotiator remains flexible about the means used to achieve the aim. The following are some examples of such situations.

■ If there is a problem with a disruptive employee, the desired result is ending the disruption so that everyone can resume normal working. That result can be achieved either by converting the disruptive employee to the required way of working or by dismissing this person.

■ If the problem concerns a dispute over the terms of trade with a supplier, the desired result is the resumption of supplies on acceptable terms, quality and times. This can be achieved by sourcing supplies elsewhere (with all the potential negative effects) or reaching a mutually acceptable compromise or agreement with the existing supplier.

■ If a customer has a serious complaint, the desired result should be rectifying any loss to the customer and protecting the good name of the company. It can take years to *build* a reputation and a matter of minutes to *lose* it.

Negotiation is not weakness, it is a pragmatic approach towards reconciling different views, both of which may be valid, and, for this reason, even though the desired result must be kept uppermost in the negotiator's mind, it may be necessary to dilute one or both parties' expectations, that is to move towards a compromise.

19

Preparing the ground

The desired result can only be achieved if the interview proceeds roughly along the route (there may be several options) determined in advance by the negotiator. In trying to ensure that the conversation keeps to such routes, it is essential that the negotiator plans accordingly, researches data and information, assesses the opposing viewpoints and, above all, remains flexible in approach at all times. The steps outlined in the following check-list are a basic guide.

Before discussion

1 Discover the nature of the subject that needs to be clarified.

2 Explore *all* aspects of the matter to separate the facts from the opinions.

3 List the facts you find separately from 'understandings', which may need to be confirmed by the other party before they can be accepted.

4 Get to know your adversary and try to work out what *their* desired result is and the way in which they think.

5 Determine the desired results of the two parties do not coincide, is there a mutually acceptable alternative?

If a problem is raised without warning

1 Find out the exact nature of the complaint.

2 Explain that time is needed to investigate it properly and give it due consideration.

3 Set a date/time to discuss it.

4 Ensure that the discussion is held at that date/time or before or agree a postponement at or before the time set, giving reasons for the delay.

During the discussion

1 Ensure that someone is available to take notes.

2 Introduce those present.

3 Indicate that you wish to arrive at a mutually acceptable solution.

4 Invite the complainant to put their case or, (if more appropriate) to state the facts as they see them and ask for their correctness to be confirmed.

5 Allow complete freedom of expression and time.

6 Make notes about any unclear points or queries and ask for them to be clarified at the end of the other party's presentation. Do not interrupt the flow.

7 Consider the merits of the case impartially to achieve objectivity.

8 Avoid any preconceptions based on opinions - base views only on agreed facts.

9 If consensus is not arrived at, suggest adjourning the discussion until an agreed time.

Summation and compensation

1 Consider the complainant's 'losses' - in other words, look at the case from the other party's viewpoint.

2 Consider positive alternative solutions that might ease, solve or answer the problem.

3 Make offers and obtain feedback.

4 Consider altering rules, regulations, procedures or whatever that have been found wanting by the case.

21

The critical requirement in the negotiation process is a realisation of the other party's viewpoint and assessment of their 'loss' or reaction. As previously mentioned, keeping an open mind on this subject is essential. In order for your assessment to be accurate, a depth of understanding and perception are required that experience tells us only a minority possess.

Case study 2.1
UNRESTFUL BREAK

The couple viewed their ten-day holiday as a disaster - the original hotel had been overbooked and they had been forced to live out of suitcases in a bed and breakfast studio for four days before the tour operator found them better hotel accommodation than that covered by their original reservation.

When dealing with their claim for compensation, the tour company tried to convince the couple that, because the replacement hotel had been of far better standard than the original (which was not disputed), they had already been 'compensated' for the disaster of the initial four days.

This case study evidences a failing that is particularly prevalent in, but not confined to, the travel industry. Some operators are so inept that they seem to be incapable of recognising (or unwilling to recognise) that when a holiday goes wrong, repayment of any costs involved are inadequate, virtually irrespective of their size. No single word accurately describes this failing but we could call it 'underticipation', as it is a cross between (or composite of) underestimating the very real annoyance and failing to anticipate the need for adequate compensation that encompasses more than monetary loss.

22

The all-too-prevalent attitude equates a ruined holiday to a faulty *appliance*. However, although the appliance can be replaced, normally without great loss, a holiday occupies *time*, which cannot be replaced. The failure to see such a complaint from the other party's viewpoint, in this case that the initial four days were 'lost' or 'below standard', and a negative defence of a difficult position, merely serves to aggravate the injustice in the minds of the complainants and increase their determination to win compensation. The defensive reaction - that accepting responsibility without question creates a precedent that could 'open the floodgates', simply makes the situation worse. This is because it is indicative that, as there may be many others able to claim, the product being supplied must be inherently defective. This may only strengthen the resolve of the complainant to achieve compensation, which is hardly a desired result. We need to guard against 'underticipation' and being defensive when complaints are made.

Other companies react much more positively. For example, much of the perception of high quality that rightly surrounds the name and trading reputation of Marks & Spencer is derived from their policy of making refunds or exchanges for unwanted and unused goods virtually without question.

Inevitably such a policy has a cost, but it also has a value which is attractive to the customer.

'I understand what you say, but you are wrong'

This does not mean that everything the other party contends should be accepted, as, inevitably, there will be occasions when the negotiator, while fully understanding the viewpoint and contentions of the other party, simply cannot accept them and must reject them. In this instance the desired results of the two parties are impossible to reconcile. This will even apply - indeed particularly apply on occasions - to customers. As Alan Sugar, founder of Amstrad Computers, commented in 1992, 'The customer is not always right and I'm not afraid to let them know it from time to time'. Inevitably this will be the position in which negotiators also find themselves from time to time. However, in rejecting claims or comments or refusing to accept contentions, the desired result must still be borne in mind. One can, after all, say 'No' in many different ways. If the desired result is that a relationship be maintained with the other party, then rejecting the other party's arguments must be done in such a way that face is saved, as is commitment to the joint aims. This may be difficult and yet it is essential, otherwise the time invested in the whole negotiation process will have been wasted.

23

Ensuring a positive response even though the decision is adverse, can be a difficult manoeuvre, requiring flexibility or an innovative response. This, though, is the art of negotiation - to leave both parties feeling that they have got something out of the process. This philosophy is not adopted by all companies, as some believe that negotiators should always 'go for the jugular' and extract as much as possible from each encounter. While this attitude works in the short term, it ignores the fact that the terms of negotiation tend to move in cycles. That is, the next time around, the advantage may not be with you but with the other party and the tables may be turned with a vengeance.

Running the encounter

Having accepted that confrontational encounters are, as far as possible, best avoided, negotiators will normally endeavour to adopt a positive approach by setting up the meeting in surroundings and with 'trappings' that suggest reasonableness of approach and conciliation, such as those given below.

1 A quiet room or place where the meeting will not be interrupted. If the meeting can be and is interrupted by the telephone, callers, secretary with correspondence for signature and so on, this sends strong signals to the other party that the matter being discussed is not as important as the interruption. Denigrating the importance of one party and thus, by definition, enhancing the perceived importance of the other, is hardly conducive to generating rapport.

2 Serving refreshments. This can have the effect of calming nerves or soothing annoyed or aggravated tempers. It also takes time and this can be used by both parties to assemble thoughts and consider tactics.

3 Allowing sufficient time to consider the matter fully. Indicating that there is little time available is another indication to the other party that the matter is not as important as something else.

4 Taking notes of what transpires. This can enhance the other party's perception of the value you place on the discussion of the problem.

5 Agreeing a written resumé of the conclusion of the discussions.

As indicated in the check-list a little earlier in this chapter, it may be that the initial problem encounter cannot reach a conclusion and needs to be adjourned for further consideration by either one or other party, separately or jointly. In this event, similar guidelines will need to be adopted on the resumption of the discussion.

Of course not all encounters can be engineered into the ideal progression format given above. Some will occur in open meetings, with onlookers, without notice and so on, but, in each case, it will be necessary to try to calm things down, allow thinking time, defuse explosive situations. Thus, in an open meeting negotiators might use one or more of the defences listed below.

1 Request that the other party repeat the comment to ensure that you heard it correctly. This not only helps your own comprehension but has the effect of making the party think it through again and may result in the comment being framed more reasonably or more logically. Conversely, it may, of course, simply antagonise an already annoyed person. Indeed, even the fact that the negotiator speaks in controlled and quiet tones can act as a goad rather than as balm. The other party must not feel that they are being patronised.

2 Ask that the questioner does not follow their line of questioning immediately, but instead chat about it at the end of the meeting in private. Obviously this may not work as the questioner may well have raised the matter in the meeting in order to gain the tacit support of the others present or to embarrass the negotiator.

3 Ask the others present if they share the attitude of the questioner. If so, then the matter needs to be dealt with, although even then the precepts set out in the verse under 'Anticipating responses' earlier in this chapter will need to be followed. If there is no support, then it should be requested that the matter be dealt with at the end of the session or meeting.

4 If the matter has direct bearing on the subject of the meeting, almost certainly it will need to be dealt with, but again negotiators may be wise to defer consideration until the end of the session in order to ensure that other subjects are actually dealt with.

5 If the matter is deferred to the end of the session, then

25

negotiators should ensure that it is dealt with then or a reason be given for deferring it.

Hard talking

■ ■ ■

While experience suggests that negotiations prefaced by a discovery of the facts, circumscribed by assessment of the other party's character and requirements and operated via a tactful and positive meeting will more often than not allow the negotiator to 'win' the confrontation, that is to achieve the desired result, there is no doubt that in some instances such an approach is inappropriate and will be ineffective. In these circumstances, it will be necessary to adopt a far more aggressive approach - even to the point of allowing the other party to see an apparent loss of control or temper.

26

Not only will a loss of temper convey to the other party your depth of feeling on the matter, but it can also signal to that party that, as feelings run high, an alternative strategy, or even a need to back off altogether, may need to be contemplated.

Case study 2.2
THE EFFECTIVE REACTION

David Jacobs, the softly spoken, urbane former chairman of the programme 'Any questions' was known to deal tactfully with the most forceful questions and comments made by the audience during its many years. In one edition, however, a member of the audience made what he considered to be a rude and unfounded attack on members of the panel. Rather than asking one of the panel to reply, David Jacobs rounded on the questioner, pointed out very forcefully that his comments were rude, unconstructive and unacceptable and that he had no intention of allowing the comments to be dignified with an answer.

> **Key technique**
> The use of a forceful response (genuine or false) or deliberate loss
> of temper can be a valuable negotiating ploy.

Irritation as a weapon

Both a 'controlled loss of control' as it were and deliberate
misunderstandings can be used as devices to irritate the
other party so that it loses control and thus any initiative.
When temper rules, logic and persuasion are lost, wild statements tend to abound, and the task of negotiators in attempting to overcome the disaffection and achieve the desired
result may be made easier.

Case study 2.3
'AND?'

A disaffected former fan once confronted a famous actress and berat-
ed her for her perceived attitude to family, profession and fans. She
patiently heard him out for some time and, when the tirade slowed,
gently commented 'And?'

The fan stumbled on with a further tirade, often repeating his earlier
comments and, on running out of words, again received the gentle
'And?'

He was unable to answer - he had run out of steam and the star's
refusal to respond or in any way sink to his level and lose her temper,
removed the basis for any continuation of the encounter.

> **Key technique**
> Refusing to react to provocation may defuse even the most heated
> encounter.

This reaction can be described as forcing the other party to
'punch cotton wool', as it is difficult to maintain aggression
when there is no counter or feedback. A similar effect can be
created by the use of silence (see Chapter 14).

Uncovering the case

The tactics of losing one's temper, dismissal of arguments, punching cotton wool or playing down of the other party's case, can all be powerful weapons, not simply in ensuring control of the initiative but also, in forcing disclosure of more of the 'case' at an early stage. If, in order to try to regain the initiative, the other party has to use facts or contentions (that is, other ammunition) being held in reserve, negotiators then may be left with a clearer idea of the complete problem or of the opponent's case. Indeed such tactics can also be used to test how strongly the other party really feels about the subject. After all, if the other party wishes to raise the matter but has no real commitment to it, a hard and virtually pre-emptive response may lead to its swift withdrawal. Conversely, if the matter is the subject of very real concern, a hard response will usually tend to generate an equally hard counter. Having discovered the strength of feeling, negotiators may then be able to switch tactics. It will also do no harm for a reputation for hard talking or negotiating to be attributed - so long as fairness is also acknowledged.

28

Case study 2.4
MOVING TO THE RIGHT PRICE

A manufacturer wanted to increase the price of its products to a particular customer from £2 to £2.50 per unit. The manufacturer called to see the customer, who would have difficulty sourcing the product elsewhere, and advised the customer that, due to rising manufacturing and raw material costs, the new price would have to be £3. The customer was both indignant and annoyed and a considerable discussion ensued. As a result of the discussion, the manufacturer agreed to 'reduce' the price (which had never actually been implemented) to £2.50, the level originally intended.

> *Key technique*
> Letting one's opponent feel they have had an effect on the negotiation can assist progress to the desired result

In case study 2.4, the manufacturer made it appear that the negotiations themselves, in other words the input of the other party, had an effect on the outcome of the discussion. It is estimated that this ploy works effectively in around 70 per cent of encounters. Leaving the other party feeling that they had *no* effect is unlikely to achieve continued commitment and may even create resentment, whereas leaving *both* parties feeling that *they* have won, gives everyone the best of both worlds.

3
▪ ▪ ▪

Manipulating meetings

Key learning points

1 By really and continually communicating with employees, dovetailing the methods used to particular needs, problem encounters can be reduced to an absolute minimum.

2 In open meetings, speakers need to deal with delegates tactfully yet firmly. They also need to appreciate the implications of what is said, particularly of double-edged questions.

3 Good, thorough preparation for presentations will mean you are talking from a basis of knowledge and enable a dialogue and ambience to be created that will hopefully mean that problem encounters will be avoided.

4 Antagonising the audience is to be avoided whenever possible and an appreciation of their point of view will help ensure problem encounters are unlikely to occur.

Employee dialogue
■ ■ ■

Most problem encounters with employees can be avoided or at least become very much less difficult if a dialogue is created, that is if two-way communication takes place on a regular basis. Thus, in seeking to develop rapport to make sure that everyone is working to the same end, management should structure briefings and meetings so that information is passed to the employees, but also, very importantly, feedback is generated, questions are answered and worries eradicated. This process can happen in several ways:

- by management giving briefings or presentations
- by supervisors giving briefings having themselves been briefed by top management (the cascade system)
- by holding workplace forums.

The traditional formal meetings, memos and notices often only impart information, they do not begin any form of dialogue.

During briefings and forums, however, there is the potential for people to ask questions. These can be genuine, seeking greater knowledge or further clarification, or false, seeking merely to disrupt the meeting, embarrass the speaker or to make a 'name' for the questioner. Unfortunately a group of people tends to become an entity in its own right that is different in character to the individuals that comprise it. Individually, few of those involved in the French Revolution would have dreamed of taking a person's life, but, acting together as a mob and manipulated by a few zealots, they created the 'reign of terror' that was responsible for the execution of over 8000 people, most of whom were entirely innocent.

Although the audience at a meeting or conference is not a

mob, there is no doubt that, in such a situation, some people can become more aggressive than they would be on their own, and equally, others are intimidated by their fellows, and clam up completely. Neither of these reactions are conducive to good communication, but both must be understood and allowed for by the presenter who needs to prepare as set out in the following check-list and case studies.

1 Prepare comprehensive speaker's notes together with all visual aids. For most audiences, visual aids are essential as they can relieve the monotony of the single voice, aid or recapture attention and act as a focal point, as well as clearly illustrating points made in the presentation itself.

2 Prepare notes for the audience, couched in user-friendly terms and using humour in a controlled way. Good speaker-to-audience rapport can be generated by leaving a wide margin at the side of these on the paper and inviting the audience to make their own supplementary notes in the space. This immediately gives the audience the impression that their own ideas are as valuable as the notes provided and that they are in partnership with the speaker in writing a guide for later reference.

33

3 Ensure all attending have a clear view of the speaker and the visual aid screen and that the speaker has a clear view of them. The speaker will be able to gauge both audience attention and receptivity if the audience's faces (particularly their eyes) can be seen.

4 Ensure that there are enough seats for the known number of attendees plus a few spares. Where the audience is expected to be smaller than the capacity of the venue, the audience should be encouraged to fill up the front rows by putting 'Reserved' signs on the rear rows. Avoid leaving gaps among an audience as this destroys cohesion between them and impairs feedback.

5 Start and finish on time. Unless a formal programme has been made available (in which case it should be

strictly adhered to) set out the timetable or programme before starting the presentation.

6 Break down all potential and real barriers between speaker and audience by making a few introductory, possibly light-hearted, remarks, trying to gain immediate feedback from the audience. This will depend on numbers, as with any audience consisting of 50 people, the very size of the audience mitigates against this approach. With smaller numbers, however, actually inviting the audience to introduce themselves and say where they are from can help break the ice. It also loosens tongues ready for subsequent audience participation.

7 Say when you will take questions - either during the presentation or at the end. It is preferable with informal presentations and relatively small numbers to take questions as they arise. With larger groups, however, it may be necessary to ask that questions be left to the end.

8 No matter how informal the session is made, some of the audience will still feel inhibited about asking questions, so it may be helpful to state that during any breaks the speaker(s) will remain near the rostrum (or equivalent) and will be pleased to answer questions informally face to face. This helps people who have what they think may be questions to which the others know the answer to ask them without embarrassment. This also enables the speaker to relay the question, anonymously, to the audience on resumption if they feel it covers a matter that is of general interest.

9 All questions should be treated seriously and answered with due consideration, even when they are ridiculous. Showing up a question and, by implication, the questioner as being unworthy of an answer can mean that other questioners become inhibited and also destroys rapport with the audience.

Case study 3.1
ANTAGONISING THE AUDIENCE

A speaker lecturing on employee communications displayed the front page of the house journal and asked for comments. A member of the audience commented that there was too much copy and that the point size for the font used was too small. 'Don't get technical and worry about point sizes', snapped the speaker. There was an audible gasp from the audience as the person had merely responded to the speaker's own invitation for comments. After this, there was little feedback from the audience as its members understandably felt inhibited about doing the very thing the speaker had invited them to do - telling him what they thought was wrong with the page. It was subsequently agreed that the size of type used was indeed too small, but by then the damage was done - rapport was lost and so was audience feedback. This reticence was not restricted merely to the initial subject, but lasted throughout the entire presentation.

35

Key technique
Don't ridicule (however unintentionally) in open session; it may inhibit and alienate all present.

10 If a question is asked but it is expressed in an unclear way, the speaker should restate it and ask the person whether or not the restatement puts the question correctly. If it proves impossible to find out what the questioner wants to ask, it may be better to comment 'Let's leave that for now, and we'll have a chat during the break (or after the session)'.

11 If somebody asks a question and the speaker does not know the answer, it is best to say so and say to the questioner, having taken their name, that the speaker will try to find out the answer and let them know. Telling the truth is honest and is usually preferable to trying to flannel through an answer, which will often be obvious to the audience. Its use erases any credibility that has been established and any respect the audience has for the speaker.

12 If a question is posed that shows or inadequately con-
ceals dissatisfaction or an underlying complaint, it may
be better to provide as honest an answer as possible and
to suggest that, as there are other matters to cover, it
may be better to deal with the subject in detail during a
break or after the session. This can be dangerous,
though, as there may be widespread support for the
question. If this seems to be the case, it may be better to
ask the audience how many would like to discuss the
topic. If just a few indicate an interest the 'discuss in the
break' option may be appropriate, but if there are more
than a few, it may be essential that the matter be dealt
with as openly as possible. If it is a contentious item
with ramifications outside the scope of the content of
the presentation itself it may be preferable to note the
question and to promise that the matter will be discussed fully in a separate session.

Case study 3.2
AVOIDING OPEN CONFLICT

At a meeting of employees held to present the financial results for the
previous financial year, several employees made the criticism that the
company referred in the report to both investment in new machinery
and in people and yet when they requested permission to go on training courses this was turned down by the local management. As some
of the management being criticised were present at the meeting, the
speaker needed to avoid a damaging confrontation. Accordingly he
deliberately made (and was seen to have made) a written note of the
question, stated that he had done so and proposed reviewing the matter at the end of the session. When the session ended, he called the
two or three questioners over and spent a few minutes checking out
the facts, which he later discussed with the management involved. As
a result, within a few days, a policy statement was agreed and passed
on. Trying to reach this conclusion amicably within the meeting would
have been very difficult and even a discussion in open session could
have been damaging to the authority of the local management.

Key technique
Being straightforward and not attempting to conceal anything will elicit general support.

13 Antisocial behaviour during a presentation can be very disturbing - both to the other people present whose attention will be distracted, and to the speaker who may find that their own attention begins to wander spoiling the presentation. Such antisocial behaviour can include talking to another member of the audience, humming or tapping a pencil and so on. The difficulty is that often the person concerned may be virtually unaware of the action or of the effect it is having - particularly if the presentation scenario is new to them. If a break is near then it may be acceptable to wait until the break before quietly and tactfully explaining to the person that the action is causing a problem and everyone would be grateful if they could stop. Alternatively, it may be necessary to tactfully ask them then and there to desist.

37

Case study 3.3
AVOIDING DISTRACTIONS

At a seminar with around 40 delegates, two from the same organisation, sitting in the front row, chatted incessantly and it was obvious to the speaker that, although he was not being affected too badly, other delegates were finding it difficult to concentrate. In inviting questions, the speaker positioned himself so that the chatterers were directly between him and a questioner. He was then able to say to the questioner, 'I'm sorry I can't hear you' and then to the chatterers, 'I'm sorry, but could you break off your conversation, I can't hear the question, which may affect the point you are discussing'. This was followed up by a tactful word in the next break. On that particular occasion the 'guilty parties' were very embarrassed and apologised profusely.

Key technique
The speaker must control (and be seen to control) the meeting with firmness, tact and humour.

14 Almost inevitably there will come a time when the question no one wants asked is asked in open session. While honesty and openness are all very well, there will be times when some matters simply cannot be discussed, for the best possible reasons. Saying 'no comment' is insufficient. Although it may be a convenient way not to answer, it will usually be taken as tacit confirmation of the rumour on which the question is based. Some of the sting of such a question may be able to be limited by setting the parameters for questions before the presentation. For example, stating that it will not be possible to discuss pay, or an individual's bonus package, or rumours and so on. While this may head off some very awkward questions, it may also give the impression that the speaker is holding back from full communication. However, most employees are not fools, they are quite capable of realising that at times management cannot be as open as they would otherwise like to be.

Case study 3.4
AVOIDING THE IMPLICATIONS

At the Joint Consultative Committee (JCC) meeting in a factory, one elected representative asked whether the rumour that another factory in the Group was to close was true. The Chairman knew that although this possibility had been considered, no actual decision had been made. He reminded all members that rumours should always be ignored, that senior management constantly reviewed the performance of all activities of the Group and that the Group had a commitment to open communication within the limits of always notifying those affected first, so, if such a decision were to be made, the first people to be told would be those affected and it would be entirely incorrect to discuss such a decision, had it been made, which it had not, within a meeting of another factory's JCC.

38

Key technique
Recognition that some questions may need to be avoided should be accompanied by notifying employees that this may occur. Also, double-edged questions (such as 'have you stopped fiddling your expenses yet?') need to be carefully considered, and preparing for such questions in advance may avoid the most serious problems. Further, despite everyone's sincere commitment to open and frank communication, it may be necessary to conceal the truth and preparing for this eventuality is essential.

Unwilling delegate
■ ■ ■

Not all people come willingly to a meeting - even where the sponsoring organisations have to pay for their attendance. It is not unknown for delegates to be sent on seminars and training courses who do not have the faintest idea as to why they are there or know anything about the subject matter. In such circumstances, it is perhaps understandable that some will take out their resentment at being there by displaying unsocial behaviour at the event. While their problem is not the speaker's fault, it is the speaker's responsibility to deal with it as tactfully as possible, being obliged to do so for the sake of the other delegates. Preferably the point can be sorted out at a break, quietly and without other delegates being aware of it. However often the resentment can 'bubble over' during the presentation and it needs to be handled firmly and tactfully, even if this has to be in full view of the rest of the audience.

Case study 3.5
THE UNWILLING DELEGATE

Throughout the first phase of his presentation the speaker had been aware of the growing restlessness and irritation of one of the delegates. As this delegate's fidgeting was beginning to affect the other delegates (as well as his own presentation), he felt he could not wait until the first full break to tackle him and so the following conversation ensued:

I'm sorry, Mr Turner, you seem to have a problem?'
' *Yes I have, I don't understand a word of this and I'm not sure you do either - its gobbledegook.'*
'Well I'm sorry if I haven't made myself clear. Can you indicate which part you don't understand and perhaps I can clarify it.'
'All of it is pretty incomprehensible.'
'I see, well perhaps we should discuss this problem in private, so that we don't disturb our fellow delegates. Can I suggest we all have a three minute break while Mr Turner and I try to solve his problem.' [1]

In private.

'Look Mr Turner, it seems to me that the problem is not so much that you don't understand the content, but that you have no real wish to be here. You have been fidgeting since we started. It is very distracting to the other delegates you know. I can't understand why you came along.'
'Because I was told I had to by my boss.'
'I see, well that's a matter between your boss and yourself. What concerns me, is that I have another 23 delegates who <u>do</u> wish to be here and obviously your dissatisfaction is disrupting the session - that's not fair on them is it?' [2]
'Its not fair on me either is it?'
'Well, obviously I can't comment on your boss' decision, but your company has spent over £300 for you to come along, so they must have a reason and I think you'll agree that it's up to us to try to make the best of it, isn't it?' [3] 'I'll tell you what I'll do - you try and keep up with the subject matter, but if you find it too difficult, then make notes of the points you find particularly hard to understand and, during the breaks and after the end of the seminar, I'll try to give you some further explanations. The only alternative I can see is for you to withdraw from the session, which, as you are here now, is a waste of everyone's time and would somehow have to be explained to your company.' [4]

Key techniques
[1] Stating that the problem is his places the onus on Mr Turner to justify his actions.

[2] This reasonable and logical argument places the onus on Mr Turner once more to defend his position.

[3] Another fair statement has been made and, again, the onus is on the delegate to deny or defend it.

[4] The implied threat of a 'report to the company' may emphasise the seriousness of the situation to Mr Turner.

Negotiating in meetings

Of course similar scenarios are less likely to happen during in-company presentations, as the presence of managerial rank personnel will tend to act as a deterrent. However, occasionally the resentment will be so intense that antisocial actions can occur even within the working environment.

Case study 3.6
PUBLIC DISAGREEMENTS

It was known that the Training Manager and the Works Manager had had several fundamental disagreements and, during a management meeting, the antagonism boiled over to the point that the Training Manager inferred that the Works Manager didn't really know what he was talking about. This occurred in an open meeting with around a dozen managers and the Chairman present. Following one outburst, the Chairman tapped the desk with his ruler and the following conversation occurred. The Chairman said: *'Gentlemen, I don't think personal antagonism is getting us anywhere on this subject.'*

Training Manager: *'Well, he just doesn't listen to reason.'*
Works Manager: *'It's not a question of reason, it's a question of fact.'*
Training Manager: *'You wouldn't recognise the facts, if you tripped over them.'*
Chairman: *'Now, that's enough.'*
Training Manager: *'It's just plain daft.'*

Chairman: *'You won't always get the last word you know. Now listen to me both of you, we are here to discuss production targets for the next six months and I am determined that we do this. Either both of you undertake to contribute in a positive manner or you leave this meeting immediately and I will see you individually once we have concluded here - what is it to be?'*

Key technique

The Chairman, wishing to bring both parties to their senses, puts both on the spot with this choice. Either they must swallow their pride and stay or withdraw from a management meeting, knowing that their peers will know that they then have to reconvene in a semi- or actual disciplinary meeting with the Chairman.

42

Changes
■ ■ ■

Other less formal meetings may need to be held to discuss a range of topics, from the introduction of new systems to the phasing in of new products (possibly accompanied by the phasing out of old ones). Being creatures of habit, most human beings dislike change and new ideas as these often mean additional work, more learning and unlearning and changing tried and tested ways of doing things. Not for nothing has the 'management of change' been defined as the only true function of management because if everything remained the same, there would be little need for many managerial skills. The successful management of change is essential in all companies at all times as they do not stand still - they either grow (and survive) or contract (and, ultimately, go out of business). Often, problem encounters arise because of people's adverse reactions to change. While the approaches advocated here can help move things towards a positive solution, it should not be forgotten that, had the implications of the change been fully thought through, the problems now being encountered might have been avoided. In considering changes, therefore, those responsible should ensure that all who will be affected by them are involved in the process to avoid storing up problems for the future. In the same way that adopting policies of good communication can avoid some problems, anticipating the effects of changes can also reduce the likelihood of problem encounters.

Case study 3.7
CHANGES

A company wished to move its main production facility to a new site about two miles away. It wished to keep on as much of its present workforce as possible and set up a regular briefing programme, one such briefing going like this.

That's the latest progress report and you will see that within the next two months we will start moving employees into the new premises.'
   'How will the move occur?'
   'We intend phasing it to follow the order of the production process. This means that we will move the Raw Material and Stores departments first, then Production, Assembly, Finishing and Despatch.'
   'But you said you are going to change the rates of pay at the same time as the move.'
   'That's right - as each section moves, we will adjust their rates.'
   'So, depending where you are in the process will determine when you receive your pay increase.'
   'That's right. It seemed the fairest way - as location and hours change, so too does the pay.'
   'I would have thought it might be simpler to leave the hours and the rates as they are until everyone is installed in the new premises and then once the unit is fully commissioned we can all change together.'
   'That's an idea and we will check it out with everyone to see their reaction.'

43

Key technique

It must be recognised that management do not have the monopoly on good ideas. In this instance, the suggestion from the workers was found to have overwhelming support, was adopted and saved the company a considerable amount of work. It also created a good team feeling among the workforce. Only by talking and listening to employees can such ideas be communicated.

Just telling those affected about a decision without first asking for their input can cause a geat deal of anguish and negativity. Involving people in decision making that affects them will have the opposite effect.

44

4

■ ■ ■

Manoeuvring warring factions

Key learning points

1 Anticipating negative reactions and preparing alternative courses of action will help to avoid problem encounters occurring.

2 Giving some thought to the desired result of those who hold opposing views will help negotiators work out acceptable compromises.

3 There is little point in winning one point in the encounter if the effect of this is to lose the desired result - ultimatums and threats can rebound with disastrous results.

4 Saving the face of the other party may ultimately mean that the desired result is achieved. Forcing an opponent to lose, however, almost always results in the opposite, especially in the long term.

As well as the more formal presentations referred to in Chapter 3, management will often need to talk directly to employees with the aim of changing the status quo or one member of management will need to raise a problem with a peer or senior. To overcome the adverse reaction that often greets new concepts, it is often tempting to 'sell' the change in order to win people over to the new practice and motivate them to adopt it positively.

Management will also have to deal with a variety of attitudinal problems, that, unless anticipated and planned for, can seriously affect the required reaction. In this, management will be wise to have made notes as to potential problem makers and, more importantly, to have considered and prepared a suitable response and strategy to take account of them. Three of the types likely to be encountered are:

- the 'things aren't what they used to be' old timer
- the 'its about time you listened to me' bully boy
- the 'it'll never work like that' disbeliever.

Case study 4.1
MANOEUVRING THE OPPOSITION

A company developed a new lawnmower to sell at a lower price than the product it was intended to replace, but the new product was less versatile than the original.

In presenting the new product to the sales force, the Sales Manager anticipated a backlash from Sid, a representative of the 'old school' who was not at all convinced that progress was required, particularly when the new product has had a lower capability than its predecessor. He decided to pre-empt Sid's concerns by placing them before Sid's peer group, hoping that their positive reaction would offset Sid's negative attitude and that they would help him 'sell' the product to Sid. The danger in this is that Sid might feel himself forced into a corner what is needed is willing coercion rather than forcible conversion.

After all, unless Sid was convinced about the product, it is unlikely that he would be able to sell it convincingly.

The Sales Manager introduced the discussion in the following way.

'Well everyone, we've heard the technical specifications, we've seen the new machine in action and we've seen the proposals for incentives. I hope you will agree that they add up to a significant move for the company and one that will mean a considerably improved future for us all. Any comments?'

'Ay, we've seen a lot of promotional puff, but the reality is that this new machine of yours is not a patch on the old Mark 5.'

'Well Sid, lets look at each of those points carefully. First, there is a certain amount of promotional material here as with any new product, we need to get over to everyone what the best points of the new machine are. I don't know how everyone else feels, but I would have thought that the material does achieve its purpose. How long have you been with us now Sid?'

'Thirty years - man and boy.'

47

'Quite a record isn't it. Remember how you used to sell the old Mark 1?'

'Ay, we had to describe it in words with only a roneoed technical spec.'

'And you could only get about four or five calls in each day because of the time you had to spend describing the machine and its capabilities, couldn't you? Because the calls were restricted so were your earnings, weren't they?'

'Too right, you had to see people in the evenings to maintain decent earnings.'[1]

'Well, fortunately we've moved a long way since then. You now have packs of market research information, plus high-quality pictorial specifications of the new products and video programmes so customers can see the products in action. And, of course, unlike the difficulties Sid and his mates had to put up with 30 years ago, nowadays we have our reputation for good quality, which is its own recommendation. I know these sales aids are a lot to carry around, but they are just that - aids to help you make sales, which help you earn your commission. I'm sure, Sid, you would be the first to agree that these sales aids really do help.'[2]

'Ay, but you've still got to sell the machine and you've made that job more awkward because it's not as good as the old model.'

'Again, there are several things we need to examine there, but,

before we do, let's just make it clear that we're not getting rid of the old Mark 5 machine. We are still making it and intend to make it for at least the next year or so. However, it's an old-style machine and, as you are always telling us, quite rightly, the public are always looking for something new. So, if you can still bring in the orders at a reasonable level for the Mark 5, we will certainly keep it in the list. We do think, however, that once the Mark 6 gains recognition, Mark 5 sales will tend to fall rapidly. We live in very competitive times and unless we develop new machines for new demands we will simply not stay in business. So, Sid, don't worry about your favourite machine - it will still be around for a while yet.'

'And people will still prefer it to this new machine - it's no good.'

'Well I'm not sure I can agree with you there Sid - after all, you have seen the results of the market research we carried out with a sample of the public. Yes, we have removed the middle grass height cut, but that was because those we asked said they either used the low or high cut and very rarely did they want to use the middle-cut. Taking the middle-cut and the other extras out saves us £9 on the production costs and, allowing for VAT etc., means we can shave nearly £15 off the retail price, which means we gain a price advantage over Brown's comparable model. That means we will be undercutting them rather than them undercutting us, which I know, Sid, you and others complain about.

And there is another point here as well. We all know how difficult it is to sell anything at the moment. From the research we commissioned, it seems that what the customer prefers at present is a cheaper machine. Most people are quite happy to do without extras like the middle-cut, the edger and a longer electrical lead if the price is lower. If that is what customers want, then we must give it to them or we will go out of business. Times have changed and we must change with them. Don't forget, we have made sure you won't lose out as we have increased your commission rate to compensate for the lower sales value you will generate. Are you happier, Sid?' [3]

48

Key techniques

[1] By citing one of the bad aspects of 'the old days', the Sales Manager has made Sid agree that the old days were not all good, that change can be beneficial and has tried to create a rapport with him.

[2] By acknowledging Sid's contribution over the years, the Sales Manager is granting him prestige and recognition. Using Sid's admission of shortcomings, the first part of the argument can therefore be undermined.

[3] The Sales Manager has not tried to counter Sid's negative responses (which would have generated the argument that Sid wanted and would have enjoyed, but would have gained nothing), but instead used them to display positive benefits.

Case study 4.2
NO SALE TO THE SALES DEPARTMENT

An organisation was regarded as a one-product company and the Board was very concerned that it should diversify. To this end, a Development Department had been set up and was actively sourcing new products for related markets. The Sales Manager was an expert in selling the existing main product, but was scathing about new and derivative products outside the main list. He was also furious that the new development department had not been placed under his control. At the third Executive Committee meeting in four months, new products were being suggested and, for the third time, the Sales Manager was busy shooting the ideas down, like this.

'I tell you, I've been selling longer than most of this Committee have been drawing breath and these crazy ideas that this new Department keep coming up with, will never work.'

'Fred, no one doubts your knowledge of selling widgets and we need all the sales of widgets that we can achieve over the coming years - I assume you still feel you can achieve a growth of 5 per cent compound over the next 3 years?' [1]

'Yes, I've told you time and time again, we will definitely achieve those targets - you can see the results already coming through in the latest sales
figures. What I don't want us to do is waste time and money on these no good ideas.'

'So, we can bank on the sales targets and thus the financial contribution from our traditional sales of widgets, which gives us some defence against the imports that we know will take all the expansion in our market.'

49

'Yes, yes, yes - we've been over all this before.'

'Fine Fred, but the problem is that an increase of sales of 5 per cent is OK for Year 1, just about acceptable for Year 2 but unacceptable in Year 3, because the increase in our costs will have shrunk the margin by then. Obviously we can't expect you to keep achieving compound sales increases for what is becoming a rather old-fashioned product despite the restyling and repositioning we've commissioned. As you yourself are fond of saying, salespeople need something new to talk about, don't they? [2] So, the fact is we need new products and unless we develop them now we are never going to have them in time to replace our older products as they come to the end of their expected life.'

'But these ideas are rubbish - they're never going to work in a month of Sundays.'

'Well they're certainly never going to work unless we believe in them and give them our support. Of course, even with such support some of them may not work anyway, but the purpose of this Committee is to run the business. We will not be able to keep the business expanding unless we plan for the future. In considering the financial projections it is obvious that we need several new products - these may not be ideal, but at least they are a start. What we need is everyone's considered input to improve the good points and eradicate the bad. Perhaps it would be helpful for us to set up a small working party to take the ideas forward - would you have time to spare for that Fred?' [3]

'Yes I'll be glad to examine these ideas, before they come here - at least it will avoid wasting time here!'

'Thanks Fred, I'll be chairing the working party and obviously we will welcome everyone's constructive comments. [4] I do stress, though, that as a matter of urgency we need to find several new products to take us forwards. I accept that this may mean a new way of selling and we may need to consider setting up parallel selling operations to avoid damaging the potential of our existing product - obviously we do not want to dilute the effort of Fred's team.'[5]

50

Key techniques

[1] Avoiding answering the emotive argument and dealing with the facts (the financial targets in this case) moves the meeting forwards. Reacting to the emotive comments would merely generate a negative and time-consuming argument.

[2] By highlighting the financial logic of the problem, the Chairman forces tacit, if grudging, agreement from his opponent, indicating the relatively short life left in the existing product and quoting Fred's own words at him. Fred can hardly deny any of it.

[3] Again, the Chairman refuses to become side-tracked into an argument and has moved the discussion forwards. The offer to Fred is such that he has no choice - either he accepts and then tries to destroy the ideas in Committee or he refuses, which will hardly bolster his standing as Sales Manager.

[4] Using his own appointment as Chairman of the Committee, stamps the Committee with authority and sidetracks any intention of Fred trying to steamroll the new Committee.

[5] Having used guile and logic previously, the Chairman underlines his commitment to the new idea by means of a gentle warning - that pure obstructiveness could lead to Fred's area of operation being further restricted.

Not *all* encounters are concerned with the promotion of new products, procedures and so on. Sometimes the problem may be more a question of managerial responsibilities, arising either as a result of a clash of personalities or a misunderstanding of the 'required manner' of acting. These can raise far more complicated issues than we have seen so far as often management can be placed in the position of *wanting* to agree with the subordinate and yet being unable to do so because of other pressures.

Case study 4.3
TOO MANY EDITORS . . .

Pat had been recruited to the post of Public Relations Manager in a charity where previously no single person had assumed such responsibility. Prior to her taking up the post, Pat had requested a job description. This was given to her and, in it, allocated the responsibility for the production of the annual report to her. In addition, both before recruitment and on her commencing work, all employees and advisers had been informed of Pat's appointment and told that, in future, she would be handling all external communication material. Although press releases and single-sheet publicity documents were produced by her without problems, dissension started with the production of the charity's report to its fundraisers. Pat requested an interview with the Chief Executive and the following conversation took place.

'Well Pat, what's the problem? Make it quick will you, I have a meeting at 3pm.'

'I have a major problem, but I think it will need at least 30 to 45 minutes to discuss it - can we fix a time?'

'I'm pretty booked up for the next week or so.'

'I don't think it can wait that long, but, as you are so tied up, what I could do is jot down the problem and my suggested solutions in a one-page resumé, leave it for you to read through and consider, then perhaps you could find time for a quick discussion later so we can move forwards?'

'Are you sure that's necessary? Can't we knock it on the head now?'

'No, I'm sorry, but it is fundamental and I do think we need to discuss it briefly after you've read my comments.' [1]

52

Pat then prepared a short report, outlining the problems and indicating that the current manner of working was at variance with her understanding of what her responsibilities were but she phrased things calmly and logically, not indicating her very strong feelings on the subject. Although such an indication might bolster the strength of her arguments, placing these in black and white may make them look a little like a threat, which might be counter-productive. In this it can be assumed that Pat's aim was to publish the new format report and this was the end to which she must work.

The Chief Executive now has a problem. He prepared Pat's job description, notified all involved of the new arrangements and, with the Board, approved the concept. To backtrack will destroy his credibility, but to insist that Pat proceeds with the new-style report, may deter some of the charity's backers from continuing to lend it support. He met Pat.

'Pat, thank you for your report - I had not realised the seriousness of the difficulty you had when we spoke a few days ago. This seems to throw up a number of problems, as I am sure you have realised.'

'I have realised the seriousness of its implications - but this is compounded by the urgency. Unless we know how we are going to proceed within the next 48 hours, I am not sure we can meet the

publication deadline.' [2]

'You do of course realise that this Committee represents some of our most important sponsors and we do need to keep them involved.'

'Of course, but surely this was anticipated when the Board decided to change the manner and concept of the publication, wasn't it?' [3]

'I am afraid we overlooked the point.'

'Well, somehow we need to resolve it now.'

'What do you suggest?' [4]

'Obviously the Board have decided that the report needs to be updated and have agreed the concept and approach, but equally, you don't want to antagonise the backers. I would suggest that you, as Chief Executive, send to each backer, a copy of the current proof with a note stating that, first, the Board have agreed that a new concept should be adopted; second, that, as a charity, we are trying to cut costs, so we have shortened the report as well as its timetable; third, that, to avoid typesetting costs (which can be as much as 60p for altering a comma), we need them to keep suggested alterations to an absolute minimum; and fourth, that, being under severe time constraints we need comments by (we could specify a time/date that would only allow them around 24 hours to reply).' [5]

53

Key techniques

[1] The immediate inference of these first exchanges is that the problem and even Pat herself are of relatively little importance. Either Pat can recognise the reality of the situation and try to put over in a nutshell what she's up against, risking the swift and shallow response that may be more of a 'papering over the cracks' effort rather than an attempt to really sort out the fundamental problem or she can dig her heels in and insist on being allocated adequate time, albeit at a later date. Pat's response is firm as she feels so strongly about the problem that she has nothing to lose. It will be difficult for the Chief Executive to turn her offer of a short report down as she is taking the onus for action.

The problem concerned Pat's authority and control over the corporate report. She understood, (and her job description indicated) that part of her task was to upgrade the traditional report. She believed she was to present a new concept for approval and then write and design the report in accordance with that design concept. This would mean that the report would be given a more modern format, reflecting current thinking and styles. Subject only to final content checking by the Chief Executive and Board, she would then have the document produced.

The Chief Executive and Board had approved the concept, but, as Pat finalised the copy and design for the new-style report, she had been informed by the Advisory Committee of the charity (consisting of 12 representatives of the sponsoring organisations) that they wished to oversee the content and copy and were expecting the usual five-hour meeting to read through every word, correcting and changing as they felt necessary, which had been the case previously, and that this meeting would be held prior to preparation of the final proof. Pat's problems were fourfold:

a she felt that this procedure conflicted with her previous understanding of her own appointment and responsibilities

b she could foresee that the Committee would want to make massive changes during the meeting even though the new concept had Board approval

c if there were substantial changes, then, as the document was already at proof stage, the typesetter's charges for making such alterations would mean that she would exceed the budget set by the Board for producing the report

d she was unsure that she could continue to work under these changed requirements, which are at variance with her original remit.

[2] While not reassuring Pat, at least in this way the Chief Executive has laid a foundation for genuine discussion. Pat, meanwhile, has not moved from her original position at all - in fact, she has dug her heels in to some extent by emphasising the need for a decision, reminding the CE of the publication deadline.

[3] This is really the crux of the problem and Pat uses this to put the Chief Executive on the spot. Its a double-edged question: either he must agree that it was anticipated (which begs the question 'what was decided') or he must confirm that the point was overlooked which reflects poorly on the Board's control of the situation.

[4] While the CE is being honest, this admission enables Pat to seize the initiative. However, she does this in a positive way, seeking to

move the discussion forwards. Emphasising the failings of the Board, would only have meant that the Chief Executive would have had to defend a position that would be unlikely to lead to a mutually acceptable solution. If, however, she suggests a solution that is acceptable to him, then both parties can be satisfied. If she had put forward an unacceptable solution, then this would have indicated to him that Pat considered the situation to be irredeemable, in which case, although he may have a problem getting the report finished and printed, he can maintain the status quo for the time being, leaving the situation to be sorted out in the medium term. Indeed, as Pat's terms are three months' notice, it is unlikely that she will walk out and, thus, he may even be able to ensure she oversees the report's production even though she cannot agree its content/concept. This may mean, however, that he will need to offer her other incentives.

Conversely the Chief Executive's question puts Pat on the spot. Either she can indicate that the report needs to be produced the way she initially understood it was to be produced (which leads to her running the risk of alienating the charity's backers' who are more vital than a company's customers) or she can give way and agree to operate it the way it has always been done or she can suggest some compromise solution. If she digs her heels in, she knows she risks losing her job. If she gives way completely and runs it the way it was done before, she will not be following her instincts and, indeed, the instructions (however imperfectly couched) of the Board. This actually gives her an edge over the Chief Executive, and may be the foundation for an acceptable compromise.

55

[5] This approach benefits from:

■ being positive and pragmatic

■ reminding the Chief Executive that his Board have already approved the new concept, so if they back-track they lose credibility

■ allowing all those previously involved to continue to feel involved, even if, to all practical purposes, they may not be

■ stressing the need to reduce costs, which should be a major plus point for those involved with a charity

■ making it somewhat difficult for sponsors to take offence and withdraw their support because they will still be involved

■ allowing Pat to retain most of what she understood to be her responsibilities and controls, which can be built on further in the future.

It would be unlikely that most reasonable Chief Executives would not accept this compromise, but if they did not, and if the Chief Executive decided *not* to back Pat but instead asked her to produce the report in the former way, it would not be surprising if her first report for the charity was also her last.

5

■ ■ ■

Eyeball to eyeball encounters

Key learning points

1 To find a solution to, or resolve, a problem encounter, the other party's views must be appreciated (even if they are not accepted).

2 Innovative suggestions and discussions are more likely to lead to the desired result than will imposing assumed solutions.

3 The problem encounter should not be used as an occasion for criticism - objective, positive solutions must be the aim.

In dealing with specific and one-off problems relating to a particular person, it must be realised that the description 'tough talking' may not refer so much to the need to deal positively and objectively with problems as to the need to overcome problems againsta background of subjective, psychological considerations. Nevertheless at times ingenuity can be used to resolve difficult situations without causing loss of face or distress for the people involved.

Case Study 5.1
LEFT FOOT FORWARD

The Transport Manager was bemused having studied the company's best sales representative's company car record over the last year. Although the car had only done 24 000 miles, the tyres had been replaced once and the brakepads and linings replaced twice. He reported the findings to the representative's Manager who agreed to investigate the problem. On accompanying the rep on a drive, he noticed that he used his left foot to brake and would often apply both feet simultaneously to the controls, thus both braking and accelerating. The following conversation ensued:

This car seems to have very heavy wear on its brakes and tyres, Don, is there anything wrong with the controls?'

'I haven't noticed anything - I thought it was something to do with the wheel tracking but that was checked at the last service.'

'Transport say they can't find anything wrong with the tracking or the wheels - its very strange. You don't have an unusual way of driving do you?' [1]

Later.

'Don, I wanted to have a word with you about driving. The Board have decided that everyone should attend a refresher driving course.'

'But there's nothing wrong with my driving - I'm a good driver.'

'We all think that and yet we can all learn to be better can't we?'

'I suppose so, but it seems like a waste of money to me.'

'Well our insurance brokers who run the course say that every company that uses the course sees a significant reduction in its insurance

premiums as a result, so it shouldn't cost us anything in fact, they reckon that if we gradually put all our drivers through the course we will reduce the number of accidents and so actually save money.'

'But I've hardly had any accidents.'

'Sure and let's hope it continues like that, but your repair figure is very high. Anyway, we could all get into our cars tonight and not make it home, couldn't we?'

'I suppose so - is everyone doing this then?'

'Well that is the way in which we can reduce our costs. If every driver goes through the process, the brokers reckon we can reduce our insurance premiums by half.' [2]

At the driving school.

'Don, which driving instructor taught you to drive using your left foot to operate the brake?'

'My dad taught me to drive and he said it was better to use my left foot for the brake as I'm left-handed. He said my left foot would be stronger than my right which would give more power for braking.'

'But you have power-assisted brakes in this car don't you?'

'Yes, I think so.'

'Well, with those brakes, you only need a little pressure on the pedal. I am surprised your brakes haven't been wearing out faster than normal.' [3]

'Well, the company said the repair costs were high.'

'I bet they were. Now, we'd better see what we can do to change the habits of a driving lifetime hadn't we?'

Key techniques

[1] Asking the question invites a response (this is a positive act), which is preferable to making a statement (as this may provide a defensive and thus negative response, particularly as this relates to a person's driving ability, which is a very emotive subject). The question gave Don the option of coming clean about his driving technique.

[2] Instructing the driving school to deal with the problem passes the difficulty to a professional, external driver rather than an internal manager. It may be easier for Don to take queries and criticisms from such a (remote) source.

[3] Even such an expert, however, needs to put across the criticism or correction in a user-responsive and positive way.

59

Using criticism constructively
■ ■ ■

Case Study 5.1 concerns the need to change habits. This in itself implies a criticism of the way things are. The adage 'truth hurts' is self-evident and yet, regardless of hurt, often organisations need to criticise in order to produce the desired results.

Assuming a desired result has been set by the party doing the criticising, the manner in which the criticism is communicated needs to be carefully considered. Only *constructive* criticism is likely to be beneficial and, even then, many people find the experience painful or possibly unacceptable. There are four main reactions to criticism:

- acceptance
- failure to accept responsibility
- failure to accept the whole basis of the criticism
- denial.

Acceptance of criticism

Only those who are emotionally secure, mature and committed to their own and the organisation's future are likely to be capable of hearing and accepting criticism. Equally, only such people are likely to be able to change either themselves or the situation for which they are responsible.

Case study 5.2
ACCOUNTABILITY

The Chief Executive and a manager were discussing a report prepared by the latter.

'I find it very difficult to follow this report.'
  'I thought I had covered all the angles.'
    'I'm not saying that you haven't - indeed, you have uncovered one or two aspects that haven't been fully appreciated before. The trouble

is, I find the report confusing.'

'Are you saying that it's a presentational rather than a content problem?' [1]

'I think that is so - you need to pull it apart and put it into a more logical order. It could also benefit from imposing a structure whereby each part is presented similarly and the conclusions flow into a single recommendation section.'

'Right, I see exactly what you mean.' [2]

Key techniques

[1] The Chief Executive has manipulated the conversation so that the subordinate seems to supply the answer of their own accord.

[2] The approach 'here is a problem we need to discuss and resolve' obtains positive feedback and response.

Failure to accept responsibility

If the person refuses to accept responsibility for whatever it is and slides such responsibility onto others, the negotiator may find it virtually impossible to pin the person down - at least this time.

Case study 5.3
NON-ACCOUNTABILITY

The Chief Executive and a manager were discussing a report.

'I find it very difficult to follow this report.'

'Yes, I told my people that, but they've used the data that the Sales Department gave us.'

'But it's your report isn't it?'

'Not really, all we've done is try to address the question using other people's data.'

'But you were asked to prepare this report, weren't you?'

'No, I said we could research what was available internally and assemble it for further study.'

'Right, in that case, what I'd like you to do is, as head of development, take full responsibility for everything that's in this report and

present it to the Board on [date]; check all the data and facts used and confirm that this has been done and, lastly, add a set of recommendations as a conclusion and indicate which of these would be your choice for action, giving your reasons for this.'

> **Key technique**
> The problem that needs to be overcome is that the employee is sliding away from taking responsibility for the report. Accordingly, the Chief Executive delineates the manager's accountability for what he is asking him to do very precisely. If later the manager tries to duck responsibility once again, it should be very difficult for this approach to succeed.

Failure to accept the criticism's validity

62

Here comments may be made by the negotiator, be listened to and apparently accepted by the other party, but have no effect - there is no change in attitude, approach or whatever. The criticism has not been accepted by the person and so things stay the same.

Case study 5.4
'I HEAR WHAT YOU SAY, BUT . . .'

The Chief Executive and a manager were discussing a report and had the following conversation.

'I find it very difficult to follow this report.'
 'I can't see why - I've set it out in numbered sections.'
 'The numbering is fine, but you have jumbled the content between the various sections.'
 'No, each section is separate.'
 'I know the sections are separate, but the content of several is similar or overlaps and should be dealt with as part of a single section.'
 'But they're separated in order to make it easy to understand and follow.'
 'It does not do that - you've dealt with the question of customer complaints in sections 5, 9, 10 and 19. These need grouping into one main section. You refer to stock problems in sections 6, 7, 10 and 15 -

again, these need to be grouped into one or two main sections and so on.'

'But that makes it far more difficult to lay out.'

'I don't agree. You were asked to poduce this report, so that the Board can make decisions. It is the Board's needs that you must satisfy - you need to ask yourself what do the target audience require. As a member of that target audience I am telling you that I find this report confusing. I want each aspect of the problem tackled as an entity, not spread throughout several pages.'

'I feel that it is clear as it is.'

'Don't you think it would be better if you took general headings such as "Quality," "Stock", "Customer preferences", "Customer complaints" and so on and grouped the various points under those headings?'

Key technique

The Chief Executive is making little progress here and, despite trying to coach the manager in the way he wishes the report to be presented, may need to prepare an outline for the manager to complete.

The conversation also raises questions about the flexibility of the manager and the progress the person is making in their career development. If the manager cannot take constructive criticism, it may be unlikely that personal development will be able to take place or that this person will even be able to lead their own team well.

Denial

Here the criticism is made and listened to, but then denied, virtually irrespective of what can be overpowering evidence. This is indicative of the person's commitment to filtering out criticism - in order to ensure the continuation of the status quo. Such a person believes that only they know the correct way to do things. Inherent in such a belief is, of course, the view that the person seeking to alter the status quo does not understand the situation at all. People who act in this way are mavericks and can be very destructive.

Case study 5.5
CRIMINAL RECORD

An employee had been arrested and charged on a number of inde-cency counts involving young girls. He was reasonably efficient at his work, during the course of which he did not come into contact with the public or with children. The offences had been carried out at his own home and the only connection between the offences and the compa-ny was the employee himself. The employee, released on bail, pre-sented himself for work but was referred to the Personnel Director.

'I understand you wish to return to work, Bill.'

'That's right - I'm on bail until my case comes up in about a month's time.'

'I see. Do you think it wise to come back until the case is over?'

'Why not - I'm pleading not guilty?'

'I think you ought to know, I have received many requests from other employees that you not return to work.'

'What's it got to do with them? It's my life, I haven't hurt them.'

'That may be true, but matters concerning your life are affecting the performance of this factory and, in view of the nature of the charges, it may be better for everyone if your return is postponed until after the court decides the issue.'

'But I want to work.'

'I understand that. However I am telling you that I feel it would be extremely unwise for you to return in view of the ill-feeling that is rife in the factory.'

'But I haven't been found guilty yet.'

'I appreciate that, but we must look at the realities of the situation and the reactions of the other employees. Were you to return, you would face a very hostile reaction that would affect our business and would not be in the interests of anyone, would it?'

'I suppose not.'

'What I would suggest is that we regard you as being on leave of absence until the court case and we review the matter after that, once we know the situation.'

In fact, Bill was found guilty and sentenced to imprisonment. Even from his prison cell he requested that he be allowed to return, despite the obvious problems that would result. The company replied that his several years' sentence effectively frustrated and thus terminated his contract of employment.

Key technique
The Personnel Director puts across the company's concerns to the employee politely, stating the undeniable grounds of the employee's problems, how these relate to him continuing to work and the effects on the other employees. Also, the Personnel Director avoided pre-judging Bill.

Changing contracts
■ ■ ■

The results of problem encounters with employees, involve changing the terms under which the employee works for the company. As in Case Study 5.5 above, such situations often need to be very carefully handled in order not to infringe the employees' rights. Once again having a degree of flexibility and adopting an innovative approach can help here.

65

Case study 5.6
LOSING A DRIVING LICENCE

The Sales Manager and sales representative were considering a problem that had arisen regarding the employee's performance of her duties. Having been with the company for a number of years, Susan was expecting a baby and had just been found guilty of a drink/driving offence, which meant that she lost her licence for six months. The following discussion took place in the Sales Manager's office in a meeting with Susan.

'So Susan, you can no longer perform the job we employ you to do?'
  'I don't agree at all, I can still see my customers until I start my maternity leave.'
  'But you have been banned from driving.'
  'I know I can't drive, but my mother is prepared to act as my chauffeuse for the three months up to my maternity leave. She's got a full and clean licence.'
  'I'm not sure I like that idea.'
  'Well it doesn't make any difference to the company - we have only got to ask our insurers to cover her'

'Are you sure it wouldn't be better for you to start your maternity leave early for us to have the car back and find someone to take over from you?'

'But we've already got someone organised to cover for me while I'm on maternity leave and, besides, I want my car during my maternity leave.'

'But surely you will be leaving the car with us?'

'No, my contract says I am entitled to a car and even if I can't drive it I am still entitled to it, my mother can drive me.'

Key technique

Always be prepared; it is obvious the Sales Manager had not prepared for this encounter as he did not have the facts he needed to be able to deal with the matter positively. Susan is a good sales representative and the desired result should be for her to return to normal working as soon as possible. The Sales Manager is also guilty of patronising the employee to the point of discrimination.

Constructing the interview in the following way might have been preferable.

'Well Susan, this is a difficult situation. I must remind you that the company car rules state that we expect all our drivers to take a responsible attitude towards their driving. I hope you agree and will avoid this happening again - it does not reflect well on you or the company. I hope you appreciate that I'll have to put a note on your file to that effect.'

'Yes I understand. I certainly have no intention of repeating this - apart from anything else, it's causing too much hassle.'

'Let's see what we can sort out. You are three months away from the start of your maternity leave and we need a sales representative to cover the territory until the temporary person starts - any ideas?' [1]

'Yes, I feel I can continue as my mother has agreed to act as my driver for that time - she's got a clean licence.'

'I see, so we shall want full details of her and her driving record straight away. She does realise that your call schedule will have to be maintained regardless and that it's a fairly long day. Is she fit enough?' [2]

'I'm sure she is and, as she will get used to the car during this time, she can drive it during my maternity leave, can't she?'

Key techniques

[1] Without passing the buck, the Sales Manager is involving Susan in the decision making and so her commitment is retained.

[2] This positive response moves the discussion forwards in a constructive way and yet the Sales Manager has also managed to warn Susan against lessening her effectiveness.

Innovative reactions may not only solve a problem but also lead to general progress. Thus, an increasing number of companies have policies regarding actions to be taken in the event of the loss of a driving licence, which can include the removal of the car (if an alternative driver is not available). People then know where they stand and will work to avoid getting into such situations in the first place.

Theft

67

When an employer believes that an employee is guilty of theft, an extremely awkward and embarrassing situation can arise. This is worsened by the fact that it is only rarely proven, the contention often resting on circumstantial rather than actual evidence. Obviously the negotiator in such circumstances needs to be in possession of as many facts as possible and has to assess the desired result. In such instances, the desired result, almost certainly, will be for the thefts to stop as experience indicates that once thefts start to happen, they become more frequent. Once it is known that there is a thief at large, others start to take things, believing that the 'other' thief will be blamed for their acts.

Case study 5.7
THEFT

A director was extremely concerned that the number of petty thefts seemed to be increasing and that most seemed to occur in or around the busy Sales Department. She was particularly concerned because, as a favour to a manager involved in social work, she had employed a young girl, Tina, who had a history of petty theft and, was still serving a probationary sentence. As a number of other young girls of around her age worked in the Sales Department she had placed Tina there, but she now suspected Tina was responsible so she called her to her office.

'Tina, thank you for coming down. How do you like it in Sales?'

'It's nice - the work is interesting and the other girls are fun.'

'Good, do you think you will be able to settle down here?'

'I think so - it all seems very friendly.'

'Yes, we do try to make it friendly, which is why I am so concerned about some unpleasant occurrences in and around the Sales Department. Are you aware of any problems?'

'What sort of problems? I don't think so.'

'I understand that several of the girls in Sales, plus three of the staff in Accounts, have lost money or other items from their handbags - I am surprised you hadn't heard about it.'

'So you're accusing me . . .'

'I am doing no such thing, I merely asked you if you had heard anything about it and I'll ask you again - have you?'

'Well, one or two of the girls have been searching for things they say they've lost, but they've no right to say it was me.'

'Tina, no one has said anything about you. No one knows about your past except Mr Jones and myself. We are simply concerned that we seem to have a petty thief here and, should anyone find out about your record, it could be very awkward for you, because people tend to . . .'

'Say if you've been a thief before it must be you again.'

'I'm afraid so. Have you lost anything?'

'No - I suppose <u>that</u> makes me guilty as well.'

'Not at all, but perhaps you could keep your ears and eyes open and let me know about anything unusual. We will stop at nothing to make sure these thefts don't happen again and, as you know, we always prosecute employees who steal from our premises.'

Key technique

The thefts stopped soon after the interview and, soon after that, Tina left. Accusations were unnecessary and, as there was no proof, were best avoided, but the right messages can be conveyed, as here, in an oblique way.

Compulsive resignations

■ ■ ■

Tina did not offer her resignation in the interview, presumably feeling that to do so would point to her guilt. She was prepared to bluff it out until she was ready to move on elsewhere. Other employees, however, can be so taken over by mistaken feelings of guilt that they resign on impulse as soon as there is the slightest indication of criticism - implied or direct. Very often, their resignation is not in any way a desired result, although, eventually, it may become so as the time time spent reassuring such individuals can be considerable and is all, to some extent, wasted.

Case study 5.8
IMPULSIVE RESIGNER

The manager had just blown his top on hearing that a letter sent Recorded Delivery for his attention, had, contrary to all instructions, remained in the Registered post record book for a week, rather than being passed directly on to him. Having found the letter, he was about to begin responding to its contents when the person in charge of the post room, asked to see him.

'Yes Bob, what's the problem? Sit down and get it off your chest.' [1]
'I've come to give you my resignation.'
'Oh, why is that then?' [2]
'Because of the mess over that letter.'
'I see. Well, it was certainly a mess, but that's no reason to resign. I gave you a warning to make sure it does not happen again, and that's that.' [3]
'Well, I feel responsible and feel I should go.'
'I see. Well, you are certainly responsible and must ensure that your staff deal with all their work in a responsible and efficient manner - there are procedures and they must be adhered to. Having said all that, I see no reason why you should resign.'
'I think it would be best.'
'Best for whom - for you? You will have difficulty finding another job at your age, it's not best for us as we will have to replace you and train someone else in all the systems you know first hand and it's not best

*for your staff. You have an opportunity to stress to them how neces-
sary it is that the procedures are adhered to and to train them accordingly.' [4]*

'I still think I should go.'

*'I don't - I think you will be running away from your responsibilities.
I think it best for you and for us that you face up to those responsibilities - sort that staff of yours out Bob, they let you down. Tell you what,
I'll pop down tomorrow and we'll run a briefing session on the subject
once everyone's calmed down.' [5]*

Key techniques

[1] Bob is obviously in a state and may lose his temper or even his
emotional control. As well as removing the psychological advantage
Bob will have by standing (looking down on the manager), offering
a seat will help him cope in either eventuality.

[2] A low-key response should help reduce the stress of Bob's emotional state.

[3] While disciplinary matters should not be forgotten, except when
the time expires, experienced management will try to move the relationship past such problems.

[4] The appropriateness of this kind of response depends on the circumstances. If Bob is emotional, the apparent harshness of the
retort may be too strong. If not then the harshness seeks to remind
Bob that he has responsibilities and that seeking to duck is to
ignore his role.

[5] The manager has not let Bob walk away from his responsibilities,
but, by offering to share the load, he is giving him support.

70

6

■ ■ ■

Solving performance problems

Key learning points

1 Performance counselling is best effected positively, without any judgemental overtones, objectively and positively and by setting targets to monitor performance.

2 Meeting emotive criticism with calm logic and explanation after careful examination of facts will help progress the encounter towards a satisfactory resolution.

3 Placing untrained personnel in positions of responsibility will lead to there being more problem encounters although experience they will gain may reduce the number that do occur significantly.

4 Reaching conclusions without establishing the facts may enable the other party to sidetrack the main thrust of the matter.

5 Those who wish to behave in an unacceptable or anti-social way cannot be allowed to continue to do so as this harms everyone else.

Where tough talking is required to progress problems that relate to a particular employee, an individually tailored solution may work. However, where the repercussions of a solution can affect a number of employees, negotiators must be aware of the dangers of creating a precedent and, indeed, this may be as important as finding a solution to the particular problem. Sometimes problems are as much a result of the attitudes of the person concerned as they are of the worries expressed by them and so this affects the choice of solution. A prime example of this occurs when people need to improve on their presently unacceptable performance to match a required standard and the reason for them not performing well is their personality rather than a lack of training or skills.

72

People come in all shapes and sizes and have all manner of personal characteristics - some of which can be improved by training, while others cannot. It should also be recognised that, at any one time, up to a fifth of an organisation's workforce will have a personal problem that is likely to affect their performance at work. Further, a tenth of the workforce may be experiencing a serious problem that is likely to have a considerable effect on their normal capacities for judgement and responding well to situations. It is essential to avoid making judgements until the full story is known as behaviour that is out of character can often be put down to the stresses the person is under. Support and tact rather than tough talking is needed at such times.

The disorganised manager
■ ■ ■

Such instances as those mentioned above apart, if unacceptable traits are noticed in employees, they need to be dealt with swiftly - both for the good of the organisation and for the benefit of the person concerned. Such traits can take a variety of forms - a classic one being the disorganised procrastinator. This type of person reminds me of the story of the committee member who felt he should not serve on the committee any longer as he was concerned that he constantly put things off, delayed finishing jobs he said he would do for the committee and so let the members down. Having made the decision to come off the committee because of his procrastination, he then put off telling the secretary that he didn't want his name to be put forward for re-election and was promptly re-elected!

Case study 6.1
THE DISORGANISED MANAGER

A director was very concerned at the apparent inability of his subordinate to organise her day, despite various coaching sessions. Eventually he called him into his office.

73

'Jane, I want to run through the priorities for next week.'
'Right, fire away.'
'Don't you think it might be better to get your diary?'

Later.

'Now, I am very concerned that we seem constantly to miss deadlines and overrun set time limits and so on. What I'd like you to do is to list all the things you have to do next week.'
'What, now?'
'Yes, right now. You need to get into the habit of planning ahead, so, first of all, list everything. Then put them into an order of priority - to make it easy, try giving each item a rating, say, 5, meaning it has a high priority, running down to 1, meaning it has a low priority.'
'What happens if I have more than 5 items?'
'I expect you will have, but there's nothing to stop more than one item having the same grading. Having listed everything, insert the items into the days you have available so that they will act as a guide to what you expect to be doing next week. I expect other things will intervene but at least you'll have a reminder of the importance of the items that have not been dealt with so far. Then, each day, cross out what has been achieved, which will give you the 'leftovers', which must be added to the following day's tasks.' [1]
'Is that it then?'
'No. I also want you to start writing a monthly report on what you

and the Department have accomplished in the last month, and at the end I want you to set down what your priorities are for the following month - in order of importance and setting a time limit for their completion. Then, at the end of the month, we'll review the priorities you set yourself and see how well you did.'

'Is that all?'

'I think you'll find it will be quite a lot, but there is one thing more. I want you to clear your desk every night. Usually your aim should be to deal with most of the items that hit your desk during the day, but obviously there will be, say around a quarter that may have to be left. If you leave the mass of data on your desk to mount up inevitably more and more items will be lost or will be overlooked.'

'Righto.' [2]

'I think I must stress the importance of all this Jane. You are good at the job, when you can get on top of it. The trouble is, you are rarely on top of it. You really need to make these suggestions work if you are to continue in the role. I'll jot down a resume@ of what we've agreed and let you have a copy.' [3]

74

Key techniques

[1] The manager is forcing Jane to use the act of writing to formulate her priorities and, in stipulating that Jane must enter everything in her diary, the manager (through Jane) is creating a record that will be available later to provide factual back-up.

[2] The manager is concerned that Jane is just casually accepting what needs to be done. This prompts him to emphasise its importance and insert some steel into the interview in the last exchange.

[3] Compiling and providing a copy of what was agreed will help make Jane accountable for what happens subsequently.

The barrack-room lawyer
■ ■ ■

In nearly every company there is a person who, knows what is 'right', what 'rights' attach to employment and insists on such 'rights' being observed, regardless of the law. This does not mean that obligations can be ignored, merely that, in most instances, it is impossible to make black-and-white decisions - there can be many shades of grey. Circumstances can and do alter cases. Unfortunately, very often, the barrack-room lawyer's perception of what is right and appropriate is coloured by their innate sense of grievance, which, in the worst cases, can verge on paranoia. This sense can be so strong that they cannot be reasoned with.

Case study 6.2
EXPLAINING POLICY

When a company made a number of its shop staff redundant, its policy was to make a basic redundancy payment to everyone leaving their service. However, some shops were sold as going concerns (thus most of the staff would enter new employment or be continuously employed, without a break). Other shops were sold as empty units (thus the staff would not benefit from immediate or continuous employment). To try to balance this, an additional redundancy payment was made to those staff who would not immediately enter new employment.

When a director visited one of the shops in Newcastle, however, a furious employee came up to him and the following exchange took place.

'I've been waiting to see you, I'm hopping mad about this redundancy.'

'I see, I'm sorry to hear that Miss, Mrs . . .? Let's mention your difficulty to the Manager and then go into the staffroom or office to try to sort this out, shall we?' [1]
They moved to the staffroom and the Manager of the shop joined them.

'Now, shall we sit down and find out what the problem is. We appreciate that this is a difficult time for everyone and we do want to try and avoid as many problems as possible.' [2]

'Well, I don't think this redundancy thing is at all fair - I've really lost out.'

'I see, well let's check exactly what has happened first.' [3]

The director discovered that Miss Jones had been given a letter terminating her employment in common with the rest of the staff. The problem might have stemmed from errors in the records leading to an incorrect calculation, or from an inconsistency in the treatment of Miss Jones' case compared to that of her colleagues or something else. Either a few minutes could be spent checking the details or the following shortcut could be taken.

'Is the problem connected with the letter, the calculations or what?'

'No, I'm not getting as much as my twin sister and we're on the same grade, we joined together - and it's not fair.'

'I see, well, on the face of it that does seem unfair - what does your sister do?' [4]

'She's a counter assistant, too, at Hexham, but she's going to get twice as much as me.' [5]

'Ah well that is because Hexham is being sold as a vacant property so they will all be unemployed after the closure, whereas this shop is being sold as a going concern, so you will still have a job.'

'But I would <u>prefer</u> to have the money.'

'I think you are missing the important point about redundancy pay. Once she leaves our employ, your twin sister - what's her name by the way?'

'Kate.'

'Once Hexham is sold, Kate will not have a job. The doubling of the redundancy pay for her is in recognition of the fact that it may be some time before she gets another job. On the other hand, although you will be leaving our employ on the same date, your shop will continue in business and you will keep your job. Wouldn't you agree that having a job is better than not having one at the moment - particularly here where there are few jobs?'

'But I would prefer to have the money - I've worked for the company for five years, I think I deserve some consideration.' [6]

'Well, let's look at those two points. First, I can see the initial attraction of the double payment, although, of course, it will not necessarily last long. As far as getting some consideration from the company, I think you are forgetting the fact that the company is giving you a redundancy payment, even though it has managed to sell this shop as a going concern. That is party in recognition of the service each employee has contributed. After all, redundancy payments exist to provide a financial bridge between one job and another. Although some people will be lucky enough to move from one job straight to another, others will not be so lucky and may spend a considerable time out of work. The purpose of the redundancy payment is to help those people who have difficulty getting a new job to manage while they are out of work. Now, this is not a problem you are going to have because

you will get a single redundancy payment even though you will still have a job. Kate may have twice that amount, but she has no job and may well need to rely on the redundancy payment while she tries to find another job. [7] I appreciate that you may not like the situation and might still prefer the double payment but that simply does not apply to employees at this branch. We have tried to structure the policy so that everyone is treated as fairly as possible, I do hope you can understand this?'

Key techniques

[1] As the encounter took place on the shop floor, the first thing the director wished to do was to move to a private area away from both public and other staff members. Having an audience may add to the potential embarrassment and make it difficult to defuse the confrontation. Using the words 'I', 'sorry' and 'shall we' helps to create a rapport and break down initial hostility. The inference is 'OK, there's a problem, but together we can sort it out', but referring to the problem as 'your difficulty' gently underlines where the responsibility lies. It is the *employee's* problem that the *company* will try to help sort out. Asking for the employee's name, is a further attempt to create a rapport and to make the procedure comfortably informal.

They then moved to the staffroom and the Manager joined them. The Manager, who is directly responsible for the employee, must be involved to avoid breaking the chain of command.

[2] Sitting everyone down should relax all concerned. Interestingly, this effect is one of the reasons for seating greater portions of the crowd at football matches as it seems that aggravation and violence occur more naturally when those involved are standing. The required informality could be assisted by offering refreshments, especially if the employee is really agitated or upset. The legendary British cup of tea actually has several beneficial effects:

■ it diverts attention from the confrontation to a neutral, hospitable act

■ it gives time for the initial anger to cool slightly, and

■ it enables both parties to marshal their thoughts.

[3] Before attempting to reach a solution, the facts need to be established. Thus, the first step in this direction is to establish exactly what has been said to the employee - after all, it may be a simple misunderstanding.

[4] The onus has been placed on the employee to justify the apparent unfairness. Obviously, assuming the twins did start on the same day and are on the same grade, it seems logical that they should receive the same redundancy payment.

[5] Establishing the facts demonstrates the reason for the different payments. The other shop is being sold as a property deal and so, at completion, the staff will be unemployed, whereas the Newcastle unit is being sold as a going concern and so staff will be kept on.

[6] This is the real complaint. Although the company's argument is sound, there may be no way of converting the employee to the logic of the plan. In this case, there may be no point in trying to make Miss Jones enthusiastic about the company's logic - it is best here to try to convince her that the logic is fair even though it may not satisfy her.

[7] The director has patiently explained the logic behind the policy adopted. It would be difficult for anyone except the most awkward employee to do anything but agree with the argument. If, however, the person still argues, it might be necessary to explore the possibility of the employee transferring to another branch.

The inexperienced supervisor

■ ■ ■

Very often, people placed in positions of authority may lack sufficient training in handling the situations they face in their supervisory roles. Their responses may be immediate reactions rather than calm assessments of facts and of alternative means of handling them to achieve the desired result.
end of page

Case study 6.3
JUMPING TO CONCLUSIONS

The Manageress of the shop, who was also its owner, was justifiably annoyed because for the sixth or seventh time she had come back from her break to find sweet wrappers on the floor behind the counter. Although she had given her assistant permission to take one bar of chocolate from the stock to have with her cup of tea while she held the fort for her in the shop, it seemed that this concession was being abused, so she had a word with her.

'Have you helped yourself to more than one bar again?' she demanded testily of her assistant.

'What do you mean "again" ', was the reply, as a queue began to form.

'That's the fourth time this week I've come back to find wrappers on the floor behind the counter after the break.' To the next customer, 'Thats 60p, please.'

'But I've only been here twice this week [1] - how dare you accuse me of stealing in front of all these people.'

'I did not accuse you of stealing.' [2]

'Yes you did, in front of all these people you said I had been helping myself - that's defamation of character, I could sue you for that.' [3]

With the benefit of thought and/or experience, the conversation might have been better conducted as follows.

The Manageress returns from her break to find the sweet wrappers and the assistant serving four or five people. She calls another assistant who is filling the shelves in the shop.

'Paula, could you serve please - Mrs Thompson could you pop into the staffroom?'

In the staffroom.

'Mrs Thompson, I noted as I went into the shop then that there were a number of wrappers on the floor behind the counter, do you know why?'

'No.'

'I see. I have noticed previously that when I have left you in charge behind the counter, when I have returned from my break that there are wrappers on the floor - have you any explanation?'

'I expect they're from the free issue of chocolate for the break.'

'The rule regarding free issue is that you are allowed one item per break - it would seem from the wrappers that more than one item may have been taken. Was anyone else behind the counter during my break?'

'No, I was on my own, but the wrappers could have been dropped by anyone before the break.'

'You know my rules are that the floor must be kept clear and it was certainly clear when I started my break, so I can only conclude, if no one else was behind the counter during my break, that you must have dropped them - is that reasonable?' [4]

Key techniques

[1] Attempting to resolve the problem without thought or considering the facts almost inevitably creates problems. In this case it will not only lead to problems between employer and employee, but the conversation was also overheard by customers. The mistakes made by the Manageress in this case were several:

- this is potentially a disciplinary matter, yet she has not waited to conduct it confidentially, the counter of a busy shop is just not the right place for such a discussion

- she has made several assumptions rather than seeking information

- her original comment is a statement rather than a question - indeed it is virtually an accusation of theft - 'helping yourself' is an emotive phrase

- as, to most listeners, the accusatory nature of the statement is clear, it is at least arguable that the reputation of the assistant is being impugned

- the facts that would make or break the case have not been checked and it may be that exaggeration has entered the commentary because, if the assistant really is stealing, then she could only have carried this out twice at the time stated so referring to four instances is either incorrect, an exaggeration or indicative that someone else may at least be partly at fault.

Even if the assistant is totally in the wrong and is thieving, the conversation has been so badly handled that the rights and wrongs of the theft have been overshadowed and the structure of the encounter can be used by the assistant to challenge the validity of the conversation.

[2] Being too swift in action or comment tends to result in a response that passes the initiative to the complainant.

[3] The twin mistakes of, first, acting without thought and, second, speaking in a public area has rebounded to the extent that (even though she may be entirely in the right with her accusation) the Manageress could well be faced later with a civil court action.

[4] By proceeding logically, not making assumptions, refraining from making accusations and concentrating on one particular instance where proof is supportive, in this alternative scenario, the Manageress takes, and retains, the initiative.

81

The addict
■ ■ ■

People in employment, indeed people generally, are far more aware of personal rights and what can be called 'personal space'. Nowhere is this more likely to be potentially a problem than when it is necessary to deal with an addict within the working environment. The nature of the addiction - nicotine, alcohol or other drugs - is immaterial because the effects on fellow employees can be considerable. Unfortunately, because the substance is addictive, the person may, despite earnestly wanting to break the habit, find this extremely difficult, if not impossible.

Case study 6.4
ALCOHOL PROBLEMS

An accountant was accustomed to having a liquid lunch at the local pub. A director was concerned at a number of repercussions that had arisen because of this habit and so he had a chat with him.

'Michael, I wanted to have a word with you about your lunchtime

arrangements. I understand that you always have lunch at the local pub - is that right?'

'Sure, I have a few beers and a sandwich down there.'

'How do you get there and how many is a few?'

'I pop down in my car. I suppose I have three or four pints usually. I'm never late back.'

'Yes, I appreciate that you only take the allowed time - I'm not worried about that. What concerns me is that you are driving a company car after a drinking session and that you then start the afternoon's work having had a fair number of drinks.'

'It doesn't impair my work ability.'

'I agree that I haven't noticed any problems with your work, but what does concern me is the attitude of your staff.'

'Why, has someone complained?'

'No one has complained - that's the trouble. I think most of them think its a bit of a joke, although others don't think driving a car after having downed a few pints is any laughing matter and I must say I agree with them.'

82

'Oh, I see.'

'I'm not sure if you do. You see you are a manager and, as such, have a position that should command the respect of your staff. If your actions are such that you are not earning such respect, then your position as a manager is threatened. Indeed, it goes further than that because their respect for management generally lessens because we are seen to be condoning such actions by not taking any action.'

'Oh.'

'In addition, should you need to discipline a member of your staff after lunch, you will do so with your breath smelling of beer, which I would think undermines the authority of that meeting. Your authority is being undermined. Can I suggest that you think about it for a couple of days and we have another chat next Monday?'

Key technique

The director has not taken any disciplinary action, merely conveyed certain facts and views that the accountant is now left to mull over. Obviously he will expect some reaction at the next meeting, but if this comes from the accountant, it is likely to be more effective than any further disciplinary action from the director. Self-judgement and analysis is usually more effective than imposed requirements.

A number of companies have adopted a 'no alcohol' policy and in such cases, the above type of encounter becomes somewhat simpler. The employee could simply be requested to follow the company's rules, emphasising again the advantages of adopting the policy.

7
∎ ∎ ∎

Handling awkward attitudes

Key learning points

1 Mutual respect for one another is essential - assuming that the other party is incapable of rational or original thought will destroy all chances of progress towards the desired result.

2 Persuading somebody that another viewpoint to their own is worthwhile is likely to be more effective, in the long term, than when such a change has been forced.

3 Keeping alternative options in mind gives you some flexibility, which is very useful as you move towards a desired result.

Often problem encounters are caused by attitudes that are expressed without thought for the effect they will have or the reaction that could result. So far, the need for carefully assessing the other party's viewpoint, as well as the desired result, has been continually stressed. Antagonism, leading to the total frustration, in every sense, of the desired result, is often caused by either a deliberate or unconscious lack of comprehension of the other's needs and sensitivities. In *The Water Babies*, Charles Kingsley refers to the 'loveliest fairy in the world . . . Mrs Doasyouwouldbedoneby', inferring that treating other people as you would like to be treated is all important. For those dealing with people, this would appear to be an obvious and basic requirement to guide their actions, yet it is amazing how far from such a golden rule some negotiators can stray.

86

How to patronise and infuriate people
■ ■ ■

As indicated, before, negotiators (and all supervisors and managers for that matter) should neither underestimate intelligence nor overestimate knowledge. Most people are quite capable of understanding the most complicated information so long as it is explained in straightforward language. Failure to credit people with intelligence infuriates them and can lead to unnecessary barriers going up that block the way to a desired result. Jargon can be defined as a refuge for the lazy and the insecure and so should be avoided. Jargon is a refuge for the lazy in that its user cannot be bothered to explain the item in clear language. It is the refuge of the insecure because it can provide a barrier behind which its users can shelter, trying to protect their importance by using words that only the initiated will comprehend.

Managers who assume that their employees are incapable of rational thought, cannot be trusted with responsibility or will be unable to deal with problems or bad news, will be hampered by their own misconceptions if they allow these assumptions to be communicated to their staff. Indeed, such managers are as foolish and inexperienced as the person who always claims to know what his staff are thinking - ignoring the principle that staff are capable of thinking on several levels. Both assumptions are founded on the sometimes baseless view that management know better than their employees and must take all their decisions for them. Such a patronising attitude can sow the seeds of its own downfall.

Case study 7.1
NEVER PATRONISE

At the time of the annual pay review, the Factory Manager and the Accountant had discussed what could be afforded for the 1000 strong workforce and arranged to meet the union representatives to discuss the situation. The meeting, convened in the Factory Manager's office, was opened by the Manager distributing copies of his script, which he then proceeded to read, word-for-word, to the meeting.

'Well there we have the figures that the company can afford. We see no great advantage in endless discussions over the figures and think you should consider them and put them to your members. I'd like us to meet again in a week's time and hope we can get agreement then. Thank you.' [1]

A week later.

'We have considered the offer you made last week. We feel it is unacceptable and cannot recommend it to our members.'

'I see but is it not for your members to decide whether they should accept it or not?' [2]

'No, they delegate decision making to us and we negotiate on their behalf. We have discussed the offer and feel that the increase in rates of pay is insufficient.'

'But it is all the company can afford.'

'Well, we don't accept that that is entirely correct and, in any event, we feel that there is another way this can be dealt with.'

'There can't be another way - we have set out what the company can afford, trade is difficult and your members must accept this. It is up to

us to decide how we can trade.'[3]

'Our members do realise the difficult conditions - they know sales are down, they can see the stockroom and they know there's an over-time ban. They have to manage their weekly budgets in the same way that the company does, but <u>they</u> can't cut margins to try to improve sales as they only have one commodity to offer - so many hours per week.'

'Quite, and the only rate we can afford for those hours is £3.60.'

'We cannot accept that - we believe it should be a minimum of £3.80 per hour.'

'But there is no way we can afford that.'

'There is and we are prepared to put it to our members. [4] If we assume that you can afford £3.60 per hour, that gives a total cost for the workforce per hour of £3600, plus payroll costs. We believe that the rate should be £3.80 and, if you can only afford £3600, that means you need to lose around 50 people out of the workforce of 1000. To get the rate for the job, we are prepared to work with you to find where we can save that number of jobs. We feel we can achieve the same output so you will benefit from added productivity.'

88

'Are you saying you are prepared to put your own members out of work in order to achieve the rate of pay you want?' [5]

Key techniques

[1] The meeting would have been better held in a more neutral place - the Manager's office is not such a place.

Reading aloud a note that has already been distributed is tanta-mount to indicating that it is questionable whether the attendees can read!

Lack of perception of the other side's viewpoint and their need to show purpose (in this case, the need for the union representatives to show that they could gain value by negotiation) is both conceited and a failing.

[2] This is patronising and pointless. The union must be allowed to manage its affairs the way it wants, and challenging this right just aggravates to no purpose.

[3] Approaching the problem with a closed mind, as the Manager is here, may allow the conversation to *proceed*, but ensures that it will not make *progress*. Assuming that there is only *one* solution insults the other party, who may well have ideas of their own.

[4] Because the Manager had no idea about what the other party's viewpoint is, he lost the initiative.

[5] The union negotiators had moved a long way towards achieving their desired result by being very clear about their purpose, bolstered by their research and the facts they have collected. They were helped towards their desired result by the Manager letting them seize the initiative because of his own lack of preparedness and condescending attitude.

Case study 7.2
NEVER ASSUME

There had been a number of pay snatches locally and so the company agreed to a suggestion made by the local police that an armed police officer should be located in the pay office during the two days in which the Christmas and New Year pay, plus Christmas bonus would be paid out.

The concept was 'sold' to the employees, (although it was not discussed with them) on the basis that this would be for their protection as much as their money and 'it was a great idea, wasn't it'. As it certainly seemed a good idea to management, a director was taken aback when one of the staff asked to see him about it.

What's the matter Maureen?'
'Everyone in the pay office is very unhappy about this added protection for the Christmas pay delivery.'
'Why is that - you will be better protected than you are normally.'
'Oh yes, except that if there is a raid, we could all be caught in the crossfire!'

Key technique
Thinking through suggestions and anticipating the responses of the workers, or, better still, obtaining feedback from dialogue with them about it, could have avoided this situation occurring. Being presented with a *fait accompli* irritates many people. Being able to exert some choice over one's own destiny results in far greater rapport.

Making assumptions
■ ■ ■

Much of what employers are required to implement *vis-à-vis* their employees, is actually imposed on them because of various agencies of the state. Although the means by which the state itself tests reactions in advance of legislation is improving, nevertheless, very often companies have no choice *but* to implement it as best they can. In such circumstances, perhaps it is understandable, although certainly not excusable, if they, in turn, say to their employees, 'We don't like it, you may not like it, but we've got to do it anyway'. Attractive though it may be, this kind of shortcut can sometimes turn out to be a rather long diversion, requiring considerable guidance to redirect things back to the correct route.

90

Case study 7.3
SICKNESS PROBLEMS

Since employers were given the responsibility for paying statutory sick pay on behalf of the state, employees have been required to self-certify their first seven days of sickness. The payments made on behalf of the state for such sickness benefits could be recouped from subsequent National Insurance contributions. However, the Department of Social Security made it clear that only if such payments were made to *legitimate* claimants could reimbursement be claimed. Thus, the onus for checking sickness claims was placed on the employers who, in turn, required supervisors to do this. Supervisors were very concerned and their representatives met with the Personnel Director.

'I understand you are unhappy about the new system for recording and paying state sickness that we explained last week.'

'Yes, we are unhappy about signing these new forms stating whether or not the sickness is genuine.'

'I see, why is that?'

'Because we're not doctors and cannot judge sickness accurately. We think their doctors should sign them.'

'Well, let's look at the facts. How long do you think the average person's doctor sees them each year?'

'I don't know, about 10 minutes I should think.'

'OK, let's accept that it is a pretty short length of time compared to the 30 hours or so each week that our supervisors see their staff - so who should know the person better?'

'The supervisor, but we know nothing about illness.'

'Fine, let's leave illness aside for a moment. The supervisor is likely to know the employee much better than the doctor, which is why the state wants us to check the validity of the employees' claims. Now, do you think most supervisors know their staff well enough to suspect when things aren't quite right?'

'Most of the time, but not necessarily when it comes to illness.'

'OK, so we are agreed that supervisors do tend to know their staff fairly well and an experienced supervisor will often know when an employee is lying.'

'Oh yes, that's part of the job.'

'Quite and, really, that's all these new forms ask of you - as supervisors, not as medical practitioners. They simply ask you to confirm whether or not you think that the explanation given as to the reason for absence is fair or not.'

'But we don't know if the sickness is genuine.'

'Quite and no one is asking supervisors to comment on this. Everyone knows there are malingerers. You may not be able to prove it, but, if an explanation seems unsatisfactory to you, then you simply say so on the form. The onus is then on the employee to prove that the absence, in fact, was genuine.'

'But we're being put in an awkward position.'

'I can see your point, but I am not sure I agree - you are being asked to supervise your employees, nothing more. You are asking for an explanation for the absence as you have a perfect right as a supervisor to do. All the State is asking is for you to confirm whether or not you feel that the explanation is reasonable or not. Obviously, if you don't sign the form, someone else has to, which could undermine your authority - something you are often, quite rightly, concerned about.'

Key technique

Despite being in a difficult position, the Personnel Director has sought to explain what is being required, using logic and patience and reminding the representatives of the basics of their responsibilities. It should be mentioned, however, that sometimes such a patient, logical approach can actually irritate the other party, so the approach needs to be tempered by the situation.

Persuasion is better than force
■ ■ ■

Because the advantages of a particular course of action seem crystal clear to one person, or to one layer of management, this does not necessarily mean that it will be acceptable to another party, to those lower down the chain of command or at the sharp end. Dealing with a problem encounter by pulling rank, may simplify the decision process, but it will definitely complicate the implementation.

Case study 7.4
FORCING THE ISSUE - AND LOSING

Some shops were having considerable difficulties - sales of traditional products were at a standstill yet costs were rising. The Chairman therefore decided that the shops should start selling biscuits as an additional line. He summoned a meeting of the managers.

'Now you all know our problems - static sales, rising costs, lower profits. We can't afford to stand idly by and watch our business go down the drain, so I have decided that you are going to start selling cakes and biscuits.' [1]

'We did that ten years ago, and it didn't work.'

'It'll never work, people don't expect us to sell cakes and we'll never get them to learn that we do.'

'We haven't got the space to display the products.'

Key techniques

[1] As the Chairman has already made the decision, there seems little point in holding the meeting - the decision could have been communicated by memo. Convening a 'meeting' raises expectations that various views will at least be listened to and respected. Raising expectations only for them to be disappointed is worse than not raising them in the first place.

[2] To counter the negative reaction, the Chairman insisted that his decision be carried out and was subsequently dismayed to find that few shops were displaying the new products. Because the views of the managers responsible for the shops had not been converted

positively to the Chairman's idea, they had had a decision foisted on them, they had individually decided that the new idea was not going to work and so ensured that it did not.

An alternative, much more successful scenario could have gone like this.

■ the Chairman could have seen each manager during previous shop visits and finding a shop with spare space, chatted about filling it with an additional range so that, almost spontaneously, the concept of selling cakes and biscuits could have been developed, each manager, to some extent, feeling that it was their own idea, thus gaining their genuine commitment to the idea

■ the Chairman could have asked for suggestions for new product ranges (which almost certainly would have then included the cakes and biscuits concept) and invited the managers to choose perhaps two with which to experiment

■ the Chairman could have offered some sort of bonus or other incentive for the manager who achieved the best results in each area and/or all areas

■ the Chairman could have allowed himself apparently to be talked out of the idea, but then invited the managers to make alternative suggestions to halt the down sliding of profit figures of the shops and if no alternatives were suggested, this would strengthen the case for trying his idea.

Applying power rather than persuasion may work on occasion but it seldom works as effectively as self-generated commitment.

Assumptions may backfire
■ ■ ■

My first boss's retort to my answer 'I assumed . . .', was 'you're not paid to assume - find out!' This is a good guideline as all too often what we assume or take for granted turns out to be false or at least misleading. While such assumptions can be excused in a new recruit, experience shows that management is not immune from making just such a mistake, although, needless to say it should be guarded against.

Case study 7.5
EMPLOYMENT IS NOT OWNERSHIP OF PEOPLE

A company had been taken over and the management of the acquiring company had visited the factory, but, apart from nodding 'hello' to the various managers, the new Managing Director had not introduced himself or asked that the managers be introduced to him. The Group Personnel Manager found that many of his responsibilities had been removed and passed to the Personnel function (the wife of the Managing Director of the new group holding company). So he sought and found an alternative position and handed in his resignation to the Managing Director, who was horrified or at least said he was.

94

'Why are you leaving?'
'Because I have been offered a better job.' [1]
'But why - you have a future here?'
'What future?'
'You are the only qualified personnel executive in the group - the group needs your expertise.'
'I was not aware it needed any such thing - this is the first conversation we have had since the takeover.'
'But surely you realised that we would want you to stay and oversee the function.'
'No I didn't and, if that is the case, it is the first time it has ever been indicated, indeed, the reverse seemed to be the case as much of my former responsibilities have been passed to your head office departments.'
'But I would like you to stay on.'
'I'm sorry, but I have agreed to join my new company as soon as you will release me.'
'We will hold you to your contract.'
'I have given you the notice required by my contract. I was hoping to be able to leave earlier, but, if you insist, obviously I shall honour the contract - although I must point out that my workload has dropped considerably so you are hardly getting value for money.'
'Are you sure there is nothing we can offer you to change your mind?' [2]

Key techniques

[1]   It is essential that the answers to the questions should provide information to take the discussion forwards. In this case, the question is imprecise, inadequate and inconclusive. In addition, as it seems that the company might want the leaver to remain, a foundation for the deal offered later should have been laid here by the Managing Director indicating regret at the decision.

[2]   Given that the company does want to try to strike a deal, a far more positive manner was called for from the outset, for example:

'Hi Bob, come and have a chat. I've just heard you want to leave us. I'm horrified and wonder if there is anything we can do to get you to change your mind?'

Insults fail to win favours

■ ■ ■

While irritating occurrences may be unplanned and unhelpful to the point of being unacceptable, very often an instant intemperate reaction may be the last way of achieving the desired outcome. Once again, taking time to calm down and to think things through may be the best way in which to achieve that outcome.

Case study 7.6
HOW NOT TO WIN FRIENDS . . .

At short notice an agency had arranged to supply a client with a named temporary employee on a specified date, which the client then tried to bring forward. On learning that the employee was not available until the original date, the client decided to withdraw her offer. In taking this decision she became liable for a small administration charge, which was deducted from the return fee. Her husband telephoned the agency and had the following conversation.

'As you've been unable to supply this person we need, I want the whole of our fee back.'

  'As I explained to your wife, the fee, less our normal administration charge has been sent to you.'

'That's not good enough, your service is appalling, you've been unable to supply this person, you've taken our money under false pretences and I want it <u>all</u> back.'

'I'm sorry, I do not accept any of that. We have your wife's written acceptance of our terms and it was she who changed her requirements after registration. The young lady cannot start until the original date, two weeks after the date your wife now specifies. We offered to find someone else in the time available but your wife said that this was not acceptable and opted for the return of her fee.'

'I think that's a disgraceful way to run a business. You've supplied poor-quality temporary staff in the past and now you're charging us for doing nothing.'

'I don't think that is the case - the previous arrangements were satisfactory, as your wife has indicated on each occasion. This time we carried out a great deal of work and, additionally, tried to help at short notice to satisfy changes indicated by your wife. We were still prepared to find an alternative, but this was not acceptable to her.'

'Hmmm, well, I'll tell you what, let's start again. Can you take the refund back and try to find us an alternative employee?'

'No, bearing in mind the comments you have just made, I'm not prepared to do that.'

Key technique

The desired result sought by the client's husband was a favour from the agency, even though it had acted strictly in accordance with its terms, to which his wife had previously signed her agreement. Starting the conversation by complaining and then insulting the agency is unlikely to make the agency want to do him a favour.

Sharp aggression
■ ■ ■

The ultimate trial of tough talking can occur when the real aggression surfaces during an interview and when it is least expected. Instinctive reactions may then be the best way in which to attempt to deal with the situation.

Case study 7.7
MAKING THE POINT

The Personnel Manager was carrying out a disciplinary interview with an employee whose attitude was not really conducive to the interview making any real progress.

'You do realise that the whole problem with your supervisor comes down to his complaint that your attitude is negative.'
    'So?'
    'And your answer to that question illustrates the point we are trying to make. We are here trying to help you settle down and become a useful employee - is that what you want?'
    'Dunno.'
    'Then I suggest you need to decide whether you want to work here or not because if you don't, we are all wasting our time. We have other employees and would prefer to spend time helping them.'
    'I'm not stopping you.'
    'But you are stopping some of these other employees settling down, getting on with their jobs and earning their pay. The supervisor is spending so much time trying to help you, he has not got time to spend on them. You're not stupid, you're mature and its time you sorted yourself out.'

97

Drawing a six-inch long knife from his trousers, the employee said threateningly:

'Are you telling me you are going to sort me out?'
    'Don't be so bloody silly - put that knife away before someone gets hurt and you land yourself in <u>real</u> trouble. I've just said that you are not stupid but you go and do a stupid thing like that. Waving that around will get you nowhere apart from in prison. We want to help you, otherwise we would not be spending time trying to find out what's wrong.'

Key technique
The casual dismissal of what was a real threat came instinctively from the Personnel Manager and was generated by his irritation at the lack of progress and the employee's stupidity. Presumably the genuine irritation that came across in the spontaneous answer was one reason the employee did as he was requested (fortunately!).

8

. . .

Customer care –
firm but fair

Key learning points

1 Reacting defensively or dismissing customers' complaints does not answer their complaints, it simply loses customers.

2 Terms form the basis of the contract between the two parties and should not be casually dismissed.

3 Positive customer care policies, seeking to retain customers, are not only more cost-effective than sourcing new customers, but also enhance the reputation of the organisation.

Case study 8.1
3000 SALES REPRESENTATIVES

In endeavouring to motivate employees to improve productivity, and reduce inefficiency and waste, the Director made two related suggestions. First, that all 3000 employees think of themselves as salespeople - even if they never saw a customer, in order to encourage an awareness that all attempts in this direction ultimately lead to sales. Second, that all employees realised that it was the company's customers who generate everyone's pay and only if the company satisfied its customers would it be possible for pay and continued employment to be provided.

Analysis of production subsequent to this policy being adopted revealed that returns fell from 10 per cent to 4 per cent, while a survey of customer satisfaction showed a corresponding rise.

Key technique
Involving staff in this way aids both the perception of the problem by those targeted and the ultimate accomplishment of the plan.

Unfortunately, the fact that employees' pay is totally dependent on customer satisfaction is often overlooked and may even be countermanded by defensive reactions to legitimate customer queries or complaints. This sort of attitude towards customer queries is widespread in the UK and is quite the opposite of reactions on the Continent and in the USA. This does not mean, like the saying, that the customer is always right - sometimes their complaints are unjustified and unreasonable and must be resisted. Very often, however, their comments are cast aside in a totally unreasonable way. Regardless of the correctness or otherwise of the complaint, the person dealing with the situation needs to be tactful and diplomatic and, as we have seen from other encounters earlier, it is also important to have all the facts immediately to hand.

Case study 8.2
THE CUSTOMER IS WRONG

This was the second order placed by this particular customer. The first had been a somewhat rushed order for Christmas gifts and this second one was in response to a discount flyer the company had produced to try and generate trade in the low demand part of the year. Following its standard practice, the company had produced and invoiced 10 per cent more than the number of items actually ordered. The customer telephoned to query this.

'I am very surprised to see that the order, which I requested for delivery by 1st April, was delivered late without any apology and, in addition, you have supplied and charged me for 10 per cent overs.'

'That is in accordance with our standard conditions of trade shown in our catalogue - I'll send you a copy.' [1]

After receiving the catalogue, the customer telephoned again.

'I queried your charging for the overs on my second order and the late delivery and you have sent me your catalogue. However, I would point out that your discount flyer makes no reference to any such conditions. In addition, you have ignored the fact that the order was delivered late. Also, in reading through the catalogue, I have realised that you overcharged my first order last Christmas as you charged for overprinting, which is not referred to for the goods I ordered.' [2]

The matter was passed to a director.

'We are sorry to hear you are unhappy with the company [3a], our offer sheet was rushed out and we overlooked the requirement to refer to our terms, we will be mindful of this in future to avoid any such chances of misunderstandings [3b]. We enclose a credit note for the cost of the overs. Do accept our unequivocal apologies for the late delivery, which, under any circumstances, should not have occurred [3c]. You are correct in identifying a discrepancy in our catalogue. Unfortunately this was noticed after the printing had been completed, but it was felt that our customers would appreciate that, even though it does not state this, the additional charge would apply [3d]. We feel it is unreasonable of you to stress this point [3e]. We hope that with this explanation you will feel more sympathetic towards us and the efforts we make on behalf of our customers.' [3f]

'I note all that and accept that mistakes do happen, but when they do, the correct course of action is for the company to accept res-

ponsibility, not to try to evade it.'

'But there was no deliberate attempt to mislead you - yours is the only query that has been raised regarding the charge for overprinting - and we feel it is unreasonable. We would appreciate it if you would settle your account.' [4] and [5]

Key techniques

[1] Treating a genuine customer query in this dismissive way, as well as ignoring one of the points raised, merely stores up trouble for the future.

[2] The irritation caused by the dismissive approach is the direct cause of the customer investigating further. The company must either try to justify the three matters or to negotiate (rather than impose) a way out of it.

[3] This dismissive response seeks refuge from the facts in unnecessary and totally 'flowery' wording, the effect of which is merely irritating. Plain language without jargon, flattery or 'flowery' phrases is preferable and more effective. In addition the comments slide round the facts - the customer had a genuine grievance that, despite all the words, has not actually been answered. She was not unhappy with the company (3a), but is unhappy with its unprofessional service, particularly as she is being forced to waste time trying to sort out its mistakes. This makes the last comment (3f) totally illogical. As it is the customer who has suffered, why should the company (3e) expect sympathy? By its own admissions (3b, c and d), the company is in the wrong in each case.

[4] This is a response that could work, although there is considerable risk of it coming unstuck. No one has said that the mistake was deliberate, while reasonableness is an opinion the two parties are unlikely to share. Whether the customer believes that hers was the only query or not is irrelevant - it is a *real* query and a *real* overcharge to her, and arises from the contract between her and the company. However, the onus is now with the customer regarding the settling of the account. If she fails to settle even in part, the company could take legal action to recover the amount, with all the attendant inconvenience and costs (which in the circumstances it is unlikely to recover), but it does leave the customer the option of deducting the disputed amount from the account when settling it, which would then place the onus for further action on the company.

On the other hand, the customer, because the order was delivered late, could insist that the company take the whole order back, which is the last thing the company would want.

[5] The company has failed to appreciate its goal and lost sight of the desired result. The result should have been a satisfied customer after raising a legitimate matter of concern, avoiding a returned and wasted order. A more positive approach initially would have saved a minor annoyance turning into a legal dispute.

Postcript: The customer was bemused to find exactly the same wording appearing in the company's new catalogue the following year and reported the matter to the Trading Standards office.

Pride comes before conciliation

■ ■ ■

103

Very often it seems that pride in a certain view (indefensible though it may be) can actually prevent more positive, conciliatory reactions occurring. Pride certainly seems to create a kind of blockage that stops a person seeing things as they are so that they end up trying to argue their way out of a situation when they are, in fact, wrong. Also, they do not see that the time would be better spent moving the things forwards rather than covering up past mistakes. This inevitably leads to confrontational situations where the conversation takes a destructive turn when it could otherwise be far more constructive. It can take many years to build a good reputation yet only a few minutes disputing the indisputable with the wrong person can mean that this is lost.

How best to deal with customer complaints

■ ■ ■

It is clear from all this that people who have to deal with customers need to be trained properly. The following guidelines briefly set out best practice for customer complaint encounters.

1 Discover the relevant facts - customer, order, payment record and so on.

2 Listen carefully to the complaint, noting all relevant information.

3 Check any facts volunteered or disputed by the customer.

4 Be courteous at all times.

5 Only if the complaint is straightforward should you attempt to suggest a solution.

6 In non-straightforward cases, thank the customer for bringing the matter to the company's attention, apologise for any inconvenience and say that you will find out what can be done.

7 Set a time limit by which the customer will receive an answer or further contact (and ensure that you do in fact stick to it or explain why if more time is needed).

8 Investigate the complaint and be objective about the validity of the customer's case. Think about what options there are to solve the problem and have a fall back option in case the customer refuses to accept the first suggestion.

9 Consider any precedent that might be created because of your choice of settlement and weigh up the pros and cons of the solution with regard to any possible publicity (although it is often said that there is no such thing as bad publicity, this is not true for cases where poor or faulty products are exposed or the safety of the consumer is risked).

10 Try to conclude the dispute harmoniously, so that the reputation of the company is enhanced rather than damaged.

Discretion within pre-set limits should be granted to those dealing with customer complaints so that minor grievances can be settled swiftly. In Case Study 8.2, the amounts in question were £4 for the oversupply and £50 for the unauthorised overprinting cost. Had the person the customer spoke to first suggested an immediate credit of, say, £15 for both the oversupply and the fact that the order was late, the dispute over the £50 might never have arisen. This said, a junior or untrained member of staff handling such a situation for the first time should not be left to cope alone should the dispute develop into a more difficult situation. This applies whether the organisation is responding to or initiating the negotiation.

Drawing the sting

It should not be forgotten that often the simple fact that someone has taken the trouble to listen to and make a note of the complaint may be sufficient to 'draw the sting' from the complaint. Thus, without doing anything more the problem has already been reduced from the original burning issue to a more minor irritation. The reverse is also true, that refusing to accept the terms of the complaint at all only serves to inflame what may already be a contentious issue.

Case study 8.3
LISTENING IMPROVES QUALITY

There had been a number of complaints regarding the quality and choice of the food available in the staff restaurant over a number of years. The new Personnel Manager had become aware of these and had invited two people who have made most complaints to come and see her to discuss the matter.

'I understand that you are very concerned about the restaurant.'
'You bet we are - we've been on about the quality and poor choice for ages but no one seems to take any notice and nothing gets done.'
'I see. Well, I'm new so, if you can bear repeating all the problems, I will certainly consider them and see if we can do something about at least some of your complaints. I must first say that I, too, am very con-

cerned about the restaurant because its finances are in my budget and we do not seem to be getting value for the money we are investing.'

The complaining employees then outlined the main causes of their concerns during a fairly long meeting and, in turn, the Personnel Manager set out the financial problems the company was experiencing. It was agreed that a Catering Committee should be set up to consider ways and means of improving the situation. Before it convened for the first time (and before any action had been taken regarding the complaints), one of the complainants sought out the Personnel Manager to thank her for the improvements that have already been put into operation.

Key technique

Listening constructively to complaints rather than dismissing them out of hand creates a situation where it seems to the employees that improvements have already been put in place whereas, in fact, nothing has yet been done! Subsequently, considerable improvements were made and a regular process of price increases was introduced in order to bring the subsidy back under control. Even though this raised the costs to the employees, because the initiative had been seized and those affected were involved, the policy of reducing the subsidy was accepted without murmur. The fact that improvements were introduced as promised obviously helped this policy to be accepted.

Creating barriers

In Case Study 8.3 the rationale was to listen, learn and involve in order to create a climate in which change could take place. Both sides had concerns and, by exchanging and discussing these, a reasonable compromise was reached. Had the Personnel Manager dismissed the employees' complaints, as had her predecessor, and concentrated instead on the need to reduce the subsidy (presumably by increasing prices alone) it is likely that there would have been a considerable backlash. Forcing matters through without preparing the ground first will almost inevitably create resentment, which can be so severe as to defeat the intent.

Case study 8.4
GETTING THE TERMS RIGHT

Having advertised regularly in a magazine for some years, an agency was advised that the owners of the magazine had changed. Subsequently, during the UK recession, the agency decided to suspend advertising for two issues and received the following phone call in reply to its letter informing the magazine of this intention.

'We note that you wish to suspend your advertising. As you are cancelling your advertisement, I must advise you that there will be a cancellation charge and, in addition, you will be required to repay your series discount.' [1]

'But we have never agreed any terms with your company.'

'Yes you have - the terms state that late cancellation incurs a 25 per cent charge and cancellation of a series means that the series discount has to be repaid.'

'I am sorry but I must disagree - you are referring, incorrectly, to the terms issued by your predecessors. No terms have been issued by your company.'

'For the pittance of commission I am paid, I am not going to provide new terms for the one instance where an absence of goodwill leads to this kind of problem.' [2]

'That is completely irrelevant. Normally this would be a question of contractual commitments, but in this case there is no formal contract. However, leaving this aside, even if we accept your predecessor's terms, they do not set out the charges as you have indicated. Only if there is late cancellation is there a charge and, although we would understandably lose the series discount, those terms do not indicate that the customer must repay the discount that was given earlier.'

'You have cancelled late.'

'I am sorry, but I cannot accept that - we told you of our decision more than six weeks before publication date.'

'We need to know six weeks before copy date.'

'But that is not what your predecessor's terms state - they refer to six weeks before publication date. I gave you notice over three months before one publication date and over six months before the other.'

'Well, we rely on the goodwill of our customers and I don't accept this kind of close analysis of terms.'

'But the terms govern the contract and, besides, it is your analysis of these terms that has led to this discussion. The analysis was totally incorrect, hence our querying it. I repeat that we gave several months' *notice of suspension of our advert, having advertised every quarter in your magazine for several years. As a customer of long standing I feel we are entitled to better consideration than that evidenced by this conversation.' [3]*

Key techniques

[1] This is not the best way to talk with a long-term advertiser and customer.

[2] Anger and frustration may be understandable, but it does not solve the problem - it makes the situation worse. Seeking to obtain sympathy as a technique is curious, but is surprisingly widespread. It is rarely effective.

[3] If debating or relying on terms then, first, it is essential that you completely understand what they mean, second, that the terms are actually applicable in this case and, third, that they are quoted correctly. Losing one's temper, for whatever reason, will almost certainly result in losing the argument. It is far better if 'caught on the hop' to say, 'Sorry, there seems to have been some misunderstanding here, I will look into this further and come back to you.'

Customer injury

The above examples show the kinds of difficulties that can occur regarding contracts. The situation becomes even more complicated when injury has been caused to a customer. The company's keenness to maintain its good name and be seen to be doing the right thing can clash with what its public liability insurers feel it is best to do, which will be that nothing be done or said to indicate an acceptance of liability as this could mean that they will not be able to avoid liability. In such cases, the company needs to clear with its insurers what can be done and said as, almost inevitably, there will be public pressure, perceived or real, for it to take some action and as soon as possible.

Case study 8.5
THE LIABILITY PROBLEM

An elderly lady tripped over a delivery box left in an aisle in a shop and broke her wrist. The shop had a high profile locally and was concerned to be seen to be acting in the best possible way, although they were aware of the interest of their Public Liability insurers. Accordingly, they sent a bouquet of flowers and chocolates from the shop staff (rather than from the company that owned the shop) with a note wishing her a speedy recovery. The shop's Manageress checked regularly with the lady's family as to her progress. In every contact with them, very neutral language was used.

Key technique
The conflicting interests of the shop's high public profile and genuine concern for an injured customer and its insurer's aversion to any admission of liability must be considered and reconciled.

Obviously in this instance no interview took place - and, in fact, no action was ever taken as the lady made a good recovery and she and her family were very appreciative of the sincere interest and good wishes of the shop's staff.

Inevitably, some accidents do not result in such amicable situations and, despite its sincere wishes, the company may have its hands tied because of its potential liability in dealing with the matter. Those who may be involved in dealing with such complainants must be aware of this dimension.

Case study 8.6
SAFETY FIRST

A toy chain sold a considerable number of 'pocket money toys' - small value items that children could buy with their own money. Included in the range were scissors suitable for small children, which were described as 'safety scissors'. A customer called in at the company's Head Office with a complaint regarding the scissors. He was seen by the Company Secretary who having been alerted by the shop to which the customer had gone in order to find the name and address of the

Head Office realised that there might potentially be a problem.

'Hello Mr Robinson. Thank you for coming to see us - it is always nice to see our customers, even when the reason for them coming is a complaint or query. Now, what's the problem?'

'It's these scissors your Croydon shop are selling - my son has cut his mouth on them.'

'Oh, I'm sorry to hear that. What's his name and how old is he?'

'Peter and he was two last week.'

'Is it a bad cut - did it need stitches?'

'Well no, but it drew blood and he was upset for a couple of hours.'

'I hope he is better now . . . [1] . . . how did he get hold of the scissors?'

'They were one of his birthday presents we bought from your shop.'

'I would have thought two was a little young to be playing with scissors, surely children of that age tend to put everything in their mouths don't they, I know mine do?' [2]

110

'But the packaging states that they are safety scissors, so we thought they were safe.' [3]

'Well the description "safety" refers to the fact that the blades them-selves have no points and both blades, except the cutting edges, which are blunt of course, are covered in plastic. As I am sure you know, unlike knives, the blades of most scissors are actually fairly blunt.'

'How can scissors be blunt - they cut?'

'They actually cut only because of the scissor movement of the two blades - one against the other. With these scissors, the manufacturers protect everything else but obviously cannot stop the scissor move-ment, otherwise they would not be scissors at all. We call them safety scissors in the same way that the manufacturers of safety pins name their pins safety pins. Safety pins are actually very much sharper than our scissors. The "safety" description refers to the fact that the sharp point of the pin is protected from the user - particularly small children and babies. Despite its name, the safety pin is sharp - indeed, far sharper than any part of Peter's scissors. Obviously, despite the pro-tection that is part of the safety pin, you would never give one to your child to play with would you?' [4]

'But surely you should put on your packaging that they should not be given to young children.'

'We sell several thousand of these scissors each year and this is the first time we have heard of a child cutting himself with them. Obviously, if there is anything we can do to avoid even this single occurrence, we

*want to examine it. I must say that we appreciate your coming here and
telling us of this incident and hope that Peter has now fully recovered.
What we would like to do is offer to reimburse your expenses for coming here and to give you these sweets, which Peter can definitely put
in his mouth, and we hope he enjoys them.' [5]*

Key techniques

[1] As a result of a deliberate effort, the tone of the conversation is
friendly and the attitude is positive. The customer has been made
welcome and concern has been expressed at the injury, although
no indication of acceptance of liability has been given. Using the
name of the child personalises the conversation.

[2] Using a rhetorical question invites the father to agree with the
statement, even though it contains an implied criticism of Peter's
family's actions. Including a reference to the Secretary's own children creates an opportunity for rapport through shared experiences
and makes it clear that the ways of children and the need to protect
them are known and appreciated first hand.

111

[3] This is awkward - the double-edged question. Accepting that the
ages should be on the packaging could be taken as an admission of
liability, while dismissing it, would undermine the view of the company as a responsible and sensible retailer that is sought. Care is
needed in dealing with such questions or comments and here much
of the real point is ignored.

[4] Using another rhetorical question progresses the discussion,
while the allegation that the scissors cannot be safe has been covered by the reference to a far more widely known product also used
in connection with children. Such innovative thinking is very valuable in these circumstances and demands pre-interview consideration.

[5] Without appearing too pushy, the Secretary seeks to conclude
the interview. Mr Robinson has a complaint, but the company has a
reasonable defence. Offering reimbursement of expenses and a
small gift should settle the matter. Obviously if it does not, then the
company, mindful of its Products Liability insurers, requirements,
may have to withdraw from further discussion and leave it to the
insurers. Dealing with the matter by interview (rather than by writing)
may actually benefit the company and its insurers as there is no
written record of what happened.

Customers as owners

The increase in the number of private shareholders, particularly as a result of the large privatisation issues, means that there are now a considerable number of consumers who are also shareholders (a point that is further addressed in Chapter 10). As shareholders, they are able to attend the public meetings of companies and can raise questions at these meetings - at which the press are invariably present. While such meetings are not intended to allow shareholders/customers to vent their spleen regarding poor customer relations, nevertheless, they do provide a forum for the public airing of such items and, with the press present, can be the means by which publicity is obtained for a pet gripe.

Case study 8.7
WASHING DIRTY LINEN

Even Marks and Spencer, the UK's premier high street retailer, has fallen foul of public embarrassment at an Annual General Meeting. At its 1990 AGM, a questioner wanted to know why it was impossible to buy swimwear at one of the chain's seaside resort shops. The answer was that, by a mistake, the branch had been left off the computerised stock allocation system - a mistake that had by then been rectified. Because of the company's high profile, several national newspapers immediately featured the story prominently.

Key technique
Mistakes do happen so there is little point trying to justify them. Ready acceptance and admission, followed by speedy restitution or recompense (where appropriate) is both positive and likely to be appreciated.

No great damage was done to Marks and Spencer as a result of such publicity - indeed, by its good-humoured handling of the question, it is arguable that the company's reputation for quality was enhanced. However, the case demonstrates how easy it is for publicity to be given to straightforward mistakes. Imagine how much more attractive to journalists are stories of poor or questionable service, products or customer care. Accordingly, those trained to deal with customers and complaints need to be briefed as to the potential for adverse publicity arising from their actions in this area and to be mindful of the ever-increasing legal and consumer protection elements. Both as customers and shareholders, individuals are far more aware of their rights and far more prepared to exercise these rights. Also the move towards commitment to 'charters', setting out obligations and rights can only increase such awareness. Some, however, still seek to gain publicity for their case, virtually regardless of its merits. While precedents need to be borne in mind, a more positive approach to solving problems and making amends as soon as possible is desirable. After all, the purpose of the business is to satisfy its customers, as an unsatisfied customer is unlikely to be a repeat customer. One of the obvious lessons of the recession is that customers may be difficult to retain and it is certainly easier to obtain repeat sales from a customer who has been satisfied in the past than it is to generate new customers.

113

9

. . .

Empowering suppliers for added value

Key learning points

1 Working in partnership with suppliers can help reduce costs and problems, which will in turn reduce the incidence of problem encounters.

2 Quality as much as price can cause problem encounters and so the ways in which these problems are resolved must itself be of good quality.

3 Trade and terms of trade tend to be cyclical - hard bargaining on one occasion may rebound later, whereas a reasonable compromise may be a sound investment in terms of future negotiations.

4 Being objective and truthful in dealing with suppliers is better than being subjective and/or subjecting them to unsubstantiated hype.

Although some companies continue to regard their suppliers rather like a necessary evil, albeit a very useful source of working capital, increasingly the bigger, more forward-looking ones, realising that there is an essential need for partnership between the suppliers and themselves, are developing a different approach. This entails working *with* the supplier to develop a very real and ongoing partnership that recognises the joint interests of the two parties and seeks to move both the relationship and their trade forwards.

This is not simply a question of achieving a better working relationship in order to avoid problem encounters and the need for tough talking, but goes further than that to explore better (and more economic) ways of bringing raw materials and so on, into the production process for mutual benefit. The phrase 'the easiest way to make more money . . . is to stop losing it' is apposite here, as the following illustration of the relationship between costs and profit indicates.

For a company making a 10 per cent profit on sales:

- reducing its costs by £1 saves it needing to generate £10 in sales
- reducing costs by 10 per cent without impairing sales will add 90 per cent to the bottom line profit
- increasing sales by 10 per cent and reducing costs by 10 per cent will result in a tripling of profits
- reducing costs may also enable selling prices to be lowered, increasing demand and still further increasing profits.

Obviously reducing the incidence of problem encounters will also help to lower costs and reap other benefits. Such cost reductions can also be achieved by striking individual deals and sourcing one-off alternative suppliers. However, negotiating with them may not be as cost effective as developing ongoing relationships and jointly improving the quality and cost of the items to mutual benefit.

Joint interests

■ ■ ■

For both suppliers and purchasers to have a real interest in continuing the relationship - suppliers as a means of continuing demand for their products; purchasers as a means of satisfying their demand for raw materials, services or finished goods - there must be ongoing and constructive dialogue, as well as a consensus in relation to the terms of trade, regarding price, quality, reliability, delivery and so on. This is not something that happens automatically or can be achieved instantly; it requires a state of mutual trust and respect that almost inevitably takes time to create. Further, such relationships can only exist if *both* parties feel that they are getting something out of the deal and if the various positive factors that bind them together are maintained or only varied with mutual agreement. Inevitably where such circumstances do not exist, relationships often break down and conflicts occur.

Case study 9.1
REDUCING THE QUALITY

The Director of a manufacturing company had traced current production problems to raw materials. Having eliminated three of the four constituent materials from the enquiry as not guilty, the investigation had been narrowed to one remaining item. Detailed analysis of this item revealed that the actual strength was below that required in the specification. The Director requested that the supplier's representative call.

'Thank you for calling by. We have had considerable trouble with production and have had to carry out detailed analysis of the raw materials we use in our product. As a result of that analysis it seems that the strength of product supplied by your latest two batches is 10 per cent less than that laid down in our specification.'

'Oh, I don't think that can be right.' [1]

'Well, I can assure you it is right according to our laboratory. We have analysed everything in the production process and the analysis of your product shows 10 per cent less strength. When we replicated the production process with everything else the same, but using some of your product surplus from an earlier batch, our production output was up to par, which it is not with the current batch.'

'Are you sure the tests are correct?'

'Of course we are and I need input from your production people immediately. Our production is being severely impacted, we are having to use extra amounts of your product, plus an additional stabilising compound in order to achieve acceptable output. This is expensive and we are preparing a claim for compensation.'

'Well, we cannot be held liable for that.' [2]

Key techniques

[1] Don't make this first mistake. The representative calls into question the efficiency of the manufacturer's analysis, while he cannot be certain that his own manufacturing unit have not let him down. It would have been preferable for his first reaction to have been to soothe the customer and promise to check the matter urgently.

[2] Avoid these further mistakes. In questioning the tests again and seeking to evade liability rather than keeping his company's position neutral until he has checked, he may be starting to destroy the supplier-customer rapport. The facts have been stated and constructive input - so far lacking - has been requested.

Avoiding confrontation
■ ■ ■

The initial reaction of some might be to criticise the attitude of the Director in Case Study 9.1, preferring that the representative (and thus the supplier) be treated far more strictly for their actions. The problem with attempting to do this in the initial stages is that it can very quickly reduce the discussion to a heated argument or even a full-blown row, that does not get anyone anywhere. What, though, is the Director's desired result? There must be several of these - some of which will involve the supplier and some of which may not, including:

■ resumption of supplies from the representative's company of the full-strength product to allow a return to output at budgeted costs to be achieved, as quickly as possible

■ recompense for the costs incurred

■ ongoing commitment from the supplier to provide the required raw material as specified and to be more positive in their dealings with the manufacturer.

Attaining either of the first two desired results calls for goodwill on the part of the supplier, which will not result from a row. The calm building of a case, without emotive reactions, will help both parties to avoid making instinctive negative reactions and form the basis for a later equitable claim. The third desired result is ongoing supply on terms (in the widest sense of the word) acceptable to the manufacturer - whether this be from the existing supplier or from another will depend very much on the type of response the supplier gives regarding the first two aims. If the supplier reacts constructively, offers a commitment to making amends and ensuring that there is no repetition of the failing, a continuing relationship may be possible. Even so, the manufacturer might understandably want some assurances from someone at a senior level in the supplier company.

Case study 9.2
THE SAGA CONTINUES

The representative reported back to his boss - the Director of the supplier company.

'You told him what?'

'I said I didn't think their quality problems were anything to do with our raw materials.'

'But they are one of our oldest and biggest customers - you should have either asked to call me from their offices to check the position or *noted as many details of the problem as possible, then returned here to discover our side of the story. Then you could have reported back with the benefit of our input.'*

'But that would have been admitting that it was our fault.'

'Not necessarily. It is more likely that it would have been seen simply as an attempt to gather together all the facts. It would certainly have been better than telling them they don't know what they are talking about. Anyway the responsibility, if not the problem, is our fault - we have reduced the strength.'

'When?'

'About a fortnight ago - and you were briefed on this fact at the sales conference last month. You should have anticipated this problem as we did highlight it then. We don't run those technical sessions for fun, they are to tell you representatives in the field that there are potential problems here. Next time there's a session I want to see you making notes.'

'But I'm no technical expert.'

120

'Quite and, if so, how could you say to the purchaser that their tests were wrong and that the fault did not lie with our product? What you should have referred to was our note to all customers that went out in February, advising them of the change of strength. You need to concentrate far more on the job - selling our products is not like selling pegs you know.'

Key technique

Here the Director uses what was originally a discussion about a customer's problem as a disciplinary session. There seems no doubt that had the representative paid closer attention to the briefing, his response to the customer might have been positive rather than dismissive. Keeping the matter low key at this stage means that the Director has retained sufficient flexibility to be able to return to it later, even though he has already administered a verbal warning.

Marshalling the facts

■ ■ ■

The problem the suppliers' Director has is not that the product's strength has been lowered but that the Director of the manufacturing company seems to have missed the earlier advice circulated regarding this point. The next contact with him may need to be handled tactfully, particularly as the company concerned is one of his company's biggest customers.

Case study 9.3
THE NEXT STEP

'John, it's Bill from Chemsupply. I understand you have a problem with your product that you feel is attributable to the strength of our No. 2 powder.'

'Yes, it doesn't match the specification and we've had to add extra materials in order to meet the quality standards we need. We've checked everything out and it does seem that the latest batch of your powder is under strength, but your representative denies its anything to do with you. I am pretty annoyed about both the problem and his attitude I don't mind telling you.'

'I'm very sorry about that. I have had a word with him and he realises he did not handle the problem too well. [1] The output problem is related to our powder, but we would have thought you would have realised this straight away.'

'I'm not sure I follow you - why should I have done that?'

'If you recall, we advised you a month ago that we would be reducing the strength.'

'I don't remember that.'

'Well, I did wonder if you had overlooked the point. We had a brief chat about it at the last pricing meeting - we said we needed to increase the price by around 15 per cent because of increased costs of extraction in Africa and the way the exchange rate had moved against us. You said you could not accept a price increase at the moment - do you recall that?'

'I do - we simply can't pass on that sort of price review to our customers at this time - the recession is really killing demand.'

'You don't need to tell us that! Because you were unable to accept our price increase, we said that, in that case, we would have to incor-

121

porate a substitute emulsifier that would have the effect of reducing the strength to between 8 and 11 per cent. This would enable us to hold our price but, obviously, could have knock-on effects for some processes. Our other customers have accepted the position and have altered their processes accordingly. I am sorry that it seems to have caught you on the hop as it were, but I hope you can recall that we did warn you.' [2]

Key techniques

[1] Most communication is verbal and talk is both cheap and unrecorded. Offering an instant apology rather than adopting a defensive, reactionary position can help disarm the complainant. An apology should kick start the development of rapport.

[2] This demonstrates the value of not arguing too strongly initially. One can always crank up the indignation, but backpedalling after a very strong complaint means that the initiative is lost and enables the other party to build up their case.

[3] Making notes of verbal conversations (at or immediately after the occurrence) can be invaluable. The notes police officers make at the time of an incident (but not subsequently) are accepted as evidence, and a similar presumption of accuracy can be helpful if recollections of events, agreements, arguments and so on are queried later.

People in glass houses ...
■ ■ ■

The Director of the manufacturing company's problem now is that of weighing up the costs of the additional working and products that need to be added to the process to meet the standard against the supplier's required price increase. The pros and cons should, of course, have been considered at the time the supplier gave him the choice. However, there may be an additional social dimension to the problem in that the Chairmen of the two companies are members of the same golf club and play together regularly. In the circumstances, it is not inconceivable that the next time they play, the supplier's Chairman will pull the leg of the manufacturer's Chairman about what has happened. This needs to be taken into account as disputes have a habit of attracting attention from people some distance from those actually involved. In such circumstances, the Director of the manufacturing company may have cause to be doubly thankful that he did not really pitch in hard against the representative, but instead waited for the full facts to be uncovered.

Case study 9.4
AN ADDED DIMENSION

The Chairman of the manufacturing company, calls the Director into his office and they have the following conversation.

'John, I was talking to Chemsupply's Chairman yesterday and we seem to have made a bit of a mess of this pricing/strength decision.' [1]

123

'We certainly haven't covered ourselves with glory! We needed a price freeze to maintain our finished goods price in today's market and their only way of helping us achieve that was to reduce strength. It's my own fault, but somehow the agreement that if they didn't get a price increase we would reduce strength didn't register. We've had to incur additional production expense to maintain the quality required. I'm assured the additional costs are slightly less than the cost of their price increase, although there is an adverse cash flow effect in this as well.'

'I see. Are we sure our own pricing policy is correct?'

'We have been through all this - if we increase prices, we will lose sales and market share.'

'But we've increased our costs, so we've reduced our margin anyway. Wouldn't you sooner have maintained the margin than maintained sales? [2] After all, if we maintain quality and say to the customers "To give you this quality we need to increase the price by 10 per cent", how many customers will we lose?'

'About the same amount - 10 per cent.'

'OK - so we increase our sales value from £2 million to £2.2 million but we lose 10 per cent of the sales anyway, so we're back to £2 million. The cost of the sales will have reduced by 10 per cent to satisfy the 10 per cent fewer customers, so our margin will actually have

increased and so will our profit. You will have to adjust these figures by Chemsupply's increased price, of course, but I would be surprised if we don't finish ahead on the deal.'

Key techniques

[1] To lie about what happened is pointless - the truth will be out sooner or later - so either the Director comes clean now or he will be discredited later when it is discovered.

[2] The Chairman could have said 'I'd sooner have . . .' here, but, structuring it as a question to the Director invites him to confirm, creates a rapport and preserves his dignity. In this way, the commitment of the person being criticised is maintained and even enhanced.

All aspects and dimensions of a problem need to be examined. Working closely with a supplier may mean that *both* parties get the best deal possible. Here the manufacturer needed to increase the price to maintain the quality (even if this entailed them losing customers), because then their present margin would be maintained and they would gain financially. A similar objective analysis carried out by the manufacturer could have indicated a similar strategy and benefit.

|124|

Quality problems
■ ■ ■

Not all supplier-purchaser disagreements concern price. Many centre on quality, whether this be quality of the product, of the service or of delivery time or whatever. Sometimes it is possible for disagreements to occur purely because of a basic misunderstanding. This can be difficult to reconcile until the source of the misunderstanding is recognised.

Case study 9.5
DELIVERY PROBLEMS

A representative called to see a retailer stocking her company's products.

'I'm sorry to see that your sales are below the minimum level to qualify for our quantity discount bonus.'

'That means we lose out, does it?'

'I'm afraid so - is there no way you can increase sales with a promotion, a feature in the window, local advert or something like that?'

'No, we've tried all that. The problem is not so much creating the demand, as satisfying it - you're letting us down.'

'But all you have to do is increase your order.'

'That's fine for you to say as it increases your commission, but it makes a nasty hole in our bank balance until we can sell the goods.'

'Surely as you are selling regularly that shouldn't have too much of an effect.'

'But we're <u>not</u> selling regularly, we have to sell irregularly and the customers don't like it - it destroys our credibility and we lose sales.'

'I'm sorry, I just don't understand this - if you have the products and you are a regular supplier, why should you lose custom?'

'We may be a regular supplier, but you don't deliver regularly. You claim a 48-hour delivery service, but sometimes it's 48 hours and at other times it's five days. Our customers place an order on the basis of a two-day delivery cycle and then when they come in, we have to disappoint them because you haven't delivered.'

'I see, I hadn't realised deliveries were a problem. Does the late delivery happen often?'

'Well the 48-hour delivery you promise is the exception rather than the rule in our experience.'

'But surely - although I will, of course, take the matter up with the Transport and Production people - if you advertised a five-day delivery, that would be acceptable to your clients, wouldn't it?'

'I expect it would, provided everyone else gave the same time, but you also supply Bloggs down the road and, like us, they quote 48 hours - if we start saying five days, we will get no trade at all, it will all go to Bloggs, even though, half the time, the customers will be delayed as much there as they are here.'

Key technique

The representative is on a hiding to nothing. Her only recourse is to retreat to base and try to start some action that will alleviate the very real problem being experienced by the customer. It is essential that causes of problems are clearly identified because, unless the real problem is uncovered, it cannot be solved.

Sometimes answers to questions can be coloured by subjectivity. The shopowner's answer to 'sold many widgets recently' may truthfully be 'yes - they're in great demand' if he has sold five in the last five minutes while he has been behind the till. The correct answer, though, may be 'No - there's very little demand' if the only interest for the last week has been in the five he has just sold!

Approaches to problems
■ ■ ■

Agreeing a particular price or cost may well be the subject of tough talking. In this the culture or attitude of each company you deal with will determine the approach that is likely to be successful. Some take the view that their interests are best served adopting a very hard approach, being determined to squeeze every last penny possible out of companies they contract with, while others feel that a constructive partnership should be fostered and will be in the best interests of both parties. The latter approach tends to be one for long-term relationships; the former for short-term ones only.

Those organisations adopting the tough approach must realise that as the terms of trade tend to move in a circle, during the next negotiations, the other party may be able to apply equal pressure as recompense for 'losing out' last time. In *The Nice Company* (Bloomsbury, 1990), Tom Lloyd puts forward the idea that companies that constantly seek to impose their own parameters (however defined) on others - in other words, act 'nastily' - will, ultimately, lose out because there will be progressively fewer companies over which they can exercise such power. Conversely, 'nice' companies - those seeking to agree compromise targets that are mutually acceptable to both parties - will tend to survive and prosper.

Case study 9.6
BUYING CERTAINTY

During a year when the UK insurance market was weakened by a number of new American insurers entering the UK market, looking for business, a company could have saved a small amount on its premium by moving from its existing insurers of long standing to one of the new US companies. Instead it remained with its previous insurers and agreed a smaller premium increase than the insurers had planned. The process was repeated the following year. In Year 3, the US insurers withdrew from the UK market and the market rates hardened against motor risks. The company, facing what would otherwise have been a large increase in its premium, was able to negotiate another small increase.

The process was not only cost effective, it was also beneficial in terms of budgeting. Had the company changed to the US insurer in Year 1, by Year 3, when that insurer was no longer around, the company would have been wanting to return to its former insurer, but it would have lost the goodwill it enjoyed previously and would have had to pay a much higher premium at a time when alternative quotes would have been likely to have been even higher.

127

Key technique
Such compromise negotiations that infer a degree of trust can be mutually beneficial, but, in case those individuals responsible for the agreement move on, it is as well to confirm it in writing.

Accepting responsibility
■ ■ ■

The reaction of most organisations and their staff when faced with a problem tends to be to deny responsibility, indeed, lawyers and insurers nearly always advise this in order to 'reserve the position' and, possibly, minimise any recompense required later. An increasing number of organisations are realising, however, that accepting responsibility can have considerable advantages. Certainly in terms of public awareness of problems, there must be considerable positive publicity to be gained by accepting responsibility and attempting to right the wrong - the classic stonewalling technique for accusations is not nearly so attractive. If and when the truth eventually emerges, the company will be seen to have been trying to evade its responsibilities. In *Talking Straight* (Sidgwick and Jackson, 1988), Lee Iacocca, the former head of the Chrysler car giant, recounts the following incident. The company decided to run an advertising campaign following the discovery of a relatively minor malpractice by the company. He also went on record as stating that 'selling cars that had been damaged [the malpractice that had been discovered] went beyond dumb all the way to stupid - it was unforgivable and it wouldn't happen again'. From a survey carried out immediately after the campaign and statement, it was clear right away that the public liked the fact that the company owned up to their responsibilities - 67 per cent were in favour. When the story broke originally (only three days before the response referred to above), 55 per cent of those surveyed thought the company were 'bad boys'. This attitude reversal speaks for itself.

10

. . .

Owners – defusing challenges

Key learning points

1 Rights of ownership need to be carefully defined at the start so that later problem encounters can be worked out by referring to the appropriate statement.

2 Casual dismissal of the rights of owners may have serious repercussions, some of them being well-publicised.

3 Parties to a problem encounter may have more than one relationship with the organisation, and this dimension needs to be allowed for.

4 Retaining support in problem encounters is more likely if communication bridges and respect have been built up and these are maintained willingly rather than there being any force involved.

Despite owning (or partly owning) their company, there may be occasions when owners, despite this relationship, have no right to information. They might not only think they have this right, but demand access to such information and, inevitably, these kinds of requests can pose problems. For example, shareholders in companies have legal rights to financial information but only at certain times - (when the accounts are sent to all shareholders simultaneously).

Case study 10.1
THE ONLY ANSWER IS 'NO'

One shareholder was apparently so dazzled by his ownership 'rights' that he expected to be able to demand up-to-date financial information from the company at regular intervals. The Director, fielding an awkward telephone conversation, disagreed.

'I want to know the latest financial results.'

'I'm sorry, but as I have said to you before, I cannot disclose that information to individual shareholders.'

'But, dammit, I own the company.'

'We have been over this point before - yes, you are a shareholder and you do own part of the company.'

'Well, I'm glad you don't disagree with that.' [1]

'As a shareholder you are, of course, entitled to receive the annual results. Once the results have been prepared and audited, they will be made available to you and to all other shareholders, but that won't be for some weeks yet.'

'Well, how is this year looking?'

'I'm sorry, but I can't tell you - when we have all the information, all the shareholders will be told simultaneously.'

'I'm coming round there to see about this.'

'Obviously we shall be pleased to see you, but I must repeat that we will not disclose information to one shareholder until all the figures are finished and we can tell everyone at the same time.'

'You are denying me my rights as a shareholder.'

'Not at all - you have the same rights as every shareholder and we will ensure that those rights are observed to the letter. What we are

doing is making sure everyone's rights are protected. We will do this by telling everyone the information simultaneously. In addition, although we are working on the figures now, before we publish them, they have to be audited - we would be very unwise to disclose unaudited figures, wouldn't we?' [2]

Key techniques
[1] Although this is brusque, to the point of being insulting, and could provoke a pointed reply, to do so would negate the desired effect. Rudeness is better simply ignored.

[2] The use of the rhetorical question may gain the shareholder's agreement, particularly as this follows a concessionary offer to visit the premises.

Preserving confidentiality

131

■ ■ ■

The situation described in Case Study 10.1 applies predominantly to companies. With companies listed on the Stock Exchange, since advance notification of any such information could have an effect on the price of their shares, there are requirements concerning what can and cannot be disclosed and the timing of such disclosures. Where the organisation is a partnership or some other entity, the rights of access to information may be less restrictive, but care still needs to be taken and detailed guidelines should be provided to assist those faced with the problem when pressed by enquirers.

Case study 10.2
RAILROADED

The sleeping partner dropped in to the firm and entered the office of the Director without knocking. The Director was in the middle of a recruitment interview.

'Hi Bob, just wanted the latest figures.'
The Director said to the interviewee:
'Will you excuse me for a moment, it's one of our partners - perhaps

you could glance through our sales brochure and familiarise yourself with our products while I just have a brief word with him.'

To the partner, steering him out of the office and into an empty area he said:

'I'm in the middle of an interview and I must get back immediately, I won't be free for another 20 minutes or so. Can I suggest you sit down and I'll arrange some coffee while you wait. Carol, could you get Mr Brown a cup of coffee please and then come and collect some papers he might like to see.' [1]

'It won't take long - I only wanted the latest finance figures. A couple of minutes should do.'

'Fine, but I simply can't deal with it now, I really must get back to this interview. I'll see you when I'm free in about 20 minutes.' [2]

Key techniques

[1] By seizing the initiative, propelling the partner to a neutral area, inferring that if he waits he will be dealt with in due course and arranging for him to receive some data to peruse while he is waiting, a potentially disruptive interruption has been deflected. Requesting that his secretary should come into his office for some papers gives the Director an opportunity to pass a message to the senior partner to check whether it is acceptable that the sleeping partner be given the information he seeks. Essentially the Director has created some 'thinking time' - he may be able to consider the problem even while he continues his interview.

[2] Swift reactions, again, allow the pressure to be sidestepped. By now the sleeping partner should have got the message that if he wants the information, he must wait. The alternative is not to wait and leave empty handed. In either event, the Director will have brought about his own desired result.

Other requests
■ ■ ■

It is not always apparent that you are, in fact, dealing with an owner who, arguably at least, has certain rights additional to those of other parties. This is particularly true of the larger, privatised companies or corporations where the public ownership may be spread thinly, but is certainly varied. As most such owners have relatively little individual strength, it may be felt that their ownership rights can be ignored. This, however, can be a false assumption as they have the right to attend the public showing of such an organisation - the Annual General Meeting - and may ask an awkward question, gaining equally awkward publicity. It may be thought unlikely that anything will ever come of the tiny pressure that an individual small shareholder could exercise over a mighty corporation, but, nevertheless, the publicity that such a person can attract can be the equivalent of faith moving the mountain. Certainly British Gas have experienced such attentions from shareholders trying to get themselves elected onto the Board in three successive years. Indeed, so persistent were the people concerned, the company was forced to change its Articles of Association so that the opportunity for repetition of such actions was removed. TSB responded quite differently to one of their shareholders who only exerted a little bit of pressure. The shareholder simply pointed out that British Rail did not give discounts to senior citizens on a Friday and thus it was cheaper to attend the Annual General Meeting if it were to be held on, say, a Thursday. Sure enough the TSB's Annual General Meeting was held on a Thursday the following year.

133

The response of British Gas to pressure was to fight the movement; the TSB's response to, admittedly, a much less difficult proposal was to embrace it. However, in some instances, responding poorly to requests in the first instance has resulted in very high-profile arguments that have proved costly to the company. These could have been avoided had they been more positive and objective initially.

Case study 10.3
THE CUSTOMER SHAREHOLDER

British Telecom had informed one of its subscribers of a future change in both their telephone number and exchange, but indicated that the actual change date would not be known with any degree of certainty until only a few months before the effective date. The subscriber rang the British Telecom office and the following conversation resulted.

'Look, you have indicated you will be making this change, but without saying when, which is absolutely key to us. We have a great number of changes to make to letterheads, adverts, etc., and we need to notify overseas contacts.'

'As we've already told you, it is going to happen some time in the early part of next year.'

'I know, but that is nowhere near precise enough - we need to know an actual date. We have to place overseas advertising with our phone number on it now. In addition, we have overseas customers as well as UK customers - they have got to be told of this change well in advance. If you feel unsure about the actual completion in time, why not delay the estimated date but then commit to a later date.'

'We have indicated an approximate date, we won't commit to a later date as we cannot afford to have equipment lying around idle - we need to get a good return for our shareholders.'

'Fine, but unless you satisfy your customers first, your shareholders will not be satisfied and as a shareholder myself I do not think your attitude is at all right.'

134

Key techniques

[1] Don't be patronising; assuming that saying the company needs to make a return on its investment will silence the customer. This had the effect in this case of irritating the customer shareholder to the extent that recourse was made to the office of the Chairman of this large UK company. The Chairman's office then became involved, to the embarrassment of the local office. The local office quickly learned a lesson, agreed to give three months' notice of the change and thereafter kept the customer shareholder fully informed during all the stages of the work.

[2] Failure to give due respect to enquirers can backfire and create more serious problem encounters than the one they first faced.

Ownership in other guises
■ ■ ■

The possibility that parties to problem encounters are other than they first appear to be needs to be carefully assessed by negotiators. This is particularly true in the public services sector, where traditionally there has often been an air verging on condescension regarding enquirers. Hopefully the movement towards implementing service 'Charters' in many public-sector areas will help remove this unhelpful and unfounded view of enquirers. Not comprehending the fact that the public sector exists to serve its customers and owners tends to lead to the creation of the erroneous view of the services as gifts for which their receivers should be duly grateful and that the rights of the givers of such services are somehow more important than those of its customers.

Case study 10.4
DETERMINED TO ARGUE

The householder had moved within the rating area and following earlier arrangements whereby rates were paid in 10 equal monthly amounts by banker's order set up a new order to pay the rates on the new house. The Rating Office sent reminders of the rates due - to which the householders responded by referring to the banker's order. During the second year of occupation the following took place:

135

'We have not received the rates from you for your house by the correct means.'

'Of course you have - they are being paid by banker's order as they have been for the past 11 years.'

'You haven't lived here for 11 years.'

'Not here no, but I am paying the rates for this house by bankers order from the same bank and in the same way as for my previous house in your district.'

'That's an unauthorised method of payment.'

'How can it be unauthorised when you have accepted it without question for over 11 years, and it is one of the methods of payment referred to in your guidance for payment notes?'

'You must apply again.'

'I have no intention of applying again for something that you have accepted for 11 years - where's the sense in that? You have received the rates for 6 months in this rating year haven't you?'

'Yes, but that's not the point - its an unauthorised method of payment.'

The Council then proceeded to take out a summons for non-payment of rates even though they had acknowledged that they had received every instalment correctly and payment was up to date. The householder was so incensed at being summonsed for something he was paying in any event, that he wrote to his Member of Parliament pointing out that the Council was wasting taxpayer's and ratepayer's money because of this totally perverse attitude.

Key technique

In taking this matter further, the householder also pointed out to the Council that their wages were actually partly paid by householders who deserved a more constructive and reasonable attitude. The Council had lost sight of their desired effect - the prompt payment of rates by those liable. Harassing someone who was paying correctly, when many non-payers were deserving of their debt-collection attention is foolish. Insisting that the 'right procedure' is adhered to is not necessarily cost effective, neither does it always achieve the desired result. The reality of the situation must always be borne in mind.

Takeovers
■ ■ ■

Although the threat of publicity may be the most potent sanction a shareholder or owner who is failing to receive what they consider to be adequate service from their company may have, should a hostile takeover bid be launched for the company, their power increases dramatically as both the incumbent Board and predator vie for their voting power. In these circumstances, shareholders may need to be listened to with greater attention than hitherto. However, if this is the first occasion on which such attention or requests for information have been extended to them then it may be too late to call on their support. It is essential if one wishes to rely on shareholders' support, that there has been an ongoing dialogue and a building of mutual trust in the past.

Case study 10.5
I TOLD YOU SO

The Board was trying to gain support for its defence against an unwelcome takeover bid and was canvassing private shareholders, having already canvassed the institutional shareholders. On speaking to one such private shareholder, the Company Secretary found considerable lack of sympathy where she had expected support.

'I am sorry to disturb you, the Board simply wondered if you had enough information to enable you to make up your mind concerning the bid for the company.'

'Yes, I agree with the bid - I've said for a long time that the company should be broken up and its constituent parts sold off.'

'Are you sure that is the best route for the company?'

'I certainly think it's the best route for the shareholders - and I told your Mr Haskins so at the last Annual General Meeting.'

'He's no longer with us - he's joined XYZ Co.'

'Well, XYZ Co.'s loss is your gain. I didn't have much time for him as he dismissed my ideas out of hand.'

'Your ideas are the same as the predator I assume. You do realise that there are all sorts of tax implications should this occur, that the constituent parts of the company are probably worth less than the sum of the whole and that several hundred people will be made redundant.'

'Yes, but my shares are worth 40 per cent more than they were thanks to this bid - that's what I told Haskin would happen.'

137

Key technique
In this situation there is obviously no meeting of minds. The possibility of a consensus was lost some time previously. This emphasises another consideration: regardless of the rights and wrongs of the case and no matter how firmly the negotiator believes that the reaction will go one way rather than another, sometimes the actual reaction will be a real surprise because it is influenced by a previous clash or dispute rather than the prevailing logic and so clouds present or future negotiations. Trying to negotiate in these circumstances is a little like trying to follow the legendary directions you are supposed to be given when lost in Ireland along the lines of 'Well, sure and if I was you, I wouldn't be starting from here'. In other words, it may first be necessary to create a relationship wherein consensus may be encouraged, before actually commencing negotiations.

Ownership used as a threat

■ ■ ■

In Case Study 10.1, the shareholder sought to use his relationship with the company to obtain information to which he, but not the company, felt he was entitled. There are other instances when the claim to being an owner can be used either to try to gain preferential treatment or as a threat to obtain adverse publicity.

Case study 10.6
BOTCHING THE JOB - PUBLICLY

A customer had bought an electrical appliance from a shop and the item proved to be faulty. On phoning the shop, the person who answered stated that he should bring the appliance back, and said it would be replaced. On taking it to the shop, however, the assistant who dealt with the enquiry, having given it two or three hefty slaps with his hand in an attempt to make it work, then said that if the customer left it with him, it would be repaired. The customer replied that this was not what he had been promised on the phone the day before and, having seen the item manhandled he was not at all happy about having it repaired! He requested to see the Manager, but, instead, a supervisor was called over and the following discussion took place.

'Good morning, what seems to be the problem?' [1]
   'This product is only a month old and is intermittently faulty. I rang to find out what I should do - return it to the manufacturer or to you and was told to bring it in and you would replace it. I have now been told to leave it for repair, which is unsatisfactory.'
   'Well, that is our policy, sir.'
   'But it is not what it says on your guarantee - it says here that you will replace any items found to be faulty within three months of purchase.'
   'I am afraid that is not our current guarantee, sir.' [2]
   'But it's the one you supplied with this product - it says you will replace it, I was told on the phone you would replace it and I have brought it in - making a special 20-mile journey - for it to be replaced.'
   'I see. Could I show that guarantee to the Manager, sir?'

The supervisor took the customer's guarantee and went to see the Manager - not returning for 10 minutes.

'I am sorry sir, the Manager is not around and I can't find anyone to give me a decision on this.'

'With all due respect, that is not my fault. I have made a special trip here, following phoning you for advice yesterday. I must insist you replace this faulty item or I will have to take this matter up with the Trading Standards officer and, as I am a shareholder, with your Board of Directors.'

'Can I try again to see if I can contact the Manager, sir?' [3]

Key techniques

[1] By starting positively, aware that the whole conversation is taking place on the shop floor, the supervisor attempted to defuse the situation. She was, however, let down by the non-appearance of her management.

[2] It might have been better for the supervisor to have tried to move the encounter to a more private place. By raising his voice the customer could raise the pressure on the supervisor.

[3] While it is difficult to judge whether the supervisor had made the decision on her own or whether management (having been found after all) reversed its instructions to her and whether it was just coincidence that the customer has just announced that he was a shareholder or not, the customer achieved his desired result. The same can hardly be said for the retailer - the embarrassing discussion was witnessed by several customers and there was potential damage to the reputation of this national chain. The patience and professionalism of the supervisor was the one saving grace, as the shareholder subsequently reported to the Managing Director.

139

Ownership commands little respect
■ ■ ■

Even having ownership rights in a publicly quoted company sometimes seems to cut little ice with some executives - 'That's the trouble with shareholders, they think they own the company' was one comment made to me by a company director!

The potential danger with problem encounters in this area is leaks to the media, which can turn what were fairly minor molehills into very damaging mountains.

Case study 10.7
PLEASE (DON'T) JOIN US!

A traveller was regularly using one of a chain of motels where reservations could be made by phone and paid for by credit card. He noticed a leaflet in the room inviting guests to subscribe to the operating company's own credit card, which gave priority bookings and other benefits. He applied for one and found, to his astonishment and annoyance, that his application was rejected. He rang the credit company and queried the position and the following conversation ensued.

'I'm sorry I am not allowed to go into details concerning applications for the cards.'

'I don't find that acceptable - I want to know the reason for this decision.'

'I am sorry I cannot disclose that - I cannot say more.'

'Are you saying that following your invitation to apply for the card and my having completed the application, you reject it and are not prepared to state the reason?'

'I am afraid so.'

'Please tell me immediately the credit checking company you use.'
[1]

Later.

'I have checked my credit rating with the company you use and it is impeccable. In the circumstances, I cannot see why you have not accepted the application - do you have anything to add?'

'No, I am sorry we cannot enter into discussion regarding individual applications.'

'As it cannot concern my credit rating, is it related to the fact that I said I would use it around 12 times a year - is that too low a usage? If so, this should be made clear on the application form.'

'I really cannot comment.'

Key techniques

[1] Be clear from the start. If low usage or some other factor would determine the issuing of a card, this should have been made clear on the application form. Inviting people to apply and then rejecting them without explanation is rude and damaging to the reputation of the company.

The traveller wrote to the chairman asking for an explanation and received no reply. As a result of this rudeness or inefficiency the traveller, who had shares in the operating company sold them, refused to use the chain and its associated hotels again and recounted the experience to many acquaintances. The potential damage to the operating company of this incident is considerable.

Instead of selling out of course, the traveller could have raised the matter at the Annual General Meeting of this high-profile group.

141

11

. . .

Managing media pressure

Key learning points

1 Protecting a company's name and/or reputation is of paramount importance, especially as these can take years to build and just seconds to lose.

2 Comprehensive and continual briefing must be conducted with the media, to ensure that coverage of problem encounters that do occur are more likely to be informed or accurate.

3 The subject of prospective interviews (as well as the interviewers) must be researched and the interviewee adequately briefed and rehearsed.

4 Actions (and reactions) in the event of threats and disasters need to be planned for in advance and comprehensive contingency plans should be prepared and updated as necessary.

Increasingly, companies need to develop, protect and project their desired public image. This can take a great deal of time and careful planning, although part of most reputations will be built up over time on its own, that is by virtue of the organisation being in business and trading successfully (or at least without harming those with whom it comes into contact) for a number of years. Equally, leaving it unprotected for as little as a few minutes or acting badly in a moment of crisis can destroy the reputation an organisation has built up so painstakingly over the years. Thus, in dealing with complaints and observations from the public or in attempting to project an image of the company to it, great care and tact are required and knowledge of the facts needs to be absolute. This is even more so when communication is being effected via the media, especially television. The attention span of the average viewer lasts a matter of seconds and, thus, someone being interviewed has a very short time in which to project their message. This being so, it is essential that they prepare very carefully.

Successful media interviews
■ ■ ■

If a company spokesperson is to be interviewed, preparation is essential and the guidelines given below show what things need to be thought about.

1 A complete brief must be prepared - organisation data and performance, products, problems, plans, and so on.

2 The point or aim of the interview must be discovered and appropriate responses and statements prepared, particularly if these are likely to be controversial or embarrassing.

3 The spokesperson needs to be in total control of the brief, all the facts and the prepared responses, because

otherwise the spokesperson will not feel confident enough to be able to speak knowledgeably about the subject. Any lack of confidence will tend to communicate itself to the listener or viewer.

4 Three or four simple messages or any arguments the company wishes to promote must be developed.

5 'Changes of direction' sentences need to be prepared so that if the interview leads off in one direction, the spokesperson may be able to bring it back to the message that needs to be conveyed, although this needs to be carefully done as an apparent and constant refusal to answer the question may make the interviewer far more inquisitive or confrontational, thinking you are trying to hide something.

6 Spokespeople must receive coaching in interview techniques so that they are ready for the 'off the cuff' unrehearsed question deliberately designed to catch them unawares, forcing an unprepared or unwise comment or answer.

145

7 Above all, it is important to keep calm under pressure and/or goading and be able to think quickly and laterally in order to fend off or turn round aggression and criticism.

What's the line?

Company spokespeople must discover the reason for the interview - that is what the line of questioning will be and the purpose behind it - so that a suitable 'defence' can be prepared. It is helpful to see or read previous interviews by the interviewer to discover what their style is, whether they introduce sudden traps or any other measures routinely so that the person knows what they are likely to face. All information needs to be analysed, considered in relation to the subject matter and prepared for. In this it is wise to realise that, although the logical choice of spokesperson may be an excellent chairperson, they may not be a good interviewee. In such cases an alternative spokesperson needs to be found and trained. Interviewees need to be able to think very quickly, to spot and deal with double-edged questions (those where either of the instinctive alternative answers do not put you in a good light) and to change the impact and meaning of a sentence while it is being spoken when the situation demands it. While these skills are instinctive to some, they *can* be learned and it is vastly preferable to learn them in the coaching room, rather than from bitter experience, live and 'on air'. Trial by television may be acceptable when the subject is someone generally perceived to be a crook, but is very unfortunate when someone makes, say, a genuine mistake, a misplaced attempt at humour, an inadequate reply or, through inexperience or ineptitude, does not perform well. The manner of the trial may be considered unfair, but, by then, the damage is done, the reputation will have been lost and the name tarnished.

146

Case study 11.1
LOSE YOUR TEMPER, LOSE THE ARGUMENT

In September 1992, considerable media attention was focused on the manner in which the chairpersons and chief executives of certain organisations (particularly monopolistic former public corporations) were rewarding themselves with remuneration packages that seemed to be out of proportion to their responsibilities and to those holding comparable positions in other organisations with more conservative pay policies. A number of company chairpersons were interviewed for the BBC television programme 'Panorama' which carried out a lengthy investigation into the subject. Those interviewed included one chairman of a recently privatised utility who obviously resented being called to account for the hefty increase in his own salary. The more evasive he became, the more pressing became the interviewer, to the point where the chairman decided to end the interview by walking off the set, but first indulged in a heated exchange with the interviewer, all of which was caught by the camera.

Leaving aside the complete loss of face occasioned by this lost temper and the loss of reputation occasioned by such a public examination, the chairman completely failed to implement the fundamentals of the interview situation.

1 Neither he, nor apparently his staff, had taken the trouble to construct suitable answers or defences to the questions that were likely to be asked. One must assume he knew what the subject would be (a programme of such repute is unlikely to have misled him) and thus he knew that he was likely to be quizzed on his own pay situation. With this most basic knowledge, he should have worked out a suitable defence (it might not have been too convincing but at least it would have provided some defence or explanation).

2 His staff should have prepared him for the intrusive questioning technique that he was likely to be subject to in this kind of interview, coached him to retain his good humour under stress and to avoid a situation developing where he would lose and would be seen to lose his temper.

3 He should have been made aware that simply replying 'No comment', while unsatisfactory, would at least have avoided him being caught on screen trying to disentangle himself from the microphone and get out of the studio. Refusing to answer questions makes boring viewing and the producer would have cut the interview short. Being embroiled in a heated exchange with the interviewer while trying to remove a microphone was, by contrast, compulsive, if embarrassing, viewing and was very unlikely to be edited out.

4 He should have remembered the adage 'If you lose your temper you have lost the argument'. Being seen to run away from the question immediately implied that he had no defence or explanation to offer. In the circumstances, viewers, some of whom were shareholders in the company, could hardly have concluded other than that his remuneration package was indefensibly high.

The need for research

As well as researching the tactics likely to be used by the interviewer, the interviewee needs to be in command of

147

details of all previous comments made by the company on the subject matter. This may entail some time-consuming research and cross referencing, but it is vital to ensure that there is no contradiction between what has gone before and what will be said (or, if there is, that the reason for such a change of policy or whatever is known and the interviewee can have an explanation ready explanation). Being fazed by such a question will leave the interviewee floundering, providing a negative impression of both spokesperson and company to the audience.

Treating the product carefully

For the same reason, company spokespeople always need to be very careful about how they refer to the products and, indeed, the corporate body in public. While they need to avoid excessive hype and praise, equally, it should be an unbreakable rule that if there is to be the slightest hint of criticism of the product (which itself should be the exception), then, somehow, it must be placed in context or with some redeeming features or aspects also appearing. Adverse criticism of the product by an outsider may actually benefit the marketing of the product (on the basis that there is no such thing as bad publicity), but, should a representative of the organisation question the product, such criticism can destroy it far more effectively than any competitor could.

Case study 11.2
RUBBISH THE PRODUCT, DESTROY THE COMPANY

At an Institute of Directors conference in 1991, part of which was telerecorded, Gerald Ratner, then Chairman of the retail chain of the same name, which he had brilliantly built up until it was one of the largest chains of jewellery retailers in the world, referred to some of the products being sold in his shops as being worthless (or a word to that effect), and added that, in some cases, there was more value in a prawn sandwich from Marks and Spencer than in some of his company's products. Such throwaway comments were made, to some degree, in humour but the effect on custom in the chain's units was catastrophic, particularly as the timing of the conference coincided with the nadir of the UK recession. The price of Ratner shares tumbled from 177p to 8p within a few months, Ratner himself gave up the Chairmanship of the company and resigned as a Director. At the time of writing, there are rumours that the name of the chain itself may be changed to distance the shops from the poor image resulting from the remarks.

In the case of Ratners, the cause of the damage to the product was internal. The company Chairman shot its public image in the foot. More often, however, causes of damage on whatever scale, either intentionally or unintentionally, come from without. Often competitors or even those in a business entirely unrelated to the subject's business, try to use the subject's success to promote or support their own product. At times, the link can be so vague as to barely qualify as such.

149

Case study 11.3
UNWANTED RELATIONSHIP

The Filofax personal organiser had, in the late 1980s and early 1990s a high-profile, quality image that was reflected in the price commanded by its products. A brewery local to the Head Office of the Filofax company ran a local poster advertisement linking its bitter to the Filofax brand name, without any permission being sought from Filofax. As Filofax felt that the juxtaposition of the two names was damaging to their product, they requested the withdrawal of the brewery's poster campaign.

Constant protection

It can take a great deal of time, money and effort to build up the public image of a brand or product, so protecting it as much as possible, whatever the source of potential damage is, must be a primary aim of the company. This may mean challenging the media when it runs stories that actually damage or have the potential to damage the company name or product.

Case study 11.4
PROTECTING THE NAME

The Filofax company's sales grew from £100 000 in 1980 to £7.5 million when it went public in 1987. Hardly a day passed without the product being referred to in the press or on TV - even in film titles. Inevitably this free advertising raised the public's awareness of the product - and their demand for it. Unfortunately, as so often happens, the media, which created the phenomenon, then turned against it and ran a number of stories ridiculing the product and the type of person perceived to use one. Considerable time and expense were devoted to trying to correct the damaging and inaccurate press comments about Filofax and its products in order to protect the reputation it had earned over the years.

(From the author's 'How to control your costs and increase your profits')

150

Catastrophe!

The way in which the media builds up concepts, products or even personalities, only to turn on them later, damaging or destroying them, may help them improve their circulation figures but can be disastrous for the product, company or person concerned.

'If you want peace prepare for war' runs the old saying and nowhere is this more apt than in relation to disaster or contingency planning. The concept embraces the principle that it is preferable to consider alternative actions and reactions *before* a disaster occurs, than to cobble something together in the immediate aftermath when the disaster itself sets in train a sequence of events that have a momentum of their own. Considering how much time organisations spend planning for eventualities when things go *right*, in which circumstances, if there is deviation from the aimed route, there is ample time to replan, change and alter, it is surprising how little time so many organisations devote to contingency planning for when things go *wrong*, when, often, there is insufficient time for replanning and yet an instant response is essential. Not only does the organisation need to have available an instant response in order to get its operations back on track but, almost inevitably, disasters tend to attract a great deal of media attention.

Case study 11.5
DISASTROUS EFFECTS

The Union Carbide disaster at Bhopal in India, sparked considerable public interest in the situation there but also in the safety of chemical plants generally, particularly from those living near such plants in the UK.

This led to the UK chemical industry trade association setting up a well-briefed information desk, ready and able to deal with the wide variety of enquiries from members of the public as well as from the media.

British Midland won considerable praise for the way it coped when one of its planes crashed by the M1. Their well-managed, detailed responses and reactions were not instinctive but the result of planning for such an eventuality. Planning it was hoped would never be used paid off to the company's credit when a disaster actually occurred.

In late 1991, SmithKline Beecham, makers of Lucozade among other products, were the target of alleged tampering with bottles of Lucozade in shops by the Animal Liberation Front. Not only were 5 000 000 bottles of Lucozade removed from retail outlets and destroyed, but the telephone line that the company set up to deal with enquiries handled over 1500 calls (only one from a person complaining of feeling ill). To effect this type of response at such a time, it is necessary to formulate and complete, detailed response plans and have trained staff ready to answer enquiries and complaints in a tactful yet responsive manner.

Responding to crises such as those referred to in Case Study 11.5 calls for preparation, research and a commitment of resources in advance of and in anticipation of the problem. Such consumer or media response departments take considerable time to set up, as does the training of those responsible for dealing with the enquiries. Although working to a brief giving guidance on how to answer most questions helps shape staff's responses to most questions very effectively, inevitably a hesitant or unsure tone or inflection in the voice can worry rather than reassure. In addition, the instinctive answer to some questions may immediately beg another, so questions - and their suggested answers - need to be viewed from a number of angles.

Wanted - a devil's advocate

To ensure that the answers provided are as honest as possible and yet boost confidence (within limits), it is essential to try and imagine all the worst questions that could be asked, including those the company sincerely hopes will never be asked. Playing devil's advocate in this way, producing as wide a range of questions as possible, should not only provide a list of questions but also prompt consideration, and improvement, of many current administrative procedures or the realisation that there is a lack of such procedures. Obviously, as well as sourcing the questions, it is essential to construct answers that are as detailed as possible, bearing in mind the potential problems likely to be caused by double-edged *answers* as much as double-edged *questions*.

Double-edging - the devil's alternative

In Case Study 11.7, below, the agency might be tempted to reply to the criticism made by the client that it had formed the opinion that the situation within his family was such that it was unsuitable for receiving a visitor. However, that immediately begs the question, 'If you thought that, either you should have said so or you should not have placed her with the family'. Either way, an attacking answer to the family's criticism could rebound onto the agency itself.

Similarly, in answering the shareholder's criticism in Case Study 10.5, the company could say, either: 'We have never considered selling off one or more divisions' or 'Yes, we had considered such a disposal'.

The first response invites the retort - 'Why not, it should be one of the tasks of management to manage the assets of the business in the most profitable way possible', while the alternative invites the response either of 'You are just saying that to show the Board in a good light but really it had not occurred to you before' or 'So you considered it but rejected it - why?'

In dealing with queries regarding Lucozade, no doubt SmithKline Beecham was asked why it was removing the product from the shops. Presumably, the enquirers could either have been told that the company thought they had been contaminated and were removing contaminated products, or that they had not been contaminated but were being checked all the same. Even the further alternative - that this was merely a precautionary exercise, almost invites the comment that, presumably, the company's wrapping was not tamper-proof!

153

Case study 11.6
WATER PROBLEMS

A consumer, filling his kettle, noticed that the water seemed very cloudy. He let the tap run and tried again, filling a tall glass this time so he could see it more clearly. The water remained very cloudy. Bearing in mind that there had been a number of problems in the London area, with water supplies being infected by toxic organisms, he rang his water company's emergency number and had the following conversation.

'Our water supply seems to be very cloudy.'
  'Have you tried running the tap for some time?'
  'Yes, and it is still the same.'
  'Our workmen have been in your area today so it is probably air in the water.'
  'Would air make the supply cloudy?'
  'It could do, but there's no need to panic.'

Key technique

The water company's spokesperson had not been properly briefed in terms of the words to be avoided then communicating with customers. Here 'panic' was both inaccurate and inadvisable as it, first, encourages an instinctively negative reaction from the consumer who is, after all, being a responsible citizen by checking before using suspicious-looking water and, second, the word itself is emotive and could create a feeling that the situation was more serious than is, in fact, the case - one in which panic might be appropriate! Further, inferring that the customer was panicking is both patronising and rude - even if this effect is unintentional.

As many of the questions in Case Study 11.6 have potentially double-edged answers, the full implications of each answer do need to be considered. 'No comment' is not a suitable fall-back response and should be avoided in all but the most rare situations.

The public profile

Although many organisations have a public profile in terms of potential media interest, some have an additional profile because they need to operate under a licence issued by a governmental body or in accordance with guidelines issued by such a body.

Case study 11.7
THREATS

Au pair placement agencies operate under guidelines issued by the Home Office and licences issued by the Department of Employment - a twin exposure that some seek to exploit, as the following conversation demonstrates.

'I understand that the au pair you placed with my family three months ago left today.'
   'Yes we had heard from her.'
   'So, I want to know what you are going to do about it.'
   'I am sorry, but I am sure you know from our terms that there is noth-

ing more we can do.'

'But that's not good enough - she should be here, instead of which she's waltzed off somewhere, leaving us in the lurch, for no reason at all.'

'I'm not sure if that is quite right. I understand from her that, not for the first time, you and she had a serious argument. She told me that after today's argument, she became so frightened of you, she couldn't bear to stay in the house, so she left.'

'I'm not having that - she is supposed to be here with my family. I intend taking this up with the Home Office and the Department of Employment.' [1]

'I see.'

'What do you say to that?'

'I really have no comment. Obviously you have a right to take the matter up with whomever you wish. If they ask us for comments, we will have to state what we know.'

'And that is . . . ?'

'What you have told us and what she has told us.'

155

'And you will then decide who is right - as you have done already?'

'Not at all - we try not to take sides as we are not in your house and only know what happens second hand.'

'Well, I am going to report this to the Home Office and Department of Employment.'

'As I have said, you have a perfect right to take such action as you think fit.'

Key techniques

[1] The client is seeking to use the reference to 'official' bodies as a threat. The calm response to it may have two effects:

- to cool the complainant down and allow more rational thought and consideration to take place
- to indicate, during subsequent consideration of the matter, that, as the organisation has no worries about such referral, it might be better for the client to write the episode off to experience.

[2] Refrain from any suggestion that the client should desist from reporting the case to either the Home Office or Department of Employment; even if there were some concern about this course of action, this would be an indication of weakness and give the client

the edge. Then the client might seek to prolong the discussion and gain some consideration, compensation or whatever. (Obviously such a hard line is only possible where the agreed terms indicate that the client has absolutely no case.)

Environmental issues

With the increasing importance and attention given to, environmental issues, inevitably organisations need to be ready to deal with problem encounters concerning matters that, hitherto, would have been dismissed on the basis of a 'well, that's life' attitude. Practices, procedures, materials, and so on that were formerly regarded as acceptable are now challenged and organisations must either respond by changing these so that they are then more acceptable or justify what may still be acceptable but is unwelcome. It must be recognised, too, that this movement is not going to stop and, thus, although justification may be possible today, it may not be tomorrow. The time bought by the justification process should be used constructively to phase out the subject of the complaint as attacks are likely to increase rather than decrease and it will be progressively more difficult to make justifications hold good.

Case study 11.8
SMOKE SIGNALS

A factory had been built many years ago in what had then been a 'green field' site (quite literally, as it had been surrounded by allotments). Gradually, however, suburbanisation had led to it being entirely surrounded by houses, shops and schools. Manufacturing was powered by oil-fired boilers, the exhaust of which was funnelled up a huge chimney. Normally, the emissions were clear but, occasionally, particularly if there were a draught at the base of the chimney or when the boiler was fired up, smoke would emerge from the top to the dismay and sometimes outrage of local residents.

'*Do you realise your chimney is smoking for the third time this week?*'
    '*Thank you for pointing that out. Unfortunately, despite trying to*

avoid any emissions, sometimes when we start up or if someone leaves a door at the base of the chimney open, it does give off smoke, but usually it is only for a few minutes. I'll have a word with the Chief Engineer to make sure they are following the guidelines we laid down to avoid this happening.' [1]

'Well, it's not good enough you know - this is a residential area and we don't want the smut that this smoke causes.'

'I am very sorry there have been some emissions recently - we are working towards a much cleaner process and hope to have that installed during the next shutdown.'

'But you've been saying that for some time - meanwhile all our houses and gardens, washing and cars get covered in smuts when your chimney smokes.' [2]

'I do appreciate your problems, but don't forget that the chimney and this factory were here well before the houses were built. In addition, this factory does provide employment for many of the people living in those houses - your neighbours, and, finally, the means by which we will make the process clean is very expensive and we have had to do it gradually - we simply cannot afford to do it all in one go.'

157

'I don't see why not.'

'Essentially, if we had introduced the new process in one go, we would have had to close down for over a month to do it, so we would have had to lay off all our employees - your neighbours - for at least part of that time, which I am sure they would not have welcomed - and neither would our customers. We are trying to keep everyone reasonably happy by doing it gradually.'

'But how much longer is it going on?'

'By the end of our next shutdown in a few months the whole process will have been changed and there will be no smoke at all.'

'And about time too.'

'I quite agree. Can I suggest that you and any of your friends and neighbours who are affected get together, give me a ring and we'll show you the work we've been doing, both connected with the smoke and the modernisation of the factory in general.' [3]

Key techniques
[1] Explanation of the problem may create a foundation for discussion rather than fuel irate complaints.

[2] Despite some provocation, the spokesperson remains calm and is able to make sensible and important points about being there first and providing employment for local people. This is only possible because of the steps that have already been taken to effect improvements - had this not been the case, no doubt the encounter would have been more stormy.

[3] The calm and professional way in which the company spokesperson deals with the problem (that is, their taking the matter seriously) goes some way to moving the problem onwards to a mutually agreeable solution. The successful resolution is thus part negotiation (in which the offer of a trip round the works can be an attractive carrot) and part moving the business forwards in the recognition of the need to reflect new requirements.

[4] Virtually regardless of the circumstances, the utmost patience needs to be exercised to try to placate (and satisfy) neighbours. They are unlikely to go away and can be the source of considerable (and virtually non-productive) usage of time.

Neighbours, nuisances and the good corporate citizen

159

Key learning points

1 The number of problem encounters with third parties can be reduced by forging relationships with neighbours based on mutual respect.

2 On the other hand, abusing the rights of neighbours will not only cause problem encounters, but also close off avenues to obtaining return favours.

3 Only if threats can be backed up by the action threatened, should they be used - a bluff can easily be called and, if it is found to be baseless, can destroy a preferred position.

4 All implications of a course of action should be assessed prior to it being effected.

As inferred in Case Study 11.8, a company's building is immovable and unique. Inherent in occupying a particular site, is the juxtaposition with the surrounding properties and their occupiers. In turn, this juxtaposition has allied to it a need for the company to forge an ongoing relationship with its individual and collective neighbours - that is those immediately surrounding its premises as well as those in the community at large and with the owners of the properties. It is, of course, possible to occupy a building and not become involved with immediate and local neighbours, but this policy is somewhat shortsighted because, by talking with neighbours and discovering common interests, the company may find sources of help. Some advantages of such a policy are listed below.

1 United stand in relation to a landlord common to several tenants.

2 United stand regarding matters relating to the local authority.

3 Shared vigilance as to the security of each other's property.

4 Shared knowledge on labour matters, thus avoiding overpricing and poaching.

5 Common approach in relation to problems with or raised by local residents.

6 Avoidance, or reduction of incidence and level, of potential interneighbour disputes.

7 Consensus on how best to resolve problems that may be common to all neighbours.

Parking
■ ■ ■

Of all the problems that can arise between neighbours those connected with parking or boundary disputes must form the greatest proportion. Having made efforts to foster links with neighbours, such problems can be minimised, but this can rarely avoid such problems occurring completely.

Case study 12.1
TRESPASS

A company had acquired a factory and car park and spent three months renovating and fitting out. During this time they had been aware of a number of cars belonging to employees of the neighbouring factory parking in their spaces. As these spaces would not be used until they commissioned the factory, they were content to accept the situation, but took steps to meet the management of the neighbouring factory and explain to them what they proposed to do regarding the illegal parking. The management of the other factory posted notices pointing out that the spaces belonged to a neighbour and emphasised that the bays were to be left vacant. Three times in the last few weeks before the factory was commissioned, handbills advising drivers that they were illegally parked, were left on the cars parking in these spaces and their registration numbers were noted. The handbills stated that, from a certain date, the bays would be required and that they should park elsewhere. One motorist was annoyed about this.

161

'What's the meaning of this?'
 'I'm sorry, what appears to be the trouble?'
 'This piece of rubbish I found on my car - what's the meaning of it?'
 'It's a note from the owner of the parking area where you left your car asking you to park elsewhere from next Monday as our employees will be using these bays.'
 'I've always used these bays.'
 'We know - we have a record that you park here regularly and that is the third note you have received from us advising you that from next Monday these bays will be in use by our employees.' [1]
 'I object to this rubbish on my car.'
 'I am sorry, but if you had not parked here illegally we would not have had to place the handbill there.'

'You've no right to stick rubbish on my car.'

'I'm sorry but if you park illegally, we <u>do</u> have a right to request you to stop doing so. We have not insisted on our rights for the past three months, but, nevertheless, since last January, all these bays belong to my company and you have been parked here illegally.'

'I didn't know these bays were yours.' [2]

'OK, I'll accept that, but obviously you do now, so I hope we can assume that you will not be parking here any more and that will be the end of it - is that fair?'

Key techniques

[1] Preparing the ground for action (by giving adequate notice), remaining calm and presenting the facts circumscribes the other party's room for manoeuvre.

[2] Even though this statement is an obvious lie, proving it would only aggravate the situation. The desired result is ensuring that the illegal parking does not continue.

Public trespass

In Case Study 12.1, the company had the advantage of the fact that its neighbour was prepared to help cure the problem and that the parkers themselves were fairly easily identifiable. Unfortunately, often the parkers can be members of the public visiting, for example, a neighbour. In such an instance, gaining the upper hand over the neighbour may need to be achieved in order to force them into action, otherwise they can simply deny all responsibility.

Case study 12.2
GAINING THE UPPER HAND

A company's office and car park was immediately adjacent to the spare parts counter of a neighbouring garage. The customers of the garage would often either use the company's parking spaces or double park and block their cars in (or out). The Chairman encountered one such trespasser and tackled him.

'Do you know you are trespassing by parking here?'

'I'll be gone in a moment.'

'I'm not interested in that, do you know you are trespassing here - you are actually parked in my private bay.'

'I didn't know that.'

'Presumably you can't read either.'

'Nah, I'm an animal!'

'Look, it says clearly on that notice that these bays are private.It shows our company name and my initials over the bay in which you have parked.'

'Nah, didn't see it - I'll be gone in a minute.'

The conversation (of which the above is an expurgated version) rapidly degenerated, with both parties losing their tempers, achieving nothing. The Chairman stormed into his Administration Director's office and told him to do something about this. The Administration Director phoned his opposite number in the garage and their conversation went like this.

163

'You know you have been on at us to allow you to have vehicle access over our land so you can form a rear entrance?'

'Yes, it's all agreed isn't it?'

'It's agreed in principle, but I don't think my Board will finalise it unless you take responsibility for ensuring that your visitors refrain from parking in our private bays.'

'But that's going back on the agreement.'

'Not at all, it's merely an additional term that we wish to insert in order to try to ensure that you take responsibility for what has become a major problem for us.'

Key technique

There was no way the company was going to obtain the desired result through its own actions. Using clamps might deter some customers, but would be as inconvenient to the company as to the parkers. Their solution was to pass the problem to the garage, whose need for a solution was acute.

Relationships with neighbours
■ ■ ■

The creation of informal relationships with neighbours may help to solve many problems and - even more effective - avoid many others ever becoming bad enough to be called problems. Omitting to forge such links can lead to problems ranging from a misunderstanding of intent to flagrant abuse of the rights of neighbours.

Case study 12.3
THE FAILED GAMBLE

A manager needed to site a new piece of equipment on the second floor of his office block with access via its windows. As the ground floor projected, it was impossible to gain access to the floor from the company's car park. However, alongside the property ran the car park serving the neighbouring row of shops. He decided to tell the suppliers, who were arriving very early in the morning to use the neighbour's entrance for their access platform. This was done and all went well until the machinery got stuck in the window space and a delivery that should have taken half an hour took two and a half hours. Thus, the neighbour's car park access was still blocked when their customers and staff began to arrive. Needless to say, many of the neighbours, were irrate and descended, en masse on the reception desk of the Manager's office.

'We want to see the person responsible for blocking our car park.'
'That's the man in charge of the access platform equipment.'
'He says you told him to use our access path - he didn't know it was our land and not yours. It's your responsibility not his.'
'Well, they told me that it would only take 30 minutes or so to deliver the equipment and we can't get the access tower to reach our second floor from our own car park.'
'We can see that, but who gave you permission to use our land?' [1]
'I couldn't see that anyone would mind as it was so early in the morning - it wouldn't have blocked the entrance if they'd finished the job at the time they said.'
'Blocking the car park is the problem now, but what about all the row they made when they arrived - getting the tower into position, putting

*out the supports, shouting instructions and so on woke everyone up at
5.30 a.m. - what do you say to that?' [2]*

Key techniques

[1] The manager started on the wrong foot and made the situation
much worse by trying to defend his already untenable position.
There is no way he can win the encounter. Having been caught out,
it would have been better had he come clean and apologised rather
than trying to bluff his way through and evade his responsibility for
the havoc he has caused.

[2] A more constructive procedure would have been to have sought
permission to use the car park access; to have provided some
sweetener to ensure, if there were any problems, that the resulting
backlash would be muted; and to have advised the delivery company to be as quiet as possible as they were on the land as guests and
not of right.

Having been caught, it would have been preferable for the manager
to have handled the outrage with a complete apology and an invitation into his office for a cup of coffee, rather than seeking to either
blame someone else for his shortcomings, or to justify the unjustifi-
able, which is about as effective as trying to put out a fire with
petrol.

165

Landlords and tenants
■ ■ ■

The relationship between landlord and tenant is a legal one
where the rights and responsibilities of each party have been
defined. Both have an interest in the property and a joint
interest in the continuation of the relationship, but they also
have some interests that are diametrically opposed. Nevertheless, within the legal framework and constrained by the
terms of the lease that governs the occupation, there are often
occasions when negotiation is called for (particularly when
the time comes for the rent to be reviewed) and there can then
be a need for some tough talking.

In such instancs, as in every other, it is essential for those doing the tough talking to know all the relevant facts and thus be able to argue from the basis of these facts.

Case study 12.4
THE LANDLORD LOSES OUT

Under the terms of the lease, the rent came up for review every fifth year. The agent for the landlord quoted what the tenant thought was an unacceptable figure and the following discussion of this point ensued.

'We really cannot accept that there should be any increase in the rent - the recession has severely dampened trade and we are actually making less than we made two years ago.'

'Well, we have evidence of a rent that was agreed two years ago and, adjusting for inflation, it indicates that your rent should be double what it is now.'

'That's quite ludicrous - there has been no inflation in rents in the last two years, indeed there has been a reduction. The shop next door has been empty for eight months. The landlord needs to recognise the reality of trading in the current climate. We could afford to pay, say 25 per cent more immediately or to pay a rent that increased by, say, 7 per cent each year for the five years until the next review.'

'No, we don't accept that - we will reduce our asking price to the present rent plus 50 per cent payable immediately or we will have to use the procedure under the terms of the lease to ask an independent expert for a decision.'

Key technique

This is a confrontational situation where firmness is essential. Although the tenant is being genuinely reasonable, the agents responded with a threat. Threats based on bluff can only be used once and are ineffective if called. Later the tenant called the agent's bluff and agreed to the referral to an independent expert who set the new rent at the current rent plus 20 per cent and awarded costs against the landlord.

Case study 12.5
THE LANDLORD LOSES OUT - AGAIN

The landlord was part of a large public corporation where it seemed that, in dealing with property matters, its expertise was somewhat limited and the realities of the market-place were not appreciated. The landlord requested an increase in the rent of 100 per cent after five years. This was at a time of retail buoyancy so there was certainly some justification for a sizeable increase, but not more than, say, 60 per cent. The landlord and the tenant had the following conversation about this.

'There is no way we can pay a 100 per cent increase and, on the evidence of other properties in the area, it does not seem that the market rate is anywhere near the figure you are asking.'

'That's the figure we feel the shop is worth. In view of your good payment record, we are prepared to reduce the increase by 10 per cent.'

'You are still asking for a 90 per cent increase in rent after five years, which ignores the fact that the market rate is substantially less than that figure.'

167

'Yes, we feel that the market is good and that the new rent should reflect that.'

'But the arrangement is that the rent should reflect the market rent as at the review date, not what has happened since.'

'That's our position and we are not altering it.'

'In that case, we must inform you that we will give notice under the lease to exercise the option to break the lease in six months' time.'

Key technique
The tenant knew the facts as were laid down in the lease. The threat - not a bluff but one the tenant was prepared to back up with action - was later put into operation. As a result, the landlord lost *all* income - even the existing rent - as the shop was still empty two years later.

Case study 12.6
THE LANDLORD LOSES A THIRD TIME

The landlord had the right under the lease to charge the tenant an insurance premium, which was quoted as being £17 500. The tenant's insurance brokers, however, obtained an alternative quotation for this cover of £6500. The tenant phoned the landlord and they discussed this.

'We've received this insurance premium charge for £17 500.'

'Yes, the lease provides for it.'

'Oh, we know its chargeable - that's not in dispute. Our concern is the amount of the charge. It shows a 200 per cent increase on last year - are you sure it is not a mistake?' [1]

'It's what they are charging me.'

'But we've had it independently costed by our insurance brokers who got a quote of £6500. Would you like to ring them?' [2]

'No, this is a charge from my insurer and you are obliged to pay under the lease.'

'We don't see why we should pay a charge that is three times that of an alternative quote - something is wrong here. If you won't speak to our brokers, can we speak direct to your insurers?' [3]

Later.

'We've spoken to your insurers and it appears that the charge is so great because they have loaded all your insurances this year on the basis of some heavy claims you made last year on your other properties. We have pointed out that all the fire precautions at this factory are new and that we are directly responsible. They say that they will reconsider the matter and advise you direct.'

Key techniques

[1] Collating the facts in such cases is essential - a mistake could have been made, so it is a reasonable question. However, short of asking to see the renewal note, the tenant has little option but to take the landlord's word that the charge is as stated.

[2] The facts speak for themselves and the offer to allow the landlord to speak to the brokers demonstrates the seriousness with which the tenant regarded the matter. In turn, this should have made it clear to the landlord that the matter was unlikely to be abandoned.

168

[3] If the other party will not take action, there is no reason for not trying to gain permission for the complainant to investigate further. Again, it shows the tenant's commitment to the issue. This was an unusual negotiation, but it had the desired result - an acceptable charge (the insurers reduced their premium from £17 500 to £6600).

The local community
■ ■ ■

The obligations of those operating commercially within a community to that community have been increasing over past years as the community itself has begun to realise the power and control that exists within large (and even the not-so-large) corporations. Mindful of this awareness and of the strength of opinion that can exist among the public, many of whom may be customers and part-owners in the form of shareholders, an increasing number of companies have adopted a very high-profile attitude to what they consider to be their community and environmental responsibilities. This shows itself in the company lending support to local projects, including schools, nurseries, hospitals and so on, on a one-off basis, taking the lead in all community matters, particularly where the company is the largest single employer in that community. The perception of the company as a leading light in the local community can, of course, also have unwanted repercussions.

169

Case study 12.7
TOO MUCH IN CHARGE

A local company had been requested to assist in sponsoring the near-by school. It had been pleased to donate funds and the paid time of some of its managers. The following discussion resulted when there was a meeting between representatives of the company and the school.

'We'd like to set up a career's advisory service for the pupils.'

'That's a good idea - I'm sure it will be a great help to them.'

'We thought that if you ran it within your training centre it would be ideal as you have all the equipment and so on.'

'Mmmm, that may be so, but I'm not at all sure that it's the right way to structure it.'

'Oh we thought you'd be in favour of the idea.'

'We are - as you know, we firmly believe in encouraging links between the school and industry and we are always willing to help, but I don't think you've thought this one through.'

'Do you mean you won't help?'

'Not at all - we will help, but I think you need to think very carefully how you structure this.'

'What do you mean?'

'Although we are the biggest employer in the locality, there are many others. What we can offer may be good, but it will not be what all the pupils want. If we hold the event here and staff it with our people, it will take on the appearance of being run by us and for our benefit, which will have several repercussions - none of which would be healthy.'

'Such as . . .'

'Some employers will be put off taking part if they have to come here, others may be prepared to come but will still resent the idea of coming here and, it may also be perceived that we control the other employers.'

'But that's silly - it's just that you have the ideal facilities to run it effectively.'

'No, my company's position is understandable and needs to be accepted. We will help with staffing and financially, but feel the event should take place on neutral ground.'

Key technique

Tough talking is required in the end here in order to avoid the potential backlash envisaged by the company, not just against them, but against the school.

Case study 12.8
NOT ENOUGH IN CHARGE

The local schools wanted to source more parent governors and, although a company in the area had announced that it would provide paid time off for employees who became governors, very few had come forward. In a further effort to promote the idea, the Personnel Director of the company decided to try and identify a few possibles and convert them to the idea.

'Have you seen this parent governor scheme for the local school?'

'Yes, my children go there so we had the information via their teachers.'

'Ever thought of becoming a governor?'

'Who, me? Of course not - I'm not up to that!'

'Why ever not - what do you think a governor needs?'

'Well, you need to know all about education and teaching, the National Curriculum and all that.'

'But your children are in education and they are studying according to the National Curriculum, so your family is already involved to some extent, isn't it?'

'Yes, but you need to be able to speak at meetings and express your views?'

'Well, you speak and express your views at our regular management briefings, don't you? That's not difficult. You are entitled to your viewpoint there in the same way as a governor is at meetings of the Board of Governors.'

'I'd certainly like to see more attention paid to teaching children to spell correctly rather than relying on the spellchecker in the computers they use.'

'So, there you are - you do have views. As a governor, you could put them forward.'

'But, I'm not qualified.'

'Yes you are - you are a parent, your children are in education at the school and I know that you are very keen for them to do well. What more qualifications do you need?'

'I still don't know.'

'Well, we think you'd be good at it and it would also help us as you would be part of our support of the school. The company believes strongly in these links and governors with children at the school should be best placed to have a beneficial effect on how the school is run.'

171

Key techniques

[1] Tough talking is not only needed in adversarial contexts but sometimes, as in this case, when someone's confidence needs a boost, when their instinctive reaction is that they are not up to the job. Inevitably, it is necessary to:

- anticipate all the responses (which parallells the need to source all the facts)
- try to circumvent all negative thoughts with positive ones
- convince by means of logic as well as by your faith in them
- bolster self-confidence by using examples where their expertise has been displayed.

[2] Most people undersell themselves. Indeed, in appraisal schemes, it is very often the case that subjects score themselves lower than do the people to whom they report. It is management's function to motivate, guide and encourage, which itself sometimes demands tough talking in the best interests of the person concerned.

13

■ ■ ■

Terrors, tears and tantrums

Key learning points

1 Being innovative in approach and calling on past experience are essential when dealing with the variety of problems posed during encounters.

2 Falling into the trap of using too many rhetorical questions must be avoided in order to maintain flexibility.

3 Dealing with severe personal problems requires tact and patience, respect for the individual and, above all, being generous with time.

4 The best intentions are capable of being exploited and, even when dealing with what seems to be a genuine problem, sympathy should not blot out your fact-seeking mission.

The compulsive questioner
■ ■ ■

One of the most difficult encounters can be with a person who tries to dominate the conversation or discussion by constantly contriving statements or questions that then, virtually automatically, generate answers that follow the predetermined plan of the questioner. Unless the negotiator is careful, the answers given will be the ones the questioner intended you to give and, thus, the conversation will take the contrived course set by the other party. By simply reacting according to the other's planned approach, the negotiator loses the initiative (a technique employed by many telephone sales companies - particularly those selling holiday timeshares).

174

Case study 13.1
RHETORICAL QUESTIONS DOMINATING CONVERSATION

Following his dismissal, the director rang a former colleague to prepare the ground for him to promote his case for reinstatement.

'Hi, Ian, how are sales?'
   'Not too bad, but obviously things are tight with this recession.'
   'I did say to you that you needed to keep sales buoyant didn't I?' [1]
'You did.'
   'Of course, you will be lacking my contacts now and that won't help in the current recession. You'll have lost demand from them I expect?'
   'They have been a little slow.'
   'Can't see things getting any better either - you are going to be in trouble by the end of the year unless you get sales up, aren't you?' [2]
'Its too early to say.'
   'But every month that goes by with under-budget sales is a drain on the cash flow as I said before, didn't I?' [3]
   'That's certainly true.'
   'I could contact my old customers and get them to place some orders for old times sake, which would help, wouldn't it?' [4]

Key techniques

[1] There is little Ian can do here but agree as he has not broken the chain of questions that have led to the ultimate 'statement question'. The fact that the former director said an innumerable number of things, some of which, almost inevitably, will turn out to be correct, while much of the rest were irrelevant and incorrect, is overlooked.

[2] Ian's former colleague has the advantage of having prepared his 'script' for the conversation in advance and here has seized the initiative and is leading it towards the desired result he wishes to obtain. Unless Ian breaks the chain, an ultimate 'offer' is inevitable.

[3] This rhetorical question is undeniable - facts are being delivered in a way that seeks to bolster the accuracy and prestige of the questioner.

With the logic built on in this pre-planned conversation, the director is put in the position of virtually having to agree, particularly as any possibility of gaining an order would be helpful.

In handling this kind of person, it is essential to be prepared. If, however, you are not and you cannot deal swiftly enough off the cuff with such prepared comments or questions, note the suggestions and agree to refer back to the person later, thus giving you some thinking time. The following alternative scenario could then take place.

'Hi Ian how are sales?'

'As we all anticipated, they are slow, but we're reaching a lot of new contacts and hope to rectify the shortfall in the medium future.'

'I did say you needed to keep sales buoyant, didn't I?'

'Well there was nothing original in that thought - it is basic at all times, isn't it?' [1]

'But every month that goes by with under-budget sales is a drain on cash flow as I warned, isn't it?'

'Again, that's stating the obvious and, to offset the effect, we're endeavouring to chase every new contact, but obviously we are in competition with a number of alternative suppliers. For that reason I can't keep chatting about it, I must get on. I'll give you a ring in a couple of weeks.' [2]

> **Key techniques**
> [1] This sends a rhetorical question in the other direction!
>
> [2] Practising ending conversations can be helpful. In this case, a swift resolution of the conversation before any offer is made may help. Even if it does not, however, at least it may help you retain or regain the initiative, forcing the other party into a reactive rather than proactive mode.

Making a deal
■ ■ ■

The kind of rhetorical questioning we saw in Case Study 13.1 can be carried a stage further by the persistent third party, whereby a problem encounter is structured into three phases by this person, although the negotiator sees each phase as an individual item, only realising them to be part of a cohesive strategy afterwards. In such a sequence, the third party first raises a question, indicating their preparedness to find a suitable and reasonable solution, even if it is not their own desired result. After a reasonable response or compromise has been indicated, the attitude of the party then hardens and threats are inferred if the desired result is not agreed. Finally, the party moves to the third stage where a deal is suggested.

Case study 13.2
1 PERSUASION, 2 THREAT, 3 DEAL

The first part of this structured trap uses an encounter such as is set out in Case Study 13.1 above, that is an offer, seemingly without strings - in this case, trying to assist sales demand by using personal contacts. Thus the conversation (first alternative) could have ended in the following way.

1 Persuasion
'What I can do is to speak to a few of my old contacts and get them to place orders, which will help, won't it?'

'It would.'

'I'll tell you what I'll do - no hard feelings for what has gone before, that's just business, not personal. I'll make a few phone-calls to all my old contacts and tell them that there are no differences between us and that they would be doing themselves a favour by placing their orders as before, that's in everyone's interests, isn't it?' [1]

2 Threat

One or two days after the above conversation, the former director calls Ian again.

'Ian, I've just been with my solicitor and he says that there is a cast iron case against the company for unfair dismissal and that I should take action immediately in order to protect my position, though that's not in anyone's interest, is it?'

'Not really. I thought we had agreed a compromise?'

'So did I, but he feels that to protect my interests I should take action immediately for the maximum claimable sum. Obviously the compensation awarded could hit the company hard when things are tough, but, as I am paying him for his advice, I have to listen to what he says, don't I?' [2]

'I suppose you do.'

177

3 Deal

'Ian, I've spoken to some of my contacts and I am sure that I can put together a number of orders that will help the order book now and cash flow next month.'

'Oh, great!'

'I've also had another chat with my solicitor who is adamant that there is a strong case.'

'Oh yes.'

'Mind you, it seems a bit pointless for us to argue in a tribunal when we could make the company profitable with my contacts, doesn't it?'

'I suppose so.'

'What did cross my mind was for me to drop the action.'

'That would be good news.'

'Yes, it would save aggro all round. Mind you, I think I should get something out of it. I'd suggest that, in return, you appoint me on a consultancy basis for, say, six months, to try and generate some sales during the present slump. If you pay me on commission it won't even cost you a thing.' [3]

Key techniques

[1] On the face of it, this does seem to help everyone, but, of course, the point of such an offer is to give the former director an edge that can be exploited from a different angle later.

[2] Once again, the rhetorical question is being used to force the apparently unassailable progress towards the position required. What must not be overlooked here, of course, is that the whole thing may be a bluff. The solicitor may *not* have indicated such action or, even, have been consulted at all, yet the underlying threat has been made. To counter this, Ian would need to bluff in return, responding to this threat with the retort, 'Oh really - we've also taken advice and our people think there's no case to answer', rather than referring to the compromise already 'agreed' and making the bland statement, 'You must take what action you feel correct'.

[3] This is the crunch time and, given the way Ian answered the two prongs on which the deal rests, it may be difficult for him to find suitable words to extricate himself.

178

The following is an alternative script of what could have been . . .

'Ian, I've spoken to some of my contacts and I am sure that I can put together a number of orders that will help the order book now and cash flow next month and in the following months.'

'That's fine, but we do need firm orders confirmed in writing via one of the representatives so, if you drop me a line with the details, I'll pass them on to the appropriate representative. We'll pay you an introduction fee on any orders generated, of course.'

'I've also had another chat with my solicitor who is adamant that there is a strong case.'

'As I said before, our advice is different, but you must take such action as you think fit.'

'It seems a bit pointless for us to argue in a tribunal when we could make the company profitable with my contacts doesn't it?'

'The two items are entirely separate - we can <u>both</u> benefit from any orders you can generate. If you take legal action, which, of course, may be costly for you, we will have to sort that out at the appropriate time and place. I don't see that the one affects the other in any way.'

Firmly separating the two aspects of the 'would-be' deal in this way eliminates the former director's progress to his desired result and weakens his case for compensation!

Strikes

■   ■   ■

The ultimate weapon in an industrial relations scenario is the withdrawal of labour by the workforce. Although there is no doubt that this can be an effective weapon, albeit somewhat overused, it must be accepted that if this is the only way in which a problem encounter can be resolved, in most cases it indicates a failure of one or both parties to understand the parameters by which the other is constrained. All too often, of course, the present dispute and intransigence of those involved is actually a result of what has gone before.

Case study 13.3
CUTTING OFF THEIR NOSES . . .

A factory was in the process of being sold, partly as a going concern, while part of the process was being sold to another party and the employees working on that process would be made redundant earlier than the remainder. This was a complicated process, involving delicate negotiations. Although the employees were originally kept informed by a director from head office, who visited several times, when left to their own devices, the local management seemed incapable of keeping the information process flowing. On one visit after a gap of a few weeks, the visiting director found a deputation waiting for him. The following occurred.

'We really can't go on like this - we don't know where we are.'

'I am sorry - it is a difficult process, but we have been trying to keep you all informed.'

'We haven't been kept informed at all - we have no idea what is going on. People are so annoyed they want to walk out.'

'Am I to understand that you have not been told about the latest news on the sale of the whole business as a going concern?'

'We know nothing, absolutely nothing, and people are so annoyed they want to down tools today and walk out - if they lose their money, they say they don't care.'

> 'Can you ask everyone just to hold their horses for 30 minutes until lunchtime while I check a few things out - I promise to be back to you by lunchtime and I think you know that I have always kept my word to you.'
> 'Well that's true, but we do need to know something soon.'
> 'I can understand that.'

The director found out that the local management had not kept the workforce informed, regarding this as his (Head Office's) responsibility. When the serious nature of the situation that had resulted was explained, the local manager said he was going to lunch and left the director to it!

The director immediately called a general meeting of the workforce and outlined the negotiations he was involved in to try and sell part of the process as a going concern, which would protect at least some of the jobs.

180

> 'I really can't be too specific, but we do still hope to sell the factory as a going concern, in which case many of your jobs will be saved.'
> 'How many?'
> 'If I knew that I would give you come indication, but I don't. Although the negotiations are at a final stage, they are not concluded and the new owner cannot yet say how many he will wish to employ.'
> 'How long before you know?'
> 'I expect it will be at least two weeks, but, as soon as we know, you will know - I promise you that. Please believe me when I say that the last thing the prospective owner will want to hear is that some of his would-be employees are on strike. That really could ruin the deal. I do appreciate that this is all very difficult for you, but I do urge you to be patient - it will be in your best interests. We are trying to save jobs, after all.'
> 'Not for all of us - some of us will go anyway.'
> 'That is so, but for them that's no different to the original meeting when we told you of the closure and your redundancy. We said then that _everyone_ would go unless we could find a purchaser. Having _found_ a possible purchaser, part of the case I am making to him for taking the factory, is that since we told you of the position, you have responded with better output than previously. If you stop working or strike now, it will ruin that impression and could stop the deal going through. I cannot guarantee that we will save _all_ your jobs, but I think we can save some. What I will guarantee to do is to ensure that you are informed and meet the new owner when and if the deal goes through.

I will also ensure that as soon as anything happens in future you are told. Now, is that acceptable to you?'

Key technique
The director put the facts before the workforce and allowed them to make a choice as adults. In this case, it *was* acceptable and the workforce raised a cheer, went back to work and achieved even better productivity. Half the jobs were eventually saved and, until the handover, the local management was sidelined to some extent - the director handled all the communication of the developments to the workforce. This is not an ideal managerial structure, but the circumstances dictated that such action be taken.

Tears
■ ■ ■

Dealing with temper requires tact and patience in order to try to make progress while simultaneously, trying to calm aggravated - sometimes out-of-control, emotions. Emotions can also be out of control for other reasons, particularly where news is distressing or comes as a shock, one result of this being that the person dissolves into tears. In many ways, tears are more difficult to combat than temper and often it may be necessary to postpone the encounter (if possible) until the person's emotions are once again under control.

Case study 13.4
EMOTIONAL INTERVIEWS

BEING FIRED
The Managing Director, accompanied by the company's personnel consultant, interviewed the Production Manager, who had previously been warned about his poor performance. Despite trying to deal with the matter very tactfully, immediately the Managing Director stated that, in the circumstances, the company saw no alternative but to give notice, the Production Manager burst into tears. [1]

BEING MADE REDUNDANT
The directors from Head Office had to see the entire workforce of a

warehouse in Bristol, most of whom were women. They anticipated some employees would become very emotional as this was an area of high unemployment, so they first discussed it with the senior female member of staff there. As a result, it was agreed that she should be present with them as they saw the rest of the workforce in order to offer help should any employees break down, which some did. [2]

RESTRAINING AN EMPLOYEE
Several employees were to be made redundant and, on interviewing one, she dissolved into tears and moved to leave the room. Her Manager, concerned that she should hear all the details of the package offered moved to restrain her from leaving. [3]

Key techniques

[1] Respect for the dignity of the individual is important. In this case, the consultant handed the Production Manager a handkerchief and suggested that both he and the Managing Director vacate the room for five minutes while the Production Manager composed himself.

182

[2] Anticipating and being prepared for all eventualities can help progress problem encounters, particularly where emotions can be thrown into turmoil for whatever reason.

[3] All termination decisions need to be backed up with written details so that those affected have something to refer to later when they are calmer. On no account should an employee ever be restrained - it could result in an assault charge being made.

Serious personal problems
■ ■ ■

Inevitably there will be occasions when management have to deal with encounters prompted by the personal problems of their employees, which can be very serious - including death, attempted and actual suicide, break-up of a marriage, accidents, mental and other breakdowns and so on, either of the employee or a relative. Any one of these can have a serious effect on the person involved and the discussion with them about it may be difficult to conduct due to the emotional strain the person is under.

A helpful check-list to aid you with such encounters follows.

1 Discover the facts before the encounter, including as many personal details as possible.

2 Although a one-to-one encounter may be helpful, this may be impractical if it is better that the two parties be of the same sex. However, the intervention of a third party should not be forced on the subject, who may resent this.

3 Be tactful and allow plenty of time, including the possibility of a recess for a short or longer period as necessary.

4 Provide refreshments, and allow those who wish, to smoke.

5 Ensure that the interview is kept confidential and protected from unwarranted interruptions.

6 Try to move to some solution, however skeletal.

7 In cases of ongoing personal problems, try to arrange for the person to be referred to experts - the Samaritans, doctors, solicitors and so on.

8 Take notes of what transpires, but do this in a way that does not further upset the person concerned.

9 Keep the person's immediate superior informed of progress.

10 Update them on progress as necessary.

Where a death has occurred within a family, if there are matters that need to be resolved with a close surviving relative, it may be preferable to find someone within the family, not as closely involved as that person, with whom such matters can be discussed and relayed by them to the subject at an appropriate time. However, this should only be carried out with the permission of the subject - on no account should it be *presumed* that this will be the best alternative.

Case study 13.5
A DUPLICATE WIFE

The Personnel Manager was confronted by a very emotional immigrant employee explaining that he had not been able to attend for work for the past three days as his wife had died. The Personnel Manager was very sympathetic and did everything in her power to try and ease the situation - allowing a leave of absence, an advance of pay to help cover funeral expenses and so on. However, suspicions were aroused when the grieving continued for several weeks, during which time very little work was contributed. Further investigation disclosed the fact that the wife who died was one of three regarded as 'wives' by the employee but he was not legally married to any of them.

Key technique
While not wishing to hold back the organisation's humane consideration of the employees grief, the further facts that have come to light might mean that the approach should be altered accordingly.

Tantrums
■ ■ ■

Although some tantrums are entirely understandable, others may be generated for reasons that are difficult to understand at first enquiry. When this occurs, further investigation may need to be carried out as the full facts may not be apparent.

Case study 13.6
'METHINKS SHE PROTESTETH TOO MUCH'

An agency supplied an au pair to a family in September. In early October (which was after the deadline that would enable the family to decline to continue the arrangement and obtain a free replacement), the family stated the au pair was unsatisfactory as she had been stealing. In the circumstances, the agency agreed to waive its usual terms and find a free replacement. However, the family stated that they did not want a replacement until the new year. Four days after the new au pair arrived in January, the family rang the agency with the following complaint.

'This girl is absolutely useless.'

'I'm sorry to hear that - what's the problem?'

'She is useless around the house, dreadful with the children and she hardly speaks any English.'

'Remember that we said her English was poor - that's why she has come to England, to learn the language. I can't understand why she should have any difficulty with the children, she is the eldest of eight children, so she has plenty of experience.'

'I don't care about that, you have supplied someone who is no good at all to me - I want her replaced.'

'Don't you think you are being a little premature - after all, it is quite an upheaval for a young girl to come to a foreign country and it takes time to settle down with a new family - don't you think you should give her a little time and help?'

'No, it's totally unacceptable - she's useless and so is your service. I want a replacement immediately.'

Key technique

When someone is angry like this, it is important that the facts are checked and the reason for the anger discovered. In this instance, the agency found that the previous au pair had not been stealing, that she had been perfectly happy with the family and had not left them until just before Christmas. The family had concocted the story to avoid paying a fee for a replacement. However, as the replacement was not of the same calibre as the girl they had let go, their fury knew no bounds!

Illness
■ ■ ■

The onset of illness during a problem encounter will almost certainly terminate the session, at least for the time being. Care needs to be taken in case the illness is deliberately induced in order to buy time or sympathy, and also to ensure that duress cannot be subsequently claimed in the event that attempts are made to bring the encounter to a conclusion despite the illness.

Case study 13.7
BOARD DISPUTE

The Board had passed a motion of no confidence in the Managing Director and had requested his resignation. He had indicated that this would be forthcoming, subject to certain arrangements being made to settle his contract of service. As these details were being concluded, the Managing Director collapsed and the Board Meeting was adjourned.

After 45 minutes, during which time the Managing Director recovered and took legal advice, the meeting resumed at the Managing Director's request. The following exchanges took place.

'I wish this meeting to be resumed so that we can conclude arrangements.'

The Chairman noted the request.

'In that case, you already have details of the proposed arrangements - can you agree to them?'
  'No, I want certain guarantees.'
  'I do not think that will be possible.'
  'I have taken legal advice and that is the advice I have been given.'
  'Then you have an advantage over the company as the company has not been able to take such advice. It would be preferable to agree this some other time, I feel.'

At this point, the Managing Director broke off to take a call from his solicitor. After discussing the position for some time, the Managing Director asked the Chairman to speak to his solicitor.

'I am not prepared to do that - he is your solicitor and I cannot speak directly to him, it's unethical.'
  'In view of my illness I would appreciate it.'
  'Under duress, I will speak to him, but I cannot commit to anything.'

The Chairman spoke briefly to the solicitor, remaining completely non-committal and first pointing out the unethical nature of the conversation. The meeting then resumed.

'I am very concerned that we are trying to agree these matters following the Managing Director's collapse, we might be accused of duress . . .'
  'But I do want to get this sorted out.'
  'We all do, but when you have fully recovered. Accordingly, I

propose that we suspend you from your duties on full pay pending your own recovery, and deal with this matter once you have medical clearance.'

Key technique
Some problem encounters require, despite their apparent urgency, a recognition that legal complications may render achieving the aim immediately impossible. To have acted immediately here, could have resulted in a difficult further encounter - suspension of the matter was more appropriate.

187

14

∎ ∎ ∎

Tough talking tactics

Key learning points

1 It is necessary in problem encounters to make full use of all the skills and tactics of negotiation in order to move towards the desired result.

2 A pragmatic approach to nuisance claims will help with damage limitation.

3 Silence can be a valuable ploy - it puts pressure on the other party to speak and, in speaking, to commit themselves.

Having reviewed the principles and practices of dealing with problem encounters in a range of situations and examined the application of these principles via a number of case studies, some of the basic guidelines talked about before are now highlighted so you can see how they work together.

Implicit in dealing with most of the scenarios covered by this book, is the requirement for an element of negotiation. 'Negotiating' means a conferring with others in order to find some degree of consensus, in order that the present state can be changed or the situation progressed. This can mean trying to reconcile the apparently irreconcilable, finding some common ground or adopting a compromise that may not reflect either party's ideal solution, but one that both can live with despite this. The fundamental principles of negotiation are listed below.

1 Establish the facts in order to arrive at an initial view.

2 Accept that there are two sides to every story.

3 Give due weight to the views of the other side.

4 Put your own preferences to one side in order to achieve consensus.

5 Move towards the desired result, ensuring that an entrenched position does not close off possible progress towards that end.

6 Be ready to compromise to achieve the desired result.

To achieve true consensus, it is necessary for both parties to approach the process with a similar degree of openmindedness. This, sadly, is often not the case. When such objectivity is missing, negotiation may degenerate into confrontation.

Guidelines for successful negotiation procedures
■ ■ ■

The subject matter for negotiation may be presented in either written or verbal form. The manner in which the case made is dealt with may vary quite a lot, as you can see from the guidelines for the negotiating procedure below.

Verbal discussion

1 Identify those present and their particular interests.

2 List all points that need to be covered and agree these with the other party.

3 Set a timetable for discussion - is a decision needed immediately or if not when is the deadline?

4 If an immediate decision is needed, discuss each point listed in detail, allowing all involved sufficient time to explore all the aspects and to ensure that everyone fully understands the exact status of each item.

5 If the immediate discussion is merely exploratory, each point may be covered in a more superficial way to allow the parties time to consider or reconsider their approach and/or position.

6 Summarise any decisions made or key points on which the two parties will be taking separate counsel and meeting again.

7 If additional data is to be provided, stipulate who is to provide it, to whom and by when.

8 If another meeting is to be held, set a time and the date for it.

191

Written submissions

1 Examine all aspects of the submission and list the queries arising.

2 Request clarification to answer all queries. (Such a request should be made in writing as the original submission is in writing, although it may save time to hold a meeting at this point, in which case, the minutes of the meeting should include the answers to the clarification queries.)

3 Ensure that there is full understanding of each point made.

4 Correct any false information or suppositions.

5 Assess the implications of each item contained in the quote or proposal.

6 Prepare a statement of own position, counter proposal or whatever for submission to the other party.

7 Set a time limit for responses and further consideration.

Attitudes

For both formats, the attitude of the negotiator should usually be calm and incisive, as well as, at least apparently, open-handed, although inevitably the openness may need to be a front in order to preserve tactics and ploys for use later.

Tactics for negotiations

In the discussions of the particular case studies earlier we have seen how a number of tactics and strategies work, but, inevitably, there are others, some of which are listed below.

1 **Non-disclosure** In all negotiations there is an element of bluff. Thus, either or both parties may not wish to disclose all the facts they know concerning their case or, at

least initially, what their desired result is. The timing of disclosures needs to be judged by analysing the psychology of the negotiation and of the character of the other party rather than on the facts of the matter being discussed.

2 **Misinformation** There can be a further degree of bluff in providing information to the other party and, although this nullifies the principle of negotiating with objectivity and openhandedness, it may be that the desired result can only be achieved by using such information in this way. Indeed, it may be that, by providing such misinformation, the other party is given an 'out' to agree, that is it is face-saving in character.

3 **Face-saving** Very often one party may be prepared, or even wish, to agree, but finds this difficult because it involves a loss of face This is particularly so when the negotiations have a high profile or they are on behalf of others (such as union matters). As agreement is the desired result, the other party may need to design the negotiation process to make it *appear* that both sides have gained something, regardless of the facts.

4 **Pressure** Inevitably pressure will need to be applied in some negotiations. *Latent* pressure may consist of a swift resumé of the results of the negotiations with the aim of gaining agreement to the solution, whereas *actual* pressure is an attempt to force the issue, which may put the pressured party on the defensive. It is inherently risky as any backlash could destroy the possibility of achieving the desired result.

5 **Demonstrating power** Inevitably 'pulling rank' on the other party exerts pressure simply because in this the person is exercising the strength of their position. Although it *can* work, it is risky and may lead to a damaging backlash.

6 **Threats** 'Never threaten unless you are prepared to carry out the threat'. Although this tactic indicates the

193

resolve with which the threatening party is approaching the negotiation, issuing a threat can only be done once and can, anyway, be evaded by the other party counterbluffing. If threats need to be made, then they should be introduced mildly at first, then stronger ones can be used and so on up to a major threat. The latter should never be used first.

7 **First and final offer** Implied in the idea of a first and final offer is another threat that negates the whole point of negotiation. One party is saying, in effect, 'I have no use for anything you are going to say as this is my final offer'. If it is generous, the pre-emptive offer may work, but, even so, the central idea of the other party 'justifying their own existence' is eliminated and so a face-saving tactic may also be needed.

8 **Letting the other side make the running** Like the film star commenting 'And?' at the end of the outraged 'fan's' diatribe in a case study earlier, this entails saying as little as possible - simply keeping the dialogue moving while contributing little. This is like one of the rules of interrogation: 'Let them say what they want and lead them on'. In other words, while someone is speaking more and more of their case and preferences are revealed.

9 **Keeping silent** Silence can hang heavily and few can resist seeking to fill the vacuum. Once again, in speaking, more of the other party's case is revealed and the quiet party will gain ammunition for any counter-ploys.

10 **Fishing** While remaining quiet forces the other party to speak, 'fishing' involves making statements (which can be quite outrageous comments) in order to keep the other party talking - again with the idea of drawing out more and more information about the person's case, and how deeply committed the party is to it.

11 **Misunderstanding** Fishing involves making statements to gain feedback, whereas misunderstanding involves

deliberately misinterpreting the other's comments and statements in order to test the person's depth of feeling about it and so on

12 Good guy, bad guy This is an example of applied psychology, often portrayed in dramas, where two agents, when interviewing a suspect seem to be at variance with each other. The idea is that a rapport is begun between the interviewee and the 'good guy', who then form an alliance against the 'bad guy'. The aim is to exploit the rapport that has been created in the hope that the other party will disclose more of their case to the 'friend', the 'good guy' and 'sympathetic' listener.

Handling temper in negotiations
■ ■ ■

195

The concept of a negotiator deliberately losing - or appearing to lose - their temper has already been listed as a tactic that can be used during problem encounters. However, on occasions, negotiators will be faced with problem encounters that have been forced by the party who has already lost their temper and an immediate solution to the problem is needed.

Ideally, it is preferable in such situations for negotiators to try to postpone the discussion of the problem for at least, say, an hour - preferably longer, to provide the opportunity for the temper to subside, then, hopefully the other party can discuss the matter less emotionally. Invariably, people react quite differently when they are seized by temper - they become blind to rational explanation or logic and often defy attempts at control on the part of a third party. The only person capable of restoring a degree of control is the person with the temper who may have no incentive to calm down. For similar reasons while a written response can be prepared in the heat of the moment, it should never be sent, but, instead, be amended when things are back to normal again.

On some occasions, despite phrases like, 'Calm down' or

'Come back in an hour' (which can, in fact, make the person more angry), the matter will need to be dealt with immediately, which may be difficult as the 'complaint' may be difficult to understand and the facts may be incomplete or even impossible to determine. However, bearing in mind that the logical suggestion of leaving the matter until another time may just worsen the situation, patience and perseverance during such an interview may in fact, begin to calm the subject and so the truth of the perceived complaint can be found out. All this is easy to say here, but it is not easy to accomplish. It may be helpful to follow the guidelines for dealing with confrontations resulting from lost tempers given below.

1 Remain calm yourself at all times. Once two tempers clash, then it is unlikely that any consensus will emerge - the situation will almost go from bad to worse.

2 Note down the facts, the person's opinions and any additional observations as they emerge, without comment. Commenting at this stage may just inflame the situation, while the longer the subject can talk without being challenged, the more likely they are to feel the pressure on them easing.

3 Keep the person talking and explaining the complaint or cause, asking neutral questions to try and uncover as many of the grounds for the complaint as possible.

4 Attempt to further relax the person by offering them refreshments, allowing them to smoke, or whatever, without necessarily interrupting the flow as any interruption could only serve to increase feelings of irritation.

5 After a reasonable period of time (which only the circumstances of the interview can determine), it may be possible to suggest an adjournment for say five minutes as a further cooling off period.

6 On resuming or after the initial flow of information has ceased - if no adjournment has proved possible - start

checking and correcting the facts as they have already been noted. Not only will this enable a more accurate and polished resumé of the complaint to be finalised, but, as time will have passed since the original outburst, the person is likely to be more objective about what has happened. This process can be built on by the negotiator, who can then begin to question any suspect facts or opinions and challenge suppositions and claims where these appear to be false or cannot be verified.

7 At the end of this process (points 1 to 6 may take as long as 30-40 minutes - indeed the longer it takes, the more the temper may subside, although the reverse can also be true), the negotiator should have a reasonable idea as to the complaint and may be able to suggest that, as the complainant has had time to consider their 'case', it is logical that similar time should be allowed for the negotiator to consider the problem, check facts and so on, before discussing the matter further.

197

8 If point 7 is accepted, this gives the negotiator the chance to set up an adjournment, which in itself should have a calming effect on the situation so that, on resumption, the complainant should have a more objective view of the matter. Conversely, point 7 may be rejected as the complainant wants the situation 'sorted out here and now'. In this case, the negotiator may have calmed the party down to some degree but will still need to move immediately to some decision-making process because of the state of the person.

9 In making a decision under pressure, care should be taken not to set precedents, but instead make interim decisions that can be clarified and/or approved later.

10 If an interim decision is implemented, a date and time should be set for review of the matter and implementation of a final decision.

Identifying aims
■ ■ ■

Inherent in every problem encounter, as noted in point 10 of the above guidelines, is the necessity to determine what lies ahead. The point of trying to deal successfully with problem encounters is to achieve a desired result via mutual exploration of the facts and circumstances. Obviously, at the outset, there may be two diametrically opposed desired results (one held by each party) and these need to be reconciled by negotiation and consensus until a single aim results. Once this aim is determined, however, it must both be identified and worked towards constantly. This is not only so that the process itself becomes meaningful, but so that the company or relationship gains from the whole process - in other words, so that it moves everything forwards. There is little point in investing an amount of time in what can be a very lengthy process, if no one will gain from it. This is true whether the gain actually moves the relationship forward (as consensus is necessary to achieve progress) or merely avoids worsening the situation (by reconciling disagreements or solving disputes and so on.)

Problem encounter investigation
■ ■ ■

Endemic in resolving problem encounters is the need to ensure that the desired result is identified, agreed, noted and, ultimately, achieved. This may involve more than a simple resumé of the problems and constituent factors to arrive at a solution. Where there is confrontation (and to move forwards reconciliation is needed), it is necessary to establish the responsibility for the confrontation. Often it will be obvious that certain events or lack of events, actions or inactions were the main or a contributory cause of the event. Resolving the problem encounter moves the business forward, but this only deals with half the problem. For a full resolution of the problem, not only does the desired result have to be achieved, but also an examination of the prime causes to ensure that, where these need alteration, improvement or abandonment, such action occurs. This does not imply that what is required is a witch-hunt - to establish who was responsible and then allocate blame. A more positive approach is required for two reasons, to ensure.

- that objectivity is retained and (as in the problem encounter itself) the desired result is attained, and

- that the process of raising of problem encounters is not inhibited by the fear of reprisals against those who may have been responsible for the causes.

It is often said that accidents do not happen, they are caused and, in a similar vein, it can be said that problem encounters (which in one sense can also be described as accidents, as they also disturb the way things are in a company) do not just happen, they are always *caused*.

199

In reviewing the various studies given earlier it is clear that planning and forethought would often have avoided the problem happening in the first place. Indeed, very often this point has been highlighted in the analysis accompanying the particular case study. For example, in Case Study 7.4, the Chairman had not anticipated that unless he carried his staff with him, regarding his decision he would be unable to ensure that his ideas worked as he had to rely on their goodwill to carry out his instructions. The responsibility for the failure of the concept was not that of those at the sharp end, but his own in not ensuring their commitment first. Further, in Case Study 8.4, the cause of the problem was not that the customer was being awkward, but the poor compilation and communication of the company's terms. In both examples, the person responsible for the prime cause of the problem was the very person who ultimately had to resolve the problem encounter. In other words, these encounters or accidents could have been avoided had more thought been given to the circumstances in the first place, which should provide valuable lessons for the future.

Avoiding repeating a mistake
■ ■ ■

This has to be the real value of the systematic approach to the resolution of problem encounters. Although the achievement of the desired result is extremely valuable in its own right, the company should also learn from the experience and take steps to ensure that the problem does not recur.

To do this, we first need to make sure that the prime cause(s) of each encounter are examined objectively, any shortcomings being resolved, and the implementation of change or whatever action is necessary takes place. In most cases, this can be implemented by the negotiator following up the resolution of the encounter, but in other instances more objectivity may be obtained by bringing in a third party. In either case, the overriding objective at all times should be to seek to demonstrate that the aim is to avoid the problem recurring in the future, rather than to allocate blame for what has happened in the past.

It has been estimated that accidents cost organisations between 5 per cent and 9 per cent of their turnover, which, for profit-making companies, may be as much as, or more than, the profit they make. It is likely that problem encounters cost at least as much as accidents and, as they occur much more often, could well cost a great deal more, even though such costs tend to be hidden. Americans use the image of an iceberg to illustrate that for every $1 of insured loss, there will be between $5 and $20 of uninsured losses that will impact on the company. A similar multiplier effect must apply to the losses borne in solving problem encounters. In the light of such figures, it makes sound economic sense, as well as being good practice, for companies to investigate the causes of such encounters (particularly if a number of similar encounters have occurred) in order to eradicate as many repeat performances as possible.

Prevention

The above is not meant to imply that we need to wait until a problem encounter occurs before taking action that might actually have avoided its happening in the first place. Thus, in Case Study 8.6, although the retailer saved face, putting 'Not recommended for children under 3 years old' on the packaging might have avoided the complaint arising in the first place and would certainly help avoid it happening again. In Case Study 10.3, internal guidelines that outlined how to respond positively to customer queries or even a complete customer care course, could have avoided the original enquiry developing into a complaint, the involvement of the Chairman's office and, presumably, the subsequent embarrassment the local office felt.

Constant reminders of the need to try to avoid problem encounters occurring may help improve the administration and control of companies as it requires a more holistic review of the terms, policies, procedures and attitudes of all involved, which should, in turn, improve the management skills available.

201

Disinformation
■ ■ ■

Unfortunately in trying to deal positively with problem encounters, we do not always get to play on a level surface. Logic, positive responses, commitment of time and so on can be defeated by the agents of disinformation such as rumour and hype. Rumour is usually counter-productive as it breeds unease, preconceptions and distorts facts. Rumour often abounds despite best efforts being made to establish true communication. Rumour is traditionally depicted as being multiheaded, like the mythical Hydra where two heads grew for every one that was cut off, and it is certainly two-faced, seeking to inform but only in such a way that mutual trust is undermined and unease is created in its place.

Consistent and reliable communication can play an important role in removing at least some of the credence given to rumour as an alternative information source, thereby discrediting it and removing its potential for damage.

'Hype', as it is widely referred to, is short for 'hyperbole', which is an exaggerated statement that is not meant to be taken literally. Hype seeks to project an image that it may not be possible to support in reality. Information that has been subjected to hype, may be true in essence, but can create expectations considerably outside the realms of the possible. Inevitably this creates problems when the claims or suggestions are found to be baseless. Using hype within a communication process is usually counterproductive.

202 Total communication management
■ ■ ■

Much of the move towards better communications with all parties reflects the parallel aims of the move towards improving the quality of management and performance - the standard of quality set by the British Standard BS5750. Companies that have adopted the standard have reported considerable increases on output, efficiency and productivity, as well as greater acceptance of products and services in the market-place as more customers require companies to comply with the Quality Standard. It is arguable that only if there is effective communication between all involved parties and that all problem encounters are resolved positively can any organisation embrace the precepts of BS5750. If employers do not adopt a quality approach to their employees then there is no way in which they can attain this in terms of their customers where, if possible, it is even more essential. 'People are the key to competitive advantage', argues Tom Lloyd in *The Nice Company* (Bloomsbury, 1990). Being 'nice' means being willing to think in the long term, to value reputation and to build partnerships. It is not possible to think long term without aims and standards; it is not possible to embrace quality without valuing reputation; it is not possible to build a partnership (any partnership) without communicating. The most important partnerships in this context are those between company and employee, supplier, customer and so on. Although usually these partnerships can move along without too many problems, it is when rapport breaks down, when difficulties arise, when misunderstandings occur, that the real work begins - that of dealing with the problem encounters.

Nuisance claims

■ ■ ■

The aim here has been to provide suggestions for the resolution of problem encounters that, for the most part, occur between reasonable people. It is obvious, however, that some of those raising such problems (particularly those from outside a company) may be using their complaint to try and pressurise the organisation for purely personal gain. Such individuals try to exploit any unwillingness to invest further time and/or energy to achieve a solution. Nuisance claims tend to create a 'no win' situation and may require some very tough talking in order to ensure that the company does not concede the case and thus incur costs purely on a nuisance value criteria - that is paying out to avoid a continuation of the wastage of resources. However, as long as no bad precedents are created, this could be one of those instances where it may be preferable to pay to rid oneself of the nuisance in order to avoid the continuation of the dialogue. The desired results of the two parties here are diametrically opposed. Although this may seem to challenge the principle of not giving in to pressure, it may be an essential pragmatic approach. Fighting battles one can win is one thing; fighting those you cannot, may merely result in a much greater commitment of resources. In these instances, damage limitation may be more realistic than attempting to win an almost impossible victory.

203

The management of change
■ ■ ■

Perhaps it is too much to believe that any company, except perhaps the smallest, can eradicate all problem encounters at all times. Indeed, since all companies are constantly changing, potential causes of encounters are constantly arising. It may be impossible to foresee the effect of such changes, although it could be said, too, that the successful management of change (which arguably makes up to 90 per cent of most management's responsibility) should encompass a consideration of *all* aspects of the change in order to minimise the occurrence of such encounters. Thus, in Case Study 8.4, one of the first tasks of the management responsible for the change of ownership, should have been either to adopt the previous owners' terms of business as their own or, preferably, as presumably they did not reflect the way in which they wished to control their business, to draft and promulgate fresh terms to their advertisers. The result of failure to attend to such fundamentals that rest on change is to set in place parameters or situations that make problem encounters almost inevitable and render their resolution more difficult.

204

15

. . .

Getting the ground rules right

Key learning points

1 Problem encounters can be minimised by developing and communicating policies and procedures that show best practice.

2 Considering problems in advance and with regard to policies/procedural criteria can simplify the approach and ease the way to solutions.

Tough talking

In seeking to communicate positively with customers, suppliers, employees and owners, companies need to develop detailed policies and ensure that all those responsible for implementing the policies and interfacing with those target third parties are aware of the implications, trained to respond to situations in a way that is in line with the policies and in dealing with any after-effects and implications. The advantage of developing policies is that they exist as a constant guide and criteria and may resolve many problems virtually automatically by 'designing them out'.

Case study 15.1
GETTING THE RULES RIGHT

A personnel manager was considering the little sum that was available in her welfare budget and noticed how much more had been paid out in the current year than the previous one in claims for tights 'damaged' on office furniture. It seemed that the situation was being abused so a policy statement was devised that stated that employees must take care to avoid furniture and fittings as they should expect tights to be caught by such items and that, unless the item was damaged, no further claims would be paid out. The number of claims immediately dropped.

Outline policies (see below) must be converted into detailed guidelines and check-lists for particular situations so that they are available for those at the sharp end - those who have to implement them who need to refer to these documents instantly when they are faced with a problem). Not only should this help reduce the number of difficult encounters, it should also provide some solutions.

The policy documents need to cover instances of employees dealing with suppliers, customers, public, media and owners and so on. Subdividing the document by these groups of people is helpful as each part can then be kept relatively

206

short, yet each provides sufficient data to enable the person responsible to receive the guidance they need to implement the policy.

Relationships with employees
■ ■ ■

A full employment policy will cover a whole range of personnel-related topics and is outside the scope of this book. The following outline employment policy is included here to show the sort of general commitment to communication principles that should substantially reduce the incidence of problem encounters.

1 The company recognises the individual importance of every employee and will seek to ensure that, at all times, all employees are well informed about the activities and plans of the company, to a degree that does not endanger the development or marketing of products, services and so on.

2 The company wishes to encourage the development of all employees to the level of attainment at which they will be satisfied and will also seek to inform, coach and train employees at all times.

3 The company recognises that its aims will be most effectively achieved by involving employees in decisions and developments and will endorse and encourage all means by which this can be sought. Supervision and management are expected to allow sufficient time in their schedules for active communication with those for whom they are responsible in order to ensure the active commitment of their employees and the solution of problems connected with their employment. (*Note*: The mechanism for the solution of problems might be covered by the company's grievance policy, but this commitment is much wider than that.)

4 Employees are encouraged to take a lively interest in

207

the company's activities and, should there be anything about which they have insufficient information or are unsure, should be encouraged to ask their immediate superiors. Should they not receive an adequate answer, they are encouraged to pursue their query through the grievance procedure set out in the employee handbook.

Both parties are urged to listen, with an open mind, to the views of the other to ensure that an active dialogue is achieved, to ensure that misunderstandings are explained and to attempt to achieve unity of purpose.

By doing this, the company has set the parameters for action should problems and so on occur. If it also develops a staff handbook setting out all the rules and regulations, discussions regarding subsequent transgressions can be carried out with reference to these rules. Immediately, it is not nearly so easy to say, 'I didn't know' and so the number of problem encounters should be reduced.

208

Relationships with suppliers
■ ■ ■

In the 1990s, over 60 per cent of items required to run a company are bought in. Self-sufficiency, formerly the watchword of UK companies, has ceased to operate to a large extent. Inevitably this means that the number of opportunities for problem encounters with suppliers has increased considerably, while the amount of negotiation with suppliers has also increased proportionately. The company's attitude towards its suppliers needs to be codified for the benefit of both its own negotiating or purchasing staff as well as the suppliers themselves. A basic draft of such a code follows.

1 The company will source products and raw materials from a range of suppliers, who it will regard as nominated suppliers once this relationship has been in place in excess of two years. As a matter of policy, the company will usually source from at least two suppliers, but

undertakes not to divulge the prices quoted by one supplier to another without prior written permission from that supplier.

2 All suppliers will be given detailed specifications of the product required, an indication of the timescale and price range and will be expected to provide the product (after an order has been placed) in accordance with the price, quality and other such parameters set out in the specifications.

3 All deliveries are sampled to check that they comply with the specifications and, in the event of a deviation from the specification, the organisation reserves the right to reject the whole consignment, or to renegotiate terms in the event that the materials can still be used subject to adjustment.

209

4 In the event of a discrepancy between an order and what is delivered or vice versa (such as varying of the amounts and so on), the company reserves the right to renegotiate the terms of the supply.

5 All supplier invoices will be paid on the due date in accordance with the agreed terms.

6 The organisation's terms will be supplied on demand and are printed on the reverse of both specification and order. Deviation from such terms is not permitted without prior written permission from a director of the company.

7 Each year, nominated suppliers will be requested to submit new quotations against specifications (which may be revised).

If such a policy is distributed to every supplier, once again the capacity for misunderstanding is reduced and the number of problem encounters should also be reduced as the supplier will know from the outset exactly what relationship is envisaged and what responses are expected.

Relationships with customers
■ ■ ■

The aim of a wealth-creating company is to make a profit by producing products and/or services that have a value to its customers. Companies do not stand still - they either expand and prosper or contract and, ultimately, go out of business. To expand, the company usually needs to be able to satisfy more customers each year or at least to obtain more income from the same customers each year. To achieve either (or both) it needs to satisfy its customers in terms of value, quality, delivery service and so on. An outline for a policy regarding customers follows.

1 The company commits itself to producing good quality and value products available at the time required by the customer.

2 In the event that a problem arises regarding a product, the company will endeavour to deal with the problem objectively and positively, with the aim of both solving the problem and converting a dissatisfied customer into a satisfied one.

3 All complaints - no matter what their source or basis - will be treated with courtesy and a positive attitude. This is the policy even to the extent that this may mean compensating a customer where there is no genuine complaint or where a complaint has been greatly exaggerated.

4 Customers will be treated courteously and, provided the time is appropriate, invited to tour the premises (except for any parts of the operation from time to time considered to be sensitive or secret, which will be suitably protected).

The policy to be observed in dealing with customer complaints and queries cannot be as specific as that for employees and suppliers as the relationship, while vital, as the customer in effect supplies everyone's pay, tends to be relatively loose.

However, it is essential that a positive attitude is displayed. Often complaints will be met by defensive reactions, seeking to avoid taking liability for poor service or attempting to justify inadequate standards or unsatisfactory products. Such reactions tend to be conditioned by the need not to make precedents, which overlooks the fact that precedents are of no significance if the cause of the complaint is removed.

Relationships with the public and community
■ ■ ■

Companies operate within society and, increasingly, are becoming aware that society requires them to acknowledge that, without society such companies could not operate, and that, thus, they have an obligation to society and particularly to the environment as many companies have quite a substantial impact on it. In creating an impression of itself as being part of the community, the company is effectively communicating with the community in general (with current and potential employees in particular) as without the community, of course, the company has no purpose, no staff and no customers. Such a commitment to putting something back into the community, without which the business could not operate and ceases to have a purpose, is recommended for all businesses, whatever their size. An outline policy regarding the public and the local community follows.

211

1 The company commits itself, as a responsible member of society, to treating the general public, the community and the environment within which it operates with respect.

2 The company will continue to be a member of the Business in the Community movement and to support other local initiatives, encouraging its employees to join in schemes enhancing the environment within which we operate, by means of day and block release or secondment and by encouraging employees to communicate the results of such work to other employees.

3 The company recognises the importance of environmental issues and commits itself to working towards the introduction of processes and practices that cause least harm (or, preferably no harm) to the environment. It welcomes ideas for protecting the environment from its operations from whatever source, and will work to introducing such feasible and viable ideas.

4 The company will work towards reducing or eliminating its waste and maximising its productive use of resources.

5 The views of pressure groups and those representing environmental groups will be considered objectively and borne in mind when making decisions on environmental issues.

6 Sponsorship in and links with schools. The company will endeavour to support local education establishments generally and, in detail, by . . . (etc., etc.).

7 Official agencies demanding access will be dealt with courteously and, in accordance with the access policy that determines to what information such persons have a right of access. As many agencies do have a right of access to and to obtain information from the company, a specific procedure for dealing with such requests (and for providing the information) may be needed.

Relationships with owners
■ ■ ■

The manner in which the company needs to interface with its owners will vary depending upon its type. Public limited companies have detailed obligations to their shareholders as well as to creditors and others; other limited companies have similar but fewer onerous obligations; partnerships and unlimited liability companies have still fewer onerous obligations, while statutorily authorised bodies (such as local authorities) have no legal obligations to their 'owners' (that is council taxpayers), although, increasingly, many are developing a sophisticated reporting structure to advise local residents of their actions and how the public money, for which they are effectively trustees, is spent. The manner of dealing with such 'owners' will vary according to the exact requirements of time and place and, for that reason general guidelines cannot be provided, other than perhaps the following.

1 The company recognises the right of the 'owners' to have provided to them full financial data showing the record for each financial period.

2 Such information will be provided in a format that can be interpreted by non-financial readers and arrangements will be made for a telephone hotline to be provided to answer queries arising from such material.

3 The company commits itself to full disclosure of all information, save where this would mean disclosing personal information or that which is prejudicial to the interests of the company.

213

Relationships with the media
■ ■ ■

Many companies operate in such a way that their products, manufacturing processes or services, can be of considerable public interest. This interest in the operations of both wealth-creating and wealth-consuming companies should not be underestimated. For a number of reasons, including:

■ the privatisation of formerly state-owned bodies
■ the realisation of the power and effect of companies and other bodies
■ the scandals and disasters surrounding both such organisations and their key executives, and
■ the more widespread ownership of such organisations

The attention given to them has moved from the financial

pages of newspapers to the general news pages and, indeed, often to the front page. Companies need to have a policy for dealing with the media and to train one or more spokespeople in the art of media relations. An outline company policy for this area could consist of the following points.

1 The company recognises the natural interest that will be aroused by the media on behalf of the public in its operations and will make all information, other than that which is regarded as confidential, regularly available to enquirers from the media.

2 [Name and deputy] will act as spokesperson for the company and will be briefed continually by those responsible for each [division, product and so on].

3 In the event of other employees being contacted by representatives of the media, they will be referred to the spokesperson.

4 In interfacing with the media, the spokesperson will endeavour to be truthful at all times and to ensure that such information is correctly reported.

5 Contacts with each branch of the media will be made and such contacts will be regularly briefed so that they have background knowledge of the company, which will be updated continually.

Rights to respect
■ ■ ■

The adoption of commitments and policies, which underline the importance of the fact that individuals require individual and positive treatment, involves the understanding that, at all times and in all aspects, people have a right to respect and a failure to acknowledge those rights challenges the very heart of a commitment to active communication to solve problems and achieve progress. This is evident not only in solving major problems, but also in everyday attitudes. Thus, failing to reply to correspondence, interrupting an interview to deal with a mundane telephone call, failing to provide a decision by the agreed time without adequate explanation, keeping a customer waiting on the phone without apologising and so forth, are all instances where casual and unthinking treatment of people eat away at the commitments expressed in the policies. They will only be effective if they are put into practice. Maintaining the standards we set for ourselves is an important part of implementing policies. Often it is the failure to adhere to such standards that leads to problem encounters.

Setting standards and ensuring that they are adhered to (even if they occasionally slip) produces considerable benefits for all involved. Employees who can see a commitment on paper to communication turning into an actual commitment to the community, to education and training, to treating employees as individuals with respect, to the environment and so on will, in turn, respect and feel pride for the company they work for. Employees who are able to take a pride in the achievements of their employer (which, in turn, are their own achievements) are more likely to feel committed to the company, contribute to a greater extent and have fewer problem encounters. Suppliers who are invited to become involved in the company's plans, who see their invoices paid on time and are treated as partners, are more likely to respond with keener prices and greater commitment. Customers who are treated with respect, whose legitimate complaints are met with courtesy, who know they can rely on quality and value, are more likely to become repeat customers.

215

Summary
■ ■ ■

The above policies both set out a commitment to, and act as a criteria against which to measure, future performance. In all instances, compliance with these commitments has to be effected by means of meetings, discussions or briefings. The way in which the aims included in the policies are achieved is essential to their success. The way in which the policies must be implemented have been described - that is by means of positive, open-minded, objective discussions - but the actual nuts and bolts of the operation have still to be discovered. Although inevitably it will be necessary to vary the approach to suit individual circumstances, essentially such discussions and so on must address the points listed in the checklist in Chapter 2.

An essential ingredient of the whole process is thinking time, which needs to be adequate for the purpose. In the West there is a great drive to be always getting on with things, for there to be some action. In the East the opposite holds true. The orientals set great store by thinking a problem through for what we in the West may regard as an inordinately long time, before any action takes place. This does not mean that the total time taken to implement a plan is greater, merely that more time is taken thinking the challenge, the project or the problem through, anticipating problems and alternatives, and less time in effecting the action (and sorting out problems caused by inadequate planning and thought).

Case study 15.2
FIRE!

In a complete panic, the office boy dashed into the manager's office shouting, 'Fire!, Fire!, Fire!' The manager dashed out of his office, grabbed the water bucket hanging on a bracket down the hall and ran ... but where to?

He had absolutely no idea where, how severe or what type of fire it was that he was determined to tackle. The fire could have been anything from a cigarette end smouldering in a metal waste paper bin to a raging inferno in the paint store, from the photocopier giving off smoke to the coffee machine melting its insulation, from a firework thrown into the office by schoolboys to a major fire at the largest item of plant in the factory, surrounded by tonnes of inflammable material.

More haste ...

In only one of the scenarios set out in Case Study 15.2 would the arrival of the manager with a bucket of water have been of any use. In most of the others, evacuating the building and summoning professional assistance would have been far more sensible and using water could have worsened the situation dramatically. Life-saving actions, at a time when *seconds* saved could mean *lives* saved, were impossible because the actual information available on which to base a decision was not available to the person responsible. It would have been far more helpful to have:

■ calmed the office boy down and discovered the location of the fire, its cause and size

■ decided on a suitable course of action based on that information.

The lessons from this simple example are obvious but bear repeating because recognising the need to carefully analyse a problem before moving on to find a solution to it is key to resolving most problem encounters:

■ decisions based on inadequate or absent information and/or preconceptions will almost inevitably fail

■ time spent thinking through a problem should mean that the best decision emerges from the possible alternatives

■ *preparation time* is at least as valuable as *action time*, and indeed can often be of greater value

■ time spent reflecting on things may generate innovative responses which are unlikely to emerge instinctively

■ inadequate preparation or thinking time may ultimately cause delays in action time so that, overall, the time span required is extended

Tough costing

While most problem encounters can be solved, it should not

be overlooked that in every case - whether the negotiator 'wins' the confrontation or not, the company loses because the consideration and, hopefully, solution of every problem encounter takes time and uses resources. Every encounter has a cost that has an impact on the profit or available resources of the company, directly or indirectly. However, should both parties be from the same company (for example, the problem encounter is personnel related), there is a double cost impact on that company. If the combined hourly cost of the salaries of the two employees involved is £10 and the company is making a 10 per cent profit on sales, to fund the cost of the encounter per hour requires an additional £100 of sales to be generated - tough costing indeed, particularly if the principles of the iceberg image are also applied.

While the adoption of the principles and practice set out here should help in the resolution of problem encounters, ultimately the aim needs to be to render them unnecessary - by avoiding a repetition of the circumstances that produce the encounters. That could well prove to be the greatest value of tough talking.

Index

■　■　■

the Institute
of Management

FOUNDATION

PITMAN
PUBLISHING

The Institute of Management/Pitman Publishing *Management Solution Series* provides you with all the know how you need every day of your working life. These books represent the core business skills. Not only will they help you day to day but, if you read the whole series, you will have an impressive skills portfolio to help you gallop up the career ladder.

Titles in this series:

Thinking on your feet in negotiations
Become an expert negotiator, able to handle every situation.

First things first
Time management and more.

Manipulating meetings
How to get what you want out of meetings.

Effective presentation
Become an expert at presentation, no more nerves just a lot of confidence.

How to write reports and proposals that get results
If you want your ideas to be accepted don't just write good reports, write ones that get read and get the results you want.

FOUNDATION

PITMAN
PUBLISHING

The Institute of Management's mission is to promote the development, exercise and recognition of professional management. The Institute's members include all levels of management from students to chief executives. The Institute of Management supports its own Foundation, which provides a unique range of services designed to develop, inform and advise managers in every sector of business.

What has been said about Pitman Publishing/Institute of Management Books:

"Practical guidance on a wide range of management issues"
– *The Independent on Sunday*

"They meet the need for managers to learn fast and to solve problems quickly"
– *Professional Manager*

"These books are presented in a crisp, approachable format and offer practical guidance ... The principles articulated in these books are important"
– *The Independent*

"Written in an accessible and jargon free style. Packed with helpful advice tips and tricks"
– *Business North West*

"For busy managers with little time for training, these quick to follow guides will help develop the skills to ensure they are the best in the business"
– *Jeremy Kourdi, Institure of Management*

"Certain to become a lifeline for managers"
– *Commerce Magazine*

Smoking Cessation

O R M L

OXFORD RESPIRATORY MEDICINE LIBRARY

Smoking Cessation

Dr Keir E. Lewis

Senior Lecturer, Swansea School of Medicine
and Consultant in Respiratory and General
Medicine, Prince Philip Hospital, Hywel Dda
Health Board, Wales, UK

OXFORD
UNIVERSITY PRESS

OXFORD

UNIVERSITY PRESS

Great Clarendon Street, Oxford OX2 6DP

Oxford University Press is a department of the University of Oxford.
It furthers the University's objective of excellence in research, scholarship,
and education by publishing worldwide in

Oxford New York

Auckland Cape Town Dar es Salaam Hong Kong Karachi
Kuala Lumpur Madrid Melbourne Mexico City Nairobi
New Delhi Shanghai Taipei Toronto

With offices in

Argentina Austria Brazil Chile Czech Republic France Greece
Guatemala Hungary Italy Japan Poland Portugal Singapore
South Korea Switzerland Thailand Turkey Ukraine Vietnam

Oxford is a registered trade mark of Oxford University Press
in the UK and in certain other countries

Published in the United States
by Oxford University Press Inc., New York

© Oxford University Press, 2010

The moral rights of the author(s) have been asserted
Database right Oxford University Press (maker)

First published 2010

Reprinted 2012

British Library Cataloguing in Publication Data

Data available

Library of Congress Cataloging in Publication Data

Data available

Typeset by Newgen Imaging Systems (P) Ltd., Chennai, India
Printed in Great Britain
on acid-free paper by
Ashford Colour Press Ltd., Gosport, Hampshire.

ISBN   978-0-19-955625-0

10 9 8 7 6 5 4 3 2

Contents

vi

Preface

Keir Lewis is to be congratulated on pulling together a team of predominantly younger-than-usual people to produce this book. Smoking cessation plays a vital part not only in the prevention of many illnesses but also in their treatment. Although labour-intensive it is highly cost-effective in developed countries where man-hours are expensive and will be even more cost-effective in countries where labour is cheap.

It is timely that we now have a book which concentrates on smoking cessation without neglecting prevention, pulling the evidence together for seven major disease categories and highlighting the gaps. I hope it will help draw cardiologists, general practitioners, nurses, obstetricians/gynaecologists, oncologists, psychiatrists and other health professionals (including those involved in medical education) further into the active fold which until now has been composed predominantly of chest physicians, psychologists and health prevention specialists. May it stimulate also colleagues in the developing world, where the results of the smoking epidemic will hit even harder.

Dr Ian Campbell
Chest Physician
Llandough Hospital,
Past President of The British Thoracic
Society Tobacco Committee and
Chair of its Tobacco Committee

Acknowledgements

I would like to thank each of the chapter writers and Helen Poole for also providing the real-life examples in the Appendix, Rachel Johnstone head of Medical Illustration, West Wales General Hospital, Carmarthen—for being so patient and creative in turning abstract ideas into understandable drawings. Thanks also to Peter Walton, manager Hywel Dda Health Board for co-writing the business case (in the Appendix) and agreeing for it to be published, and I am extremely grateful to Dr. Ian Campbell and Mrs. Sonia Edwards from Llandough Hospital, Cardiff for training me on smoking cessation and for their unrelenting enthusiasm.

Thanks also to Jenny Wright at OUP.

Contributors

Hazel Dixon
Smoking Cessation Specialist,
Prince Philip Hospital,
Hywel Dda Health Board,
Wales, UK

Cath Einon
Smoking Cessation Specialist,
West Wales General Hospital,
Hywel Dda Health Board,
Wales, UK

Robin Ghosal
Research Fellow, Prince Philip
Hospital, Hywel Dda Health
Board, Wales, UK

Anthony Gibson
Research Fellow, Prince Philip
Hospital, Hywel Dda Health
Board, Wales, UK

Christina Gratziou
Assistant Professor
of Pulmonary and Critical Care,
Head of Smoking Cessation
Clinic, Evgeniio Hospital
Medical School, Athens
University, Greece

Carlos A. Jiménez-Ruiz
Head of Smokers Clinic,
Institute of Public Health
and Associate Professor
of Medicine, Universidad
Complutense, Madrid, Spain

Keir E. Lewis
Senior Lecturer, Swansea
School of Medicine and
Consultant in Respiratory and
General Medicine, Prince
Philip Hospital, Hywel Dda
Health Board, Wales, UK

Helen Poole
Smoking Cessation
Counsellor, Cardiff and Vale
University Health Board,
Wales, UK

Stuart Rees
Principal Pharmacist, Prince
Philip Hospital, Hywel Dda
Health Board, Wales, UK

Elin Roddy
Specialist Registrar in
Respiratory and General
Internal Medicine, Mid Trent,
England, UK

Yasir I. Syed
Specialist Registrar in
Respiratory Medicine, Hywel
Dda Health Board, Wales, UK

Clive Weston
Reader, Swansea School of
Medicine and Consultant in
Cardiology and General
Medicine, Singleton Hospital,
Abertawe Bro Morgannwg
Health Board

Symbols and abbreviations

↓	decreased
↑	increased
ACS	acute coronary syndromes
AIDS	acquired immunodeficiency syndrome
BAT	British American Tobacco Company
BTS	British Thoracic Society
CABG	coronary artery bypass grafting
CAM	complementary and alternative medicines
CHD	coronary heart disease
CO	carbon monoxide
eCO	exhaled carbon monoxide
COPD	chronic obstructive pulmonary disease
CVD	cardiovascular disease
ECG	electrocardiogram
FEV	forced expiratory volume
FTND	Fagerström Test for Nicotine Dependence
GP	general practitioner
INR	international normalized ratio
IPF	idiopathic pulmonary fibrosis
MHRA	Medicines and Healthcare Products Regulatory Agency
MI	myocardial infarction
MS	multiple sclerosis
NHS	National Health Service
NICE	National Institute for Clinical Excellence
NNN	N′-nitrosonornicotine
NNT	number needed to treat
NO	nitric oxide
NRT	nicotine replacement therapy
RR	risk ratio
SLE	systemic lupus erythematosus
SSS	Stop Smoking Service
TED	thyroid eye disease
US	United States

Chapter 1

Epidemiology, the world tobacco epidemic

Keir E. Lewis

It is the imperative of every lover of mankind, to unite in suitable efforts to remove this rapidly increasing evil, by exhibiting its injurious effects on the health . . . and its enslaving power on the habits . . . and also, by seeking to deter others, especially the young, from acquiring this unnecessary, offensive and injurious practice.

6th Principle British Anti-Tobacco Society, 1853.

Key points

- This chapter presents an overview of smoking, its global importance, and key mortality and morbidity data.
- There are 1.3 billion smokers worldwide consuming over 5 trillion cigarettes annually.
- Smoking caused an estimated 100 million deaths in the 20th century.
- The death toll is rising with 3 million deaths predicted this year from smoking and a billion deaths expected in the 21st century.
- By 2020, all of the top 5 causes of death will be smoking-related.

1.1 Curbing the smoking pandemic: why it is important and what we can do to help

The problem of smoking is now truly global. Understanding the epidemiology of tobacco use helps us estimate tobacco-attributable risk to mankind. Due to its addictive and pleasurable properties, tobacco has been a part of the global human experience for many centuries.

Now, there are nearly 1.3 billion smokers worldwide, consuming more than 5 trillion cigarettes annually. Half will die of a tobacco-related disease. There were an estimated 100 million deaths in the 20th century, and currently we expect 3 million deaths a year attributable to smoking, rising each year with a billion deaths projected for the century ahead. Even by 2020, all of the top 5 causes of death will be smoking-related.

Estimates from developed countries suggest tobacco was directly responsible for 24% of all male deaths and 7% of all female deaths over the last 30 years, rising to over 40% in men in some former socialist economies and 17% in women in the USA.

Devastation caused by smoking is prevalent in the UK. The Royal College of Physicians described it as 'this present holocaust' highlighting in 2002, that the 'the humble cigarette is responsible for a dozen times more deaths in the UK in the past 40 years than British casualties from World War II—over 5 million'.

The United Kingdom Government, in its White Paper in 1998, declared:

> . . . smoking is the greatest single cause of preventable illness and
> premature death in the UK . . .

No precise estimate can be made of the number of deaths from smoking in developing countries, but the prevalence of smoking suggests that it will be large and it will increase as tobacco manufacturers target these countries.

1.2 What can be done about it?

Prevalence of smoking in many developed countries has fallen from all-time highs of 45% to 50% of adults just after the Second World War to between 21% to 28% adults now. This represents a tremendous public health success and is a result mainly of population-based tobacco control measures (taxation, advertising restrictions, bans in public places, etc.) and partly due to advances in nicotine dependence treatment.

However, since 1990, the rate of decline has slowed and among US adults, declined on average by only 0.39% per year with no significant drop in prevalence from 2004 to 2006. In the UK, there are worrying suggestions that smoking is increasing in teenagers, particularly girls. A four-stage model of the tobacco epidemic has been proposed by Lopez et al. Countries are at different stages of this epidemic because the peak death rates attributable to tobacco and countermeasures lag 10 to 20 yrs behind peak tobacco consumption and tobacco company promotion (see Figure 1.1 and Table 1.1).

Public legislation is key to combating the tobacco epidemic but is beyond the scope of this book. Individual treatment of smokers is also needed. On a personal level, most of us see nicotine dependence as just a 'bad habit', implying that smokers should be able to quit on their own. Most smokers do try quitting by this method, yet we all know that quitting smoking is difficult. Around 70% of smokers want to quit and over 40% try every year (usually on their own), yet only 3% to 7% can do so unaided. In contrast, a medical

Figure 1.1 A model of the cigarette epidemic

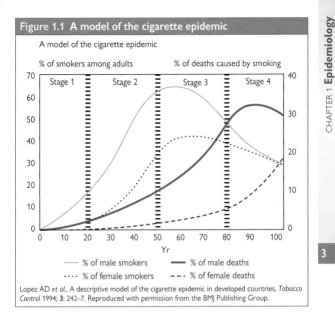

A model of the cigarette epidemic

Lopez AD *et al.*, A descriptive model of the cigarette epidemic in developed countries, *Tobacco Control* 1994; **3**: 242–7. Reproduced with permission from the BMJ Publishing Group.

Table 1.1 Examples of countries at each stage in Figure 1.1

Stage I	Stage II	Stage III	Stage IV
Sub-Saharan Africa	China Latin-America North Africa	Eastern Europe Southern Europe	Western Europe North America Australia

management concept is needed for this lethal and addictive neurological disorder, utilizing better systems of care, including behavioural modification, pharmacological interventions, telephone 'quit lines', and other services. Not infrequently smokers need help from health professionals. Nearly 70% of all tobacco users are seen at least once by a health-care provider every year, yet only 39% reported being offered any advice or assistance to quit and the majority of pharmacotherapy prescriptions are patient-instigated. Even within hospitals, a meta-analysis concluded that:

> levels of smoking cessation care are less than optimal, and the
> levels of some important care practices are particularly low.

It is evident that many opportunities to intervene in tobacco dependence are missed by health professionals. Too long have doctors and nurses been content to treat the illnesses that smoking causes without actively treating the cause. The explosion of research into smoking cessation means that lack of effective treatments is no longer a reason for failure to intervene with smokers.

The public health message to smokers needs to change from 'Quit on your own' to 'Get help from a health-care professional.'

Brief tobacco dependence treatment is effective, so every smoker should be offered at least brief intervention. Brief intervention is particularly relevant to primary care teams who treat a wide variety of patients and face severe time constraints. Intensive tobacco dependence treatment can be provided by any trained clinician who has the available resources to do so. There is a strong dose–response relationship between the intensity of tobacco dependence counselling and its effectiveness, for both healthy smokers and hospitalized patients (see Table 1.2).

Despite advances in tighter public legislation, better understanding of the genetic and neurobiological processes of nicotine addiction, and an improving evidence base for successful treatments, there are many continued failures in tobacco control. These particularly include the paucity of teaching on smoking cessation in medical schools and nursing curriculae, resulting in a lack of knowledge and confidence amongst health professionals on how to help smokers quit. Perhaps most importantly, many health professionals do not see tobacco control and treatment as their responsibility and are content to merely treat the illnesses and devastation it causes. Many health professionals may not know what stop-smoking services are available in their area, what are the most successful treatments for their addicted patients, and do not feel confident in directly helping their patients to stop smoking or how to access specialist stop-smoking services.

There are few practical books on smoking cessation geared towards general health professionals. The aim of this book is to provide a compact, practical, and evidence-based guide to update the reader on the epidemiology of smoking but also to be directly applied in different common clinical settings. We have provided general information on smoking but included sections giving key facts and tailored advice/treatment for specific groups of smoking patients.

Table 1.2 Quit rates at 1 yr by intervention	
Intervention	Rates at 1 yr
None (spontaneous quit rate)	2% to 3%
Minimal counselling (<3 min) Brief counselling (3–10 min) Counselling (>10 min)	4% 5% 8% to 10%
Interactive Internet programmes	5% to 10%
Interactive telephone programmes	10% to 25%
Group classes without medication Group classes combined with pharmacological treatment	15% to 25% 25% to 35%

Therefore, emphasis is also placed on secondary prevention—listing the benefits of stopping smoking *once already diagnosed* with that particular illness or symptom.

We have included a series of real-life case scenarios involving problems encountered in the management of particular smokers suggesting 'model' answers to common questions/challenges; we have incorporated an example of an actual (successful) business case that may be used to create a 'stop-smoking service' in secondary care elsewhere and provided references and websites to access further material.

Key reading

Forty fatal years: Royal College of Physicians (London) and Action on Smoking and Health; 2002.

Freund MC, Paul E, McElduff C, Walsh P, Sakrouge RA, Wiggers R, Knight J. Smoking care provision in hospitals: a review of prevalence. *Nicotine & Tob Res* 2008; **10**(5): 757–74.

Lopez AD, Collishaw NE, Piha T. A descriptive model of the cigarette epidemic in developed countries. *Tobacco Control* 1994; **3**: 242–47.

Mackay J, Eriksen M, Shafey O. *The Tobacco Atlas*, 2nd ed. Atlanta: American Cancer Society; 2006.

Murray CJ, Lopez AD. Mortality by cause for eight regions of the world: Global Burden of Disease Study. *Lancet* 1997; **349**(9061): 1269–76.

Peto R, Lopez AD, Boreham J, Thun M, Heath C, Jr., Doll R. Mortality from smoking worldwide. *Br Med Bull* 1996; **52**(1): 12–21.

6

Chapter 2

The physiological and psychological effects of smoking

Keir E. Lewis

Key points

- Cigarettes contain over 4,000 chemicals including arsenic, paint stripper, and at least 60 carcinogens.
- Smoking adversely affects every organ system in the body.
- Most smoking-related deaths are from lung and heart diseases.
- Particular sub-groups with high-smoking prevalence are those on lower income and certain ethnic minorities.
- Nicotine acts on cholinergic and mesolimbic (dopaminergic) central nervous system pathways.
- The $\alpha_4\beta_2$ nicotinic receptor sub-type is the main receptor mediating nicotine dependence.
- Repeat exposure to nicotine causes neuro-adaptation often resulting in tolerance; this leads to more smoking for the same pleasurable effect and more smoking needed to avoid withdrawal.
- Health benefits start within 24 hrs of stopping smoking.

2.1 The chemical content of cigarette smoke and its harmful effects in general

Cigarette smoke contains more than 4,000 chemicals including carbon monoxide, tar, cadmium, acetone, hydrogen cyanide, arsenic, and over 60 other known carcinogens. They are so designed, with all these compounds to deliver nicotine as quickly as possible to the human brain—something they do extremely efficiently (within 8 s). The faster nicotine hits the central nervous system, the greater the stimulation and therefore the more addictive the cigarette will be (Figure 2.1).

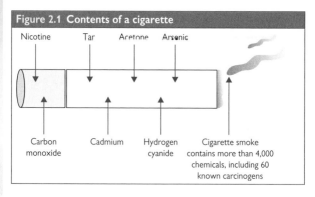

Figure 2.1 Contents of a cigarette

Nicotine   Tar   Acetone   Arsenic

Carbon monoxide   Cadmium   Hydrogen cyanide   Cigarette smoke contains more than 4,000 chemicals, including 60 known carcinogens

Cigarette smoke is inhaled because it contains nicotine, which is highly addictive. Nicotine itself has some adverse neuro-behavioural, cardiovascular, and probably carcinogenic effects but it is mainly these other chemicals, added to make the cigarette such an extremely potent nicotine delivery device, that cause the physical and mental damage, leading to so much ill health and suffering, worldwide (Table 2.1; Figures 2.2 and 2.3).

Of smoking-related deaths in the UK in 1995, 25% were due to lung cancer, 20% were due to coronary heart disease, 20% due to chronic obstructive pulmonary disease (COPD) and 13% were due to other cancers. The morbidity and other economic damage due to time off work and so on due to smoking is difficult to calculate but many diseases such as asthma, bronchiectasis, rhinitis, sleep apnoea, heart failure, and chest infections are worsened by smoking—if not directly caused by it.

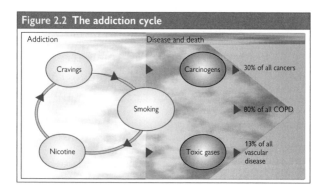

Figure 2.2 The addiction cycle

Addiction   Disease and death

Cravings

Smoking

Nicotine

Carcinogens   30% of all cancers

Toxic gases

80% of all COPD

13% of all vascular disease

Figure 2.3 Schematic showing all organs affected by smoking

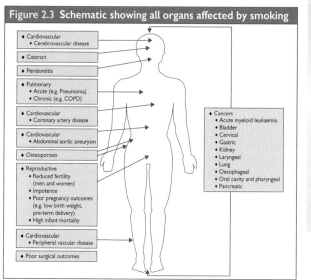

Table 2.1 Some of the known health consequences of smoking

System	Illnesses
Cancers	Acute myeloid leukaemia Bladder Cervical Gastric Kidney Laryngeal Lung Oesophageal Oral cavity and pharyngeal Pancreatic
Pulmonary	Acute (e.g. pneumonia) Chronic (e.g. COPD)
Cardiovascular	Abdominal aortic aneurysm Cerebrovascular disease Coronary artery disease Peripheral vascular disease
Reproductive	Reduced fertility (men and women) Impotence Poor pregnancy outcomes (e.g. low birth weight, pre-term delivery) Higher infant mortality
Other	Cataract Osteoporosis Peridontitis Poor surgical outcomes

Data from Department of Health and Human Services, The Health Consequences of Smoking: A Report of the Surgeon General; 2004.

2.2 Why people smoke in the first place: risk factors of smoking

Over 90% of smokers start before they are 20-yrs old. Main reasons for starting include peer group pressure, role models (children of smokers are more likely to smoke than children of non-smokers), advertising, and experimentation.

Smoking varies widely by race, sex, age, educational level, and socio-economic status. In the USA, smoking prevalence is highest in American Indians (around 36%), then blacks, whites, Hispanics, and is lowest in Asians.

In the UK, the rate of smoking for men is the highest in the 18 to 24 yrs age group (28.5%) and is slightly older for women where the highest rate is between ages 25 and 44 yrs (21%). It is lowest in both men and women over 65 yrs. Smoking prevalence varies widely in association with educational level, ranging up to 50% in those not completing schooling to lows of 6% in people with a graduate degree. In all countries, both men and women living below the poverty line smoke more frequently than those above it, so smoking is one of the biggest causes of health inequalities in our society.

Other groups at particularly high risk for being unable to quit smoking include:

- Pregnant women who cannot quit smoking during and after pregnancy
- Children and adolescents in early stages of tobacco use
- Older adults with a long history of tobacco use
- Individuals with psychiatric illness
- Chemically dependent persons (drug or alcohol misusers).

Here, the definition of a high-risk patient is someone who will have more difficulty stopping smoking on his or her own compared with other tobacco users, due to particular conditions or circumstances. As well as finding it hardest to quit, these individuals have more tobacco-related co-morbidities and poorer health for other socio-demographic reasons.

Screening tobacco-dependent patients for the following conditions will enable the clinician to anticipate particular barriers and intervene differently to achieve better quit rates:

- Chemical dependence, specifically alcohol use
- Psychiatric conditions, including major depression, anxiety, post-traumatic stress disorder, schizophrenia, bipolar or eating disorders, attention-deficit disorders (see Chapter 6)
- High nicotine dependence resulting in severe withdrawal symptoms during abstinence (see Chapter 3)
- Multiple relapses despite previous input

- Limited abstinence in previous attempts (e.g. have never quit for more than 7 days)
- Low socio-economic status or educational level, or lack of social support to change behaviour.

2.3 Why quitting smoking is so difficult: pathophysiology and psychology of smoking addiction

The essence of drug addiction is loss of control of drug use. Nicotine is the addictive drug in tobacco so an understanding of the basic and clinical pharmacology of nicotine is needed, to improve the prevention and treatment of tobacco addiction. Nicotine stimulates the sympathetic pathways of the autonomic nervous system, mimicking the natural 'fight or flight' response but in addition it acts on nicotinic cholinergic receptors in the brain to release dopamine and other neurotransmitters producing pleasure, stimulation, enhanced vigilance and task performance, and mood modulation. No other drug can cause this paradoxical response and smokers will describe a 'buzz' or 'hit' but also a calming or relaxing effect. It is particularly via this indirect stimulation of the mesolimbic pathway causing these latter effects that addiction is sustained (Figure 2.4).

There are many sub-types of nicotine receptor in the nervous system. Molecular studies and genetic studies suggest that the $\alpha_4\beta_2$ nicotinic sub-type is the main receptor mediating nicotine dependence.

Importantly, neuro-adaptation develops with repeated exposure to nicotine. Animal and human studies show increased numbers of nicotinic receptors, changes in the sub-types of nicotinic receptors, and increased neuronal plasticity in the brains of smokers compared to non-smokers. This neuro-adaptation results in tolerance to many of the effects of nicotine resulting in longer-term smokers needing to smoke more to achieve the same pleasurable effects, probably explaining why most smokers progress to higher intake.

80% to 90% of nicotine is metabolized by the CYP2A6 cytochrome enzyme system in the liver with around 10% to 20% being excreted unchanged by the kidneys. Nicotine has a short plasma half-life of around 2 hrs and this is important because of withdrawal; however, its clearance exhibits considerable individual variability that is determined by genetic, racial, and hormonal (sex) factors. Nicotine dependence is highly heritable and appears to be influenced by genes coding for some nicotine receptor sub-types, neurotransmitter genes, and genes involved in neural connectivity. Genetically slow metabolism of nicotine also appears to be associated with a lower

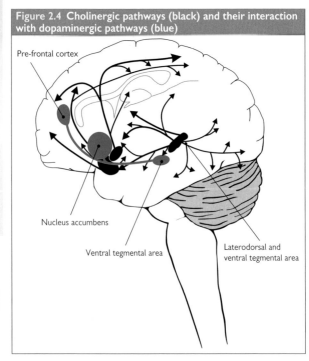

Figure 2.4 Cholinergic pathways (black) and their interaction with dopaminergic pathways (blue)

Pre-frontal cortex

Nucleus accumbens

Ventral tegmental area

Laterodorsal and ventral tegmental area

level of dependence. Pharmacogenetic studies now suggest various candidate genes and a nicotine metabolism phenotype may even influence the outcome of different pharmacotherapies, raising important concepts of personalized prescribing in smoking cessation, according to an individuals genetic make-up.

As well as deriving positive reinforcement from nicotine (and dopamine) stimulation, when smokers stop, a nicotine withdrawal syndrome ensues, characterized by irritability, anxiety, increased eating, dysphoria, and mood dysregulation, among other symptoms. Many smokers continue to smoke not actually to derive pleasure but to avoid or relieve withdrawal symptoms. Many smokers derive the most 'pleasure' from their first cigarette of the day and smoke

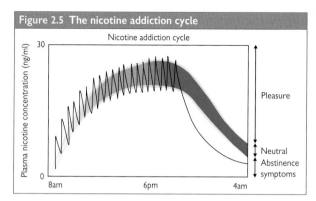

Figure 2.5 The nicotine addiction cycle

Nicotine addiction cycle

Plasma nicotine concentration (ng/ml) — 30, 0

8am   6pm   4am

Pleasure

Neutral
Abstinence
symptoms

quickly to increase plasma nicotine levels to be in their 'comfort zone', thereafter they smoke only to maintain nicotine levels within this 'comfort zone'. Shorter time to first cigarette is used as a marker for higher addiction in, for example, the revised Fagerström Score (see Chapter 3; Figure 2.5).

Conditioning also reinforces smoking; specific stimuli that are psychologically associated with smoking become cues for an urge to smoke. These include the taste and smell of tobacco, particular moods, situations, and other environmental cues. Many smokers will tell you they want to smoke only in certain situations (usually where they have smoked before). Stereotyped patterns of behaviour are associated with more dopamine release in the mesolimbic system, and many smokers exhibit a very specific and ordered ritual, for example when making their 'roll-ups'. Asking a smoker to make their roll-ups in a different way (e.g. place their tobacco tin on the other side of the table) is very challenging.

Pharmacotherapies to aid smoking cessation should ideally reduce nicotine withdrawal symptoms but block the reinforcing effects of nicotine obtained from smoking, without causing excessive adverse effects. Furthermore, given the important role of sensory effects of smoking combined with psychoactive effects of nicotine—counselling and behavioural therapies are vital alongside any pharmacotherapy.

2.4 The benefit of quitting smoking now

The most common reason given by smokers for wanting to stop is 'health.' An explanation of the benefits of quitting should be tailored to each smoker for maximal effect. Studies using generic (non-tailored) stop-smoking leaflets show a small beneficial effect only. The benefits for smokers with specific medical conditions are described in detail in Chapter 6. However, very broad useful facts to help (often 'healthy') smokers understand risk include:

- A smoker on average loses 8 to 10 yrs of life compared to non-smokers
- Life insurance companies have used studies of life expectancy to calculate that a single cigarette lowers one's life expectancy by 10.7 min. 'The price of smoking this pack of cigarettes is 3½ hours of your life.'
- Stopping smoking at any age has been shown to improve health and increase life expectancy. Table 2.2 summarizes some of the beneficial effects of quitting smoking.

Other main reasons given for wanting to stop smoking include reducing risk to family (particularly grandchildren):

- Children who live with smokers have more time off school with upper respiratory tract infections and are more likely to develop wheeze.

Table 2.2 Beneficial health changes when you stop smoking	
Time since quitting	Beneficial health changes that take place
24 h	Lungs start to clear out mucus and other smoking debris
48 h	Carbon monoxide will be eliminated from the body Ability to taste and smell is greatly improved
72 h	Breathing becomes easier Bronchial tubes begin to relax and energy levels increase
2–12 weeks	Blood circulation improves
3–9 months	Coughs, wheezing, and breathing problems improve as lung function is increased by up to 10%
1 yr	Risk of heart attack falls to about half that of a smoker
10 yrs	Risk of lung cancer falls to half that of a smoker
15 yrs	Risk of heart attack falls to the same as someone who has never smoked

Data from Action from Smoking and Health (ASH) fact sheet and McEwen *et al.*, *The Manual of Smoking Cessation* (2007).

Key reading

Benowitz NL. Clinical pharmacology of nicotine: implications for understanding, preventing, and treating tobacco addiction. *Clin Pharmacol Ther* 2008; **83**(4): 531–41.

Callum C. *The UK Smoking Epidemic: Deaths in 1995.* Health Education Authority; 1998, pp. 29–30.

John U, Meyer C, Schumann A *et al.* A short form of the Fagerström test for nicotine dependence and the heaviness of smoking index in two adult population samples. *Addict Behav* 2004; **29**(6): 1207–12.

Kuryatov A, Luo J, Cooper J, Lindstrom J. Nicotine acts as a pharmacological chaperone to up-regulate human alpha4beta2 acetylcholine receptors. *Mol Pharmacol* 2005; **68**(6): 1839–51.

McEwen A, Hajek P, McRobbie H, West R. *Manual of Smoking Cessation.* Blackwell Publishing; 2007.

Slotkin TA, Cousins MM, Seidler FJ. Administration of nicotine to adolescent rats evokes regionally selective upregulation of CNS alpha 7 nicotinic acetylcholine receptors. *Brain Res* 2004; **1030**(1): 159–63.

US Department of Health and Human Services. The Health Consequences of Smoking: A Report of the Surgeon General; 2004.

Chapter 3

Helping individual smokers to stop

Helen Poole, Hazel Dixon, and Keir E. Lewis

Key points

- All health professionals should enquire if their patients smoke and be able to offer basic advice.
- All health professionals should know how to refer patients to their local specialist stop smoking services (if the smoker is keen) rather than relying on the smoker to do so.
- Different intensities of intervention are available, with a clear dose–response effect—depending on the skill and time constraints of the heath professional.
- Various psychological approaches for behavioural support are used; all are empathic, and build on their motivation to quit to make the smoker more optimistic about a quit attempt.
- Behavioural support combined with pharmacotherapy is currently the most effective approach, achieving 20% to 30% sustained 1-yr quit rates, resulting in low 'numbers needed to treat' compared to most other health interventions.
- Follow-up sessions are crucial.

3.1 Skills that you need to have in helping your clients to stop smoking

The most important feature of any approach is to motivate the patient to stop smoking. A supportive, empathic relationship with two-way communication is crucial. Remember, many smokers already feel stigmatized and have tried to quit already. Ideally, they must be in a secure, relaxed environment where they feel able to speak openly. They should be given clear information (including literature) appropriate to their understanding but the risks of smoking and benefits of stopping should be personalized to them. The smoker needs to be helped to become optimistic about a quit attempt.

3.2 Levels of stop-smoking support and the approximate time needed for each

The National Institute for Clinical Excellence (NICE) guidelines recommends:

> Everyone who smokes should be advised to quit, unless there are exceptional circumstances
>
> and
>
> . . . smoking cessation advice and support should be available in community, primary and secondary care settings for everyone who smokes.

Various counselling techniques, based on psychological theories, have been applied but the style and intensity of intervention is determined both by individual smoker's preferences and the experience and time constraints of those available to deliver them.

3.2.1 Basic level 1 intervention

All health professionals should enquire if their patients smoke but NICE further recommends that general practitioners, community workers, nurses, dentists, pharmacists, and hospital clinicians should *all* offer brief advice. This advice could take no more than 1 to 2 min to supply key information (Boxes 3.1 and 3.2).

18

Box 3.1 Examples of brief facts

Risks:

- Smokers die on average 8–10 yrs younger than non-smokers
- Smoking kills more people per year than alcohol, illegal drugs, suicide, murder, fires, AIDS, and car accidents combined
- A cigarette contains 4000 chemicals including acetone, arsenic, paint stripper, pesticides, and over 60 known carcinogens
- Your risk of a heart attack is 2–5 times that of a non-smoker
- Smoking worsens all respiratory symptoms
- Everyday health problems include facial wrinkles, hair loss, impotence, chest infections, coughs, and colds

---

Box 3.2 Benefits

- Within 24 hrs of quitting, exhaled carbon monoxide (car exhaust) readings are that of a non-smoker
- Within 1 yr, you can halve your risk of heart disease
- Reduced risk of ear and lower respiratory tract infections in your children, grandchildren, and spouse

If smokers express a desire to stop—the health professional should know how to refer them to the nearest stop-smoking specialist, rather than advising them to 'phone a quit line' because the moment can be lost. If they do not want to stop, NICE states that they still be offered pharmacotherapy as a gateway to stopping.

3.2.2 Level 2 intervention

A higher level but still relatively basic intervention is the '5 A's approach'. It can still be delivered by any health professional and takes 5 to 10 min. It is certainly (re-)applied by stop-smoking specialists (Box 3.3).

Box 3.3 Example 5A's

Ask:
Do you smoke? Have you ever tried to stop? Are you interested in stopping?

Advise:
Prioritize information (e.g. withdrawal symptoms, weight gain), making information-specific (e.g. what smoking-related symptoms do they have), make it personal (e.g. family), make it immediate (e.g. instant health benefits), and make it positive (e.g. health gain, appearance)

Assess willingness to quit:
Motivation and readiness to quit increases abstinence rate

Assist:
Includes reviewing past attempts, helping with an action plan (e.g. diary coping with triggers), assess support needed (e.g. motivational/pharmacological, family)

Arrange:
It is important to arrange follow-up. Those who have stopped should be congratulated. Those still trying can be helped with problem solving. Those who have stopped but relapsed need to be reassured that it could take several attempts

---

3.2.3 Level 3 intervention

This involvement is more specialized, takes 30 to 60 min initially and needs follow-up appointments. Applied theoretical models here include Motivational Interviewing techniques where the relationship is client-centred and the specialist's role is to resolve ambivalence (Box 3.4).

Box 3.4 Example—motivational interviewing

'If I stop smoking I will feel better about myself but I may also put on weight, which will make me feel unhappy and unattractive.' The specialist's task is to facilitate expression of both sides of the dilemma, and guide the smoker towards an acceptable resolution that triggers change

---

Cognitive behavioural therapy techniques also require a collaborative relationship, needing active participation; they are goal-orientated and problem-focused (Box 3.5).

Box 3.5 Example—cognitive behavioural therapy

Homework task: write down the pros and cons of smoking and stopping smoking

The trans-theoretical (stages of change) model applies an integrative framework for understanding, measuring, and intervening in behaviour change, change being seen as a progression through five stages (Table 3.1).

Table 3.1 Example—trans-theoretical (stages of change) model

Stage	Key identifier	Appropriate therapy
Pre-contemplation	Does not want to quit smoking	Acknowledge their feelings and try to raise their awareness of the negatives of smoking
Contemplation	Wants to quit, but not in next month	Identify barriers to quitting, review prior quit attempts to find successes, pros, and cons of continued smoking
Action	Wants to quit within next month or has quit for <1 month	Plan quitting, avoid trigger situations; consider pharmacotherapy
Maintenance	Has quit for at least 1 month	Deal with lapses immediately, continue pharmacotherapy, analyse craving symptoms
Relapse	Quit before but now smoking on a daily basis	Identify the trigger for relapse, assess current stage, encourage to resume action

Although still widely used, there has recently been some debate over its applicability in smoking cessation. No single approach is superior and in practice, a combination of these models allows flexibility according to how the interview progresses (Box 3.6).

Box 3.6 Example—combination approaches

5A's
Raise the issue of smoking with patient
Stages of change
Provide an action plan for quitting
Motivational interviewing
Help build rapport and empathy
Cognitive behavioural therapy
Focus on goals and homework tasks, to change their behaviour

3.3 How to conduct an effective consultation session on smoking cessation

The first session with a stop-smoking specialist typically lasts 45 to 60 min, in order to cover six specific areas:

1. *Recording a smoking history.* Age started smoking, number of cigarettes per day, how soon after waking do they smoke, details previous quit attempts (see Appendix). Tobacco consumption can be recorded in pack years, that is 20 cigarettes for 10 yrs = 10 pack years, 10 cigarettes for 18 yrs = 9 pack years.

A quick and effective way to assess the smoker's level of addiction is the Fagerström tolerance/addiction to nicotine scale (see Appendix) (Box 3.7).

Box 3.7 Examples—information obtained

- If they first started smoking as a teenager, now smoke 20 cigarettes a day and start within 30 min of waking, their nicotine dependence is high. The specialist's role is to help them change their routines and habits, discuss the use of a pharmacotherapy, to help reduce the withdrawal symptoms but help them improve their self-belief and confidence in their ability to stop: 'there are 12 million ex-smokers in the UK you could be one of them.'

- Discuss previous attempts. Why were they unsuccessful, for example stress, inappropriate pharmacological aid? It is important to boost the patient's confidence and explain that this attempt could be the successful one. Also identify any strategies that the smoker felt worked well previously and encourage them to try these again.

- Ask the smoker to list as many benefits as possible that they would obtain by stopping smoking, for example health, children and especially grandchildren, finance/holiday. Keep patients positive.

---

2. *Personalize the risks of smoking and benefits of stopping.* It is important to tailor the risks and benefits to any symptoms/illness; let them know how quickly benefits can be achieved and that it is never too late to try.

3. *Exploring the smoker's personal barriers to stopping.* Assess the addiction factor in everyday life. Are they using nicotine for relaxation or a stimulant, as a time filler, stress reliever, or to reduce weight gain? Only once identified, can the smoker be helped to overcome them (Box 3.8).

Box 3.8 Examples—barriers

- Cigarettes are addictive and as difficult to stop as heroin and cocaine. Many would have experienced unpleasant symptoms when trying to quit before and these should not be dismissed
- Family life; if the patient lives with smokers, try to make their house smoke-free; explain to family and friends how important it is for them not to smoke around the quitter. Non-smoking family members can be very supportive
- If they want to relax, have a bath instead or listen to music
- If bored, do something to concentrate such as knitting, computing, or crosswords (not TV)
- Coping with stress: ten deep breaths, exercise
- To reduce weight gain, eat regular meals and snack on healthy options and is another reason to exercise

4. *Preparing to quit—withdrawal symptoms and coping mechanisms.* It needs to be explained, in advance of quitting, what withdrawal symptoms could be experienced. It is useful to give this information in a written list that may avoid further anxiety—if they do not interpret them correctly. It is important to point out that these withdrawal symptoms are normal and will pass (Table 3.2).

Table 3.2 Withdrawal symptoms and coping mechanisms

Symptoms	Usual duration	Tips
Dizziness	1–2 days	Know it will pass
Headaches	Varies	Relax
Tiredness	2–4 weeks	Exercise and sleep more
Coughing	<7 days	Sip water
Tightness in chest	<7 days	Know it will pass
Trouble sleeping	<7 days	No caffeine drinks in the evening
Constipation	3–4 weeks	Drink lots of water, eat high fibre foods
Hunger	Several weeks	Eat low-calorie snacks
Lack of concentration	Several weeks	Be prepared for this
Craving for cigarettes	Strong for the first 2 weeks, then off/on thereafter	Do something else

Once your patient has decided they want to stop smoking, they should now set a quit date and formulate coping strategies (Box 3.9).

Box 3.9 Examples—useful coping strategies

- Craving is common and they should be warned of each physical symptom
- Cravings peak at 2 min so a distraction is required
- If they always smoke in certain situations, try to change the environment, for example meet elsewhere, chew gum, or sip water in that situation
- Ask the smoker to write down the word 'success' in a diary if they had not smoked that day. If they smoked, write down reasons why and how it made them feel
- Ask them to fill a jar with water and old cigarette ends, place it in a prominent position where they often smoke, as aversion therapy; every time they get a craving, ask them to look at it and smell it and say 'this is the harm it is doing inside my body'.
- A money jar can help motivate, when a smoker gets a craving, ask them to count up their money. If saving up for a holiday get them to look at travel brochures
- To avoid weight gain, eat regular meals, snack on healthy options and exercise if possible

Ask your patient to identify a friend/family member as a source of support. Encourage them to get rid of cigarettes, ashtrays, and lighters, but if this evokes anxiety, suggest them to put cigarettes in a taped and concealed carrier bag. Hopefully, by the time they open the bag, the craving will have passed.

Pharmacological aids need to be discussed in detail, noting the advantages/disadvantages and correct dosing for that particular smoker (see Chapter 4).

5. *Relapse prevention*. This is a vital—people do relapse. We suggest that the lapse be called a 'learning cigarette'. Get the smoker to focus on how and why they smoked and start afresh, being smoke-free. Ask them to contact you or their stop-smoking specialist, if relapse occurs and make an appointment to see them early or speak to them via telephone to try and help boost their confidence in their ability to go back smoke-free.

These issues (1) to (5) are summarized in a ready to use and modifiable consultation form in the Appendix.

6. *Continuing support*. Ongoing support, in person or via telephone, can help alleviate doubts or negativity. If problems have occurred, encourage them to try alternative strategies. Recording exhaled carbon monoxide (eCO) at each appointment can act as motivator and highlight which patients are having problems. eCO readings fall to levels of non-smokers within 24 hrs of stopping and levels less than 10 parts per million are associated with beneficial health effects.

To help motivate, a reading should be compared with their reading, when they were still smoking.

Most guidelines regard a 12-month follow up is necessary to enable the patient to experience and cope with all major annual events (e.g. birthday, holiday, Christmas) without needing their cigarettes. Follow-up can also review mood, weight gain, and any pharmacotherapy side effects. Exact follow-up depends on local resources, but the smokers should also be encouraged to contact the service between appointments if needed (Box 3.10).

Box 3.10 **Example of a follow-up service as recommended by the British Thoracic Society 2004**	
*First 4 weeks	Weekly appointments
At 2 months	Telephone call or letter to encourage/support
*At 3 months	Cessation validated by eCO measurement
*At 6 months	Phone contact or cessation validated by eCO
At 9 months	Telephone call or letter to encourage/support
*At 12 months	Cessation validated by eCO
*Essential services.	
Data from British Thoracic Society Guidelines, 2004.	

Services combining all these approaches typically result in validated (eCO) sustained (over 1 yr) quit rates of between 20% and 30% and resulting numbers needed to treat of around 5 to 6. The cost per life year saved by a smoking specialist ranges from £227 to £2700, depending on the location, and exact model. This is well within the criteria recommended by NICE for commissioning and very few other health-care interventions are deemed so cost-effective in comparison.

3.4 **Conclusions**

Whatever techniques you use to help smokers, you should provide a warm, understanding relationship, showing them respect and empathy. If your patient feels supported, confident, and motivated to stop smoking, they are more likely to succeed.

All health professionals have significant influence. They can and should address smoking cessation with any smoking patients for at least 2 to 5 min and know how to refer to their nearest specialist smoking cessation service if the smoker is then willing.

See Appendix for a ready-to-use consultation form, how to adapt consultations to high risk groups and examples of real-life cases.

Key reading

Brief interventions and referral for smoking cessation in primary care and other settings. NICE public health intervention guidance no.1 2006. Available from http://guidance.nice.org.uk/PHI1/guidance/pdf/English.

Department of Health. *Smoking Kills A White Paper on Tobacco*. HMSO; 1998.

Godfrey C, Parrott S, Coleman T, Pound E. The cost-effectiveness of the English smoking treatment services: evidence from practice. *Addiction* 2005; **100**(Suppl 2): 70–83.

Prathiba BV, Tjeder S, Phillips C, Campbell IA. A smoking cessation counsellor: should every hospital have one? *J R Soc Health* 1998; **118**(6): 356–9.

Recommendations for hospital-based smoking cessation services, www.britthoracic.org.uk/c2/uploads/HospitalReportJAN04.pdf; 2004.

West R, McNeill A, Raw M. Smoking cessation guidelines for health professionals: an update. *Thorax* 2000; **55**(12): 987–99.

Wilson A, Sinfield P, Rodgers S, Hammersley V, Coleman T. Drugs to support smoking cessation in UK general practice: are evidence based guidelines being followed? *Qual Saf Health Care* 2006; **15**(4): 284–8.

Chapter 4

Pharmacological aids to smoking cessation

Stuart Rees and Keir E. Lewis

Key points

- Nicotine replacement therapy approximately doubles the chances of quitting regardless of additional support.
- Bupropion and varenicline are effective non-nicotine-based products.
- Second-line agents include nortriptyline and clonidine.
- Choice of drug is often determined by smokers' preferences which are affected by previous attempts, side-effect profiles, and potential drug interactions.
- Tobacco smoke increases the activity of several liver enzymes, so altered drug pharmacokinetics and pharmacodynamics should be considered when a patient stops smoking.

4.1 Introduction

There are a number of effective pharmacological agents to help smoking cessation. Preparations licensed in the UK can be divided into nicotine replacement therapy (NRT) and the non-nicotine-based products—bupropion and varenicline. Other, unlicensed, preparations including nortriptyline and clonidine have shown benefit but there is insufficient evidence to use anxiolytics or other antidepressants.

4.2 Nicotine replacement therapy

The aim of NRT is temporarily to replace much of the nicotine from cigarettes to reduce motivation to smoke and relieve nicotine withdrawal symptoms, thus easing the transition from cigarette smoking to complete abstinence. The first product available in the UK was NRT gum, introduced in 1979. NRT patches were introduced in the 1990s, followed by lozenges, inhalators, and nasal spray. Currently, gums, patches, and lozenges are available through many retail outlets, but inhalators and sprays are supplied only where there can be input from a health-care professional.

NRT aims to replace the nicotine from tobacco by other means of delivery: skin (patches), oral (chewing gum, sub-lingual tablets, lozenges, inhalators), or nasal mucosa (nasal spray). Liquid/powdered nicotine preparations to add to beverages and inhalers for lung delivery are being developed (see Chapter 15). Nicotine delivered by all these means is not mixed with the other carcinogens, tar, or carbon monoxide so is much safer. Indeed the Medicines and Healthcare Products Regulatory Agency (MHRA) itself admitted that:

> NRT presents a unique challenge . . . in that being the safest form
> of nicotine available it is also the most highly regulated, certainly
> when compared to cigarettes, the most deadly source of nicotine.

No current NRT delivery system can match the ability of a cigarette to deliver nicotine. Nicotine from 'fast-acting' oral/nasal products is delivered to the blood stream within minutes and it takes hours from a patch. Moreover, at standard doses, NRT produces much lower blood nicotine concentrations than smoking.

Despite these limitations, each form of NRT significantly increases the rate of cessation compared to placebo, or no NRT. The Cochrane Collaboration quotes a pooled risk ratio (RR) for abstinence for any form of NRT relative to control to be 1.58 (95% CI: 1.50 to 1.66), based on 132 trials with over 40,000 participants. This means that overall, NRT increases the chances of quitting by about 1.5 to 2 times, regardless of any additional support and encouragement. The RR for the different delivery systems of NRT is similar and is shown in Tables 4.1 to 4.5, which also summarize other product characteristics.

In 2005 the Committee on Safety of Medicines Working Group (CSM WG) on NRT recommended lifting barriers, allowing wider use of NRT in populations, including:

- Adolescents of 12 yrs and over
- Pregnant or breastfeeding women
- Smokers with underlying diseases such as
  - Cardiovascular
  - Hepatic and renal
  - Diabetes mellitus
  - Those taking concurrent medication.

Table 4.1 Pharmacological aids to smoking cessation—nicotine replacement products

Product	Dosing instructions	Side effects and disadvantages	Special warnings/ precautions for use	Risk ratio/ quitting
PATCHES				
NiQuitin and NiQuitin clear® (GSL) Step 1 NiQuitin® 21 mg Step 2 NiQuitin® 14 mg Step 3 NiQuitin® 7 mg **Nicotinell®** (GSL) Nicotinell® TTS 30 (21 mg/24 hrs) Nicotinell® TTS 20 (21 mg/24 hrs) **Nicorette®** (GSL) Nicorette® 15 mg Nicorette® 10 mg Nicorette® 5 mg **also** Nicorette® invis 25 mg (Step 1—first 8 weeks) Nicorette® invis 15 mg (Step 2—next 2 weeks) Nicorette® invis 10 mg (Step 3—last 2 weeks) All the above patches deliver the stated amount of nicotine over a 16 hour period Light smokers (<10 cigarettes per day) should start at Step 2 (15 mg) for 8 weeks and 10 mg for final 4 weeks Intended that patch is worn through waking hours (approx. 16 hrs), applied on waking and removed at bed time	**≥10 cigarettes/day** Apply 21 mg for 6 weeks, 14 mg for 2 weeks, 7 mg for 2 weeks **<10 cigarettes/day** Apply 14 mg for 6 weeks, 7 mg for 2 weeks **≥20 cigarettes/day** Initially apply TTS 30 patch **<20 cigarettes/day** Initially apply TTS 20 patch Withdraw gradually, reducing dose every 3–4 weeks Apply 15 mg patch on waking (remove 16 hrs later; usually bedtime) for 8 weeks If abstained apply 10 mg patch daily for 8 weeks followed by 5 mg patch daily for 2 weeks	Skin irritation (discontinue if severe), rash, possible sleep disturbances if worn at night, dizziness, headache, nausea, vomiting Possibly unsuitable for patients with chronic generalized skin disease such as psoriasis, chronic dermatitis, and urticaria Deliver nicotine dose slowly, do not mimic peaks and troughs achieved by smoking	Apply to dry, non-hairy skin on hip, chest, or upper arm Site next patch on different area Not applied to broken or inflamed skin Patches may be considered in patients hospitalized for *MI*, severe *dysrhythmia*, or *CVA* (initiated under medical supervision) Patches may be recommended to assist a quit attempt during *pregnancy* and *lactation*. Intermittent dosing products may be preferable as these usually provide a lower daily dose of nicotine Patches may be preferred if suffering from nausea. If patches used they should be removed before going to bed	Meta-analysis of rate of cessation using NRT v placebo or no NRT[2] 1.66 (95% CI: 1.53 to 1.81)

GSL—General Sale List; TTS—Transdermal Therapeutic System.

29

Table 4.2 Pharmacological aids to smoking cessation—nicotine replacement products

	Product (and legal class)	Dosing instructions	Side effects and disadvantages	Special warnings/ precautions for use	Risk ratio/ quitting
CHEWING GUM	**NiQuitin®** (GSL) NiQuitin® 2 mg NiQuitin® 4 mg	Use 2 mg if first cigarette of day > 30 min after waking Use 4 mg if first cigarette of day < 30 min after waking Gum should be used whenever there is an urge to smoke (using 'chew & rest/park' technique) Maximum 60 mg daily Use for 3 months then gradually ↓ use	Headache, dizziness, taste, sore mouth or throat, jaw pain, mouth soreness, increased salivation, hiccups, nausea, dyspepsia Patients need to use correct chewing technique ('chew & park') Not suitable in patients who wear dentures	Simultaneous use of coffee, acid drinks, and soft drinks may decrease absorption of nicotine and should be avoided for 15 min prior to and whilst sucking lozenge Gum may be considered in patients hospitalized for MI, severe dysrhythmia, or CVA (initiated under medical supervision) Gum may be recommended to assist a quit attempt during pregnancy and lactation. Intermittent dosing products may be preferable as these usually provide a lower daily dose of nicotine Patches may be preferred if suffering from nausea. If patches used they should be removed before going to bed	1.43 (95% CI: 1.33 to 1.53, 53 trials)
	Nicotinell® (GSL) Nicotinell® 2 mg Nicotinell® 4 mg	≤20 cigarettes a day 2 mg gum is indicated >20 cigarettes a day 4 mg gum is indicated Gum should be used for ~30 min whenever there is an urge to smoke (using 'chew & rest' technique) Maximum 60 mg daily Use for 3 months then gradually ↓ use			
	Nicorette® (GSL) Nicorette® 2 mg Nicorette® 4 mg				

GSL—General Sale List.

CHAPTER 4 **Pharmacological aids**

Table 4.3 Pharmacological aids to smoking cessation—nicotine replacement products

	Product	Dosing instructions	Side effects and disadvantages	Special warnings/ precautions for use	Risk ratio/ quitting
LOZENGES	**NiQuitin®** (GSL) NiQuitin® 2 mg NiQuitin® 4 mg	Suck one lozenge every 1–2 hrs when urge to smoke (maximum 15 lozenges in 24 hrs) for 6 weeks, then 1 every 2–4 hours for 3 weeks, then every 4–8 hrs for 3 weeks. Withdraw gradually after 3 months Periodically move from one side of the mouth to the other until completely dissolved		Slower sucking usually prevents side effects Simultaneous use of coffee, acid drinks, and soft drinks may decrease absorption of nicotine and should be avoided for 15 min prior to and whilst sucking lozenge Lozenges may be considered in patients hospitalized for MI, severe *dysrhythmia*, or CVA (initiated under medical supervision)	2.00 (95% CI: 1.63 to 2.45)
	Nicotinell® (GSL) Nicotinell® 1 mg Nicotinell® 2 mg	≤30 cigarettes/day Suck 1 mg lozenge every 1–2 hrs when urge to smoke >30 cigarettes/day Suck 2 mg lozenge every 1–2 hrs when urge to smoke Maximum 30 mg daily Withdraw gradually after 3 months	Taste disturbance, headache, dizziness, mouth soreness, paraesthesia of mouth, thirst, increased salivation, hiccups, nausea, vomiting, dyspepsia	Lozenges may be recommended to assist a quit attempt during pregnancy and lactation. Intermittent dosing products may be preferable as these usually provide a lower daily dose of nicotine. Patches may be preferred if suffering from nausea. If patches used they should be removed before going to bed	

Table 4.3 (Contd.)

	Product	Dosing instructions	Side effects and disadvantages	Special warnings/ precautions for use	Risk ratio/ quitting
MICROTAB (sub-lingual)	**Nicorette®** (P) Nicorette® 2 mg	≤20 cigarettes/day use 2 mg/h (1 microtab hourly) for patients who fail to stop or have significant withdrawal, ↑ consider to 4 mg/h (2 microtabs hourly) >20 cigarettes/day use 4 mg/h (2 microtabs hourly) Maximum 80 mg daily Gradually ↓ dose after 3 months	Unpleasant taste, hiccups, headache, dizziness, mouth and throat irritation, dyspepsia, nausea Effects wasted if swallowed		2.00 (95% CI: 1.63 to 2.45)

GSL—General Sale List; P—Sold only under supervision of a Pharmacist.

Table 4.4 Pharmacological aids to smoking cessation—nicotine replacement products

	Product	Dosing instructions	Side effects and disadvantages	Special warnings/ precautions for use	Risk ratio/ quitting
NASAL SPRAY	Nicorette® (P) Nicorette nasal spray 500 mcg/metered spray	Patient uses spray to treat craving as required, subject to a limit of one spray to each nostril twice an hour for 16 hrs daily for 8 weeks, then ↓ gradually over next 4 weeks Treatment should be limited to 3 months Daily limit is 32 mg of nicotine (64 sprays)	Headache, dizziness, cough, nausea, vomiting, dyspepsia, nasal irritation, (sneezing, running nose, watering eyes, epistaxis). Nasal side effects are common. May decline within first few days of treatment	Additionally ear sensations, increased urination, tingling or burning sensation in the head were more common compared with placebo Fastest acting product currently available and may be beneficial to highly dependent smokers	2.02 (95% CI: 1.49 to 2.73, four trials)
INHALATOR	Nicorette® (P) Nicorette inhalator (10 mg inhalation cartridge with device)	Inhale when urge to smoke For 8 weeks patient uses between 6 and 12 cartridges per day. Over the next 2 weeks ↓ number of cartridges by half, and over the next 2 weeks ↓ number to 0 by last day. Maximum of 12 cartridges per day (nicotine is not inhaled but absorbed through the lining of the mouth from the nicotine-impregnated plug in the mouthpiece)	Headache, dizziness, cough, irritation in mouth and throat, rhinitis, dry mouth, hiccups, nausea, vomiting, dyspepsia Requires more effort to inhale than a cigarette Works best at room temperature as nicotine delivery is affected by temperature	Inhalator may be considered in patients hospitalized for MI, severe dysrhythmia, or CVA (initiated under medical supervision) Inhalator may be recommended to assist a quit attempt during pregnancy and lactation. Intermittent dosing products may be preferable as these usually provide a lower daily dose of nicotine. Patches may be preferred if suffering from nausea. If patches used they should be removed before going to bed	1.90 (95% CI: 1.36 to 2.67, four trials)

P—Sold only under supervision of a Pharmacist.

Table 4.5 Pharmacological aids to smoking cessation—non-nicotine products

	Product	Dosing instructions	Side effects and disadvantages	Special warnings/ precautions for use	Risk ratio/ quitting
BUPROPION	Zyban® (POM) 150 mg tablets	Start 1–2 weeks before target stop date, initially 150 mg od for 6 days, then 150 mg bd (maximum single dose 150 mg, maximum daily dose 300 mg) Period of treatment 7–9 weeks Discontinue if abstinence not achieved at 7 weeks	Dry mouth, insomnia, nausea, headache, depression, increased risk of seizure (1:1000) May affect individual's ability to drive and operate machinery	Contraindicated in patients with a history of seizures or of eating disorders, a CNS tumour, or who are experiencing acute symptoms of alcohol or benzodiazepine withdrawal. Factors that ↓ risk of seizures include concomitant administration of drugs that lower seizure threshold, alcohol abuse, history of head trauma, diabetes, and use of stimulants and anorectics Should not be used in pregnancy or breastfeeding women Interval of ≥8 hrs between doses Take doses early in day to minimize sleep disturbance	Compared to placebo control or no other pharmacotherapy 1.94 (95% CI: 1.72–2.19, 31 trials) Abstinence at 6 months = 2.17 (14 trials) Abstinence at 12 months = 1.83 (17 trials)

| VARENICLINE | Champix® (POM) 0.5 and 1 mg | Start 1–2 weeks before target stop date 0.5 mg od for 3 days, then 0.5 mg bd for 4 days, then 1 mg bd for 11 weeks ↓ to 0.5 mg bd if not tolerated Starter pack available for first 2-week of treatment | Nausea, vomiting, constipation, headache, insomnia, vivid dreams Dizziness and somnolence Depression and suicide-related events have been reported | Advise patients not to drive or operate machinery until they know whether the drug impairs their ability to do so Health-care professionals should warn patients about the possibility of such withdrawal effects (↓ irritability, urge to smoke, depression, and insomnia) and, where appropriate, suggest gradual discontinuation Patients who are taking vareicline who develop suicidal thoughts or behaviour should stop their treatment and contact their doctor immediately Care should be taken when prescribing varenicljne to patients who have a history of psychiatric illness | Abstinence rate at 1 year: 1. Versus placebo = 2.96 (95% CI: 2.12–4.12, four trials) 2. Versus bupropion = 1.58, 95% CI: 1.22–2.05, three trials) Abstinence rate at weeks 9–12 versus NRT = 1.70 (95% CI: 1.26–2.28) No difference in continuous abstinence rates from week 9–52 (secondary outcomes) |

POM—Prescription Only Medicine.

4.3 **Nicotine-assisted reduction to stop**

The CSM WG also noted that a 'smoking reduction' indication had been authorized in ten other European countries, since 1997 and post-marketing surveillance did not indicate more or different adverse effects when used in this way. After reviewing data from seven well-designed studies, the MHRA initially licensed Nicorette® gum and inhalator for 'smoking reduction'. Microtabs are now also licensed for this indication.

4.3.1 **Combination of NRT products**

Because of the differing nicotine-delivery profiles of the various NRT products, there are considerable advantages in using more than one form of NRT to meet individual needs. For example, background nicotine levels can be maintained by a patch and supplemented by a 'burst' of nicotine from one of the oral forms when cravings become a problem. Pooled analyses suggest statistically significant advantages of combinations of long and short-acting NRT over single NRT (odds ratio (OR) 1.42, 95% CI: 1.14 to 1.76), and most guidelines (e.g. NICE, BTS) recommend combinations of NRT products.

4.4 **Non-nicotine pharmacological aids**

4.4.1 **Varenicline**

Varenicline is a new selective partial agonist at $\alpha_4\beta_2$-nicotinic acetylcholine receptors. It reduces the cravings for and decreases the pleasurable effects of cigarettes and other tobacco products by ameliorating the low dopamine release during withdrawal, but also by limiting both the dopamine release and reinforcing effects of nicotine during cessation attempts. Evidence mainly from 'healthy' smokers indicates that a 12-week course of the drug increases continuous abstinence rates at 1 yr compared with both placebo (OR 2.96, 95% CI: 2.12 to 4.12) and bupropion (OR 1.66, 95% CI: 1.28 to 2.16), leading to its licensing worldwide and recommendations, for example by NICE for use in smoking cessation. A recent open-label trial suggested that it was superior to NRT in achieving quit rates over 12 weeks but further head-to-head comparisons are needed particularly as total numbers in studies are relatively low compared to NRT. New publications are expected on its use in smokers with lung and cardiovascular disease. It is becoming increasingly prescribed as health professionals gain experience and there is increasing debate whether it should be used as first-line treatment or reserved for those who cannot use NRT or have failed to quit previously using NRT. Varenicline is generally well-tolerated with the most common reported side effects being nausea (usually mild) and sleep disturbance. Post-marketing surveillance has raised concerns of suicidal thoughts and abnormal behaviour in association with varenicline; these appear rare but have led to an update on product information by the MHRA in 2008. The update includes a warning of depression and suicidal − related events in patients using varenicline. More information will be forthcoming but early experience is favourable.

4.4.2 Bupropion

Bupropion is an atypical antidepressant, licensed in the UK for smoking cessation. Its mechanism of action in aiding smoking cessation is unclear, but the most recent Cochrane review reports that bupropion doubles the quit rate over placebo (OR of 1.94; 95% CI: 1.72 to 2.19). The most serious (occurs in about 1 in 1000) adverse effect of bupropion is seizures. Bupropion is contra-indicated in anyone with a history of seizure disorders or with a predisposition to seizures.

4.4.3 Nortriptyline

Nortriptyline, a tricyclic antidepressant, is also effective in cessation therapy. A few clinical trials suggest an effect similar in magnitude to that of bupropion with the Cochrane review quoting an OR of quitting of 2.34 for nortriptyline compared to placebo (95% CI: 1.61 to 3.41). Interestingly, both drugs seem to exert an effect independently of their antidepressant action. Nortriptyline is not licensed as a treatment for smoking cessation.

4.4.4 Clonidine

Clonidine is an α-noradrenergic agonist that suppresses sympathetic activity and is licensed for the treatment of hypertension, migraine, and menopausal flushing. Although not licensed for use in smoking cessation, clonidine has been used with a pooled (six studies) OR of quitting at 1 yr of 1.89 (95% CI: 1.30 to 2.74) compared to placebo/ no treatment, suggesting it is effective. A Cochrane review concludes that it is reasonable to consider clonidine as a second-line pharmacotherapy for smoking cessation. Its use may be limited by side effects including sedation and postural hypotension.

Trials of selective serotonin reuptake inhibitors (fluoxetine, sertraline, paroxetine), monoamine oxidase inhibitors (e.g. moclobemide), and an atypical antidepressant (venlafaxine) have shown no benefit in smoking cessation over placebo.

4.5 Medication that can be affected when a patient stops smoking

Numerous drug interactions have been identified with tobacco smoking mainly because polycyclic aromatic hydrocarbons in tobacco smoke stimulate cytochrome P450 enzymes, particularly CYP1A2. Many therapeutic drugs are metabolized via CYP1A2, so induction of this enzyme results in faster clearance and lower serum levels in smokers.

The impact of smoking cessation on medication effect is usually not considered to be of clinical significance and should not prevent a quit attempt as the benefits still clearly outweigh the risks. However, these effects are often not even considered and poorly researched.

Table 4.6 highlights some of the more significant/common interactions in order of clinical relevance (adapted from the UKMi Q&A 136.2, March 2008).

Table 4.6 Smoking and drug interactions			
Drug name	**Nature of interaction**	**Clinical relevance**	**Action to take when stopping smoking**
Clozapine	Clozapine is metabolized principally via CYP1A2 and clearance is increased in smokers. Serum clozapine levels are reduced in smokers compared with non-smokers; smokers may need higher dosages There have been case reports of adverse effects in patients taking clozapine when they have stopped smoking	High	Monitor serum drug levels before stopping smoking and 1 or 2 weeks after stopping smoking Be alert for increased adverse effects of clozapine. If adverse effects occur, reduce the dose as necessary
Theophylline	Theophylline is metabolized principally via CYP1A2. Smokers require higher doses of theophylline than non-smokers due to theophylline's shortened half-life and increased elimination. Some reports suggest smokers may need twice the dose of non-smokers	High	Monitor plasma theophylline concentrations weekly and adjust the dose of theophylline accordingly. The dose of theophylline will typically need to be reduced by about a third 1 week after stopping smoking. However, it may take several weeks for enzyme induction to dissipate. Monitor plasma theophylline concentration regularly until levels are stable Advise the patient to seek help if they develop signs of theophylline toxicity such as palpitations or nausea

Table 4.6 *(Contd.)*			
Drug name	**Nature of interaction**	**Clinical relevance**	**Action to take when stopping smoking**
Chlorpromazine	Chlorpromazine is metabolized principally via CYP1A2. Smokers have lower serum levels of chlorpromazine compared with non-smokers. A case report describes a 25-yr-old patient with schizophrenia who experienced increased adverse effects of chlorpromazine (sedation and dizziness) and increased plasma chlorpromazine levels after abruptly stopping smoking	Moderate	Be alert for increased adverse effects of chlorpromazine (e.g. dizziness, sedation, extra-pyramidal side effects). If adverse effects occur, reduce the dose as necessary.
Insulin	Smoking is associated with poor glycaemic control in patients with diabetes. Smokers may require higher doses of insulin but the mechanism of any interaction is unclear. Smoking decreases the absorption of insulin and may increase insulin resistance	Moderate	If a patient with insulin-dependent diabetes stops smoking, their dose of insulin may need to be reduced. Advise the patient to be alert for signs of hypoglycaemia and to test their blood glucose more frequently
Olanzapine	Olanzapine is metabolized principally via CYP1A2 and clearance is increased in smokers. Serum olanzapine levels are reduced in smokers compared with non-smokers; smokers may need higher dosages. Symptoms of olanzapine toxicity have been reported in a patient who stopped smoking	Moderate	Be alert for increased adverse effects of olanzapine (e.g. dizziness, sedation, hypotension). If adverse reactions occur, reduce the dose as necessary

Table 4.6 (Contd.)			
Drug name	Nature of interaction	Clinical relevance	Action to take when stopping smoking
Warfarin	Warfarin is partly metabolized via CYP1A2. An interaction with smoking is not clinically relevant in most patients. The dose of warfarin is adjusted according to a patient's International Normalized Ratio (INR)	Moderate	If a patient taking warfarin stops smoking, their INR might increase so monitor the INR more closely. Advise patients to tell the physician managing their anticoagulant control that they are stopping smoking
Benzodiazepines	Smokers taking benzodiazepines may experience less drowsiness than non-smokers. Results from pharmacokinetic studies have been mixed and the interaction, if any exists, may be due to stimulation of the central nervous system from smoking	Low	Patients may experience an enhanced effect of benzodiazepines after stopping smoking. If so, consider reducing the dose
Flecainide	Smoking increases the clearance of flecainide. Smokers appear to need higher doses of flecainide, compared with non-smokers	Low	Be alert for dose-related adverse effects of flecainide such as dizziness and visual disturbances. If adverse effects occur, reduce the dose as necessary

Since the majority of interactions are due to components of cigarette smoke other than nicotine, these interactions are not expected to occur when stopping NRT.

Key reading

Aubin HJ, Bobak A, Britton JR, Oncken C, Billing CB, Jr, Gong J et al. Varenicline versus transdermal nicotine patch for smoking cessation: results from a randomised, open-label trial. *Thorax* 2008; **63**(8):717–24.

British National Formulary (BNF). Edition 55, March 2008. London: BMJ Groups and RPS Publishing.

CSM WG, 2005. Report of the Committee on Safety of Medicines Working Group on nicotine replacement therapy. Available at: http://www.mhra. gov.uk/home/groups/pl-a/documents/websiteresources/con2023239.pdf

Gourlay SG, Stead LF, Benowitz NL. Clonidine for smoking cessation. *Cochrane Database of Syst Rev* 2004; (3) Art. No. CD000058. DOI:10.1002/1465 1858.CD000058.pub2.

Hughes JR, Stead LF, Lancaster T. Antidepressants for smoking cessation. *Cochrane Database Syst Rev* 2007; (1) Art. No. CD000031. DOI:10.1002/1465 1858.CD000031.pub3.

Jorenby DE, Hays JT, Rigotti NA et al. Efficacy of varenicline, an alpha4beta2 nicotinic acetylcholine receptor partial agonist, vs placebo or sustained-release bupropion for smoking cessation: a randomized controlled trial. *JAMA* 2006; **1**: 56–63.

Nicotine Assisted Reduction to Stop (NARS)—Guidance for health professionals on this new indication for nicotine replacement therapy. ASH, London, October 2005. Available at: http:// www.ash.org.uk/html/cessationdetail.php#reduction

Smoking and Drug Interactions. United Kingdom Medicines Information, June 2007. Available at: http://merseycare.nhs.uk/Library/Services/ Clinical_Services/Pharmacy/Smoking_Interactions.pdf

Stead LF, Perera R, Bullen C, Mant D, Lancaster T. Nicotine replacement therapy for smoking cessation. *Cochrane Database Syst Rev* 2008; (1).

'Which medicines need dose adjustment when a patient stops smoking?' UK Medicines Information Q&A 136.2, March 2008. Available at: http://www.nelm.nhs/Documents/QA136.2_%20smoking_and_drug_int eractions.doc?id=591656

Chapter 5

Non-pharmacological aids to smoking cessation

Stuart Rees

Key points

- There is not much evidence from trials about the effects of acupuncture for people trying to quit smoking.
- There is not much evidence from trials about the effects of hypnotherapy for people trying to quit smoking.
- Aversion smoking is also not recommended at present.

5.1 Introduction

A number of complementary and alternative medicines (CAM) have been considered for smoking cessation. A population survey in 1996 suggested that 15% of respondents would use complimentary therapies to give up smoking and a US survey of 1175 patients attending a tobacco treatment clinic between 2003 and 2005 reported that 27% had already tried CAM for tobacco cessation. The interventions most commonly used were hypnosis, relaxation, acupuncture, and meditation with 67% reporting interest in future use of CAM for tobacco cessation. The treatments of greatest interest for use in the future were hypnosis, herbal products, acupuncture, relaxation, and massage therapy. Female gender, previous use of conventional tobacco cessation products, previous use of CAM treatments, and a higher level of education were significantly associated with interest in future CAM use. These services are rarely offered within the National Health Service (NHS) and can be expensive, but such high levels of interest in CAM among tobacco users underscores the need to conduct stringent research in this field.

This chapter summarizes the scientific evidence from well-designed trials investigating CAM.

5.2 **Acupuncture**

Acupuncture is used with the aim of reducing the withdrawal symptoms during a quit attempt. A number of different techniques of acupuncture have been used to aid smoking cessation. These range from electrically stimulating the acupuncture needles (electroacupuncture) to using pressure alone (acupressure—no needles involved).

Several literature reviews of controlled trials of acupuncture for smoking cessation have been published with inconsistent conclusions. A Cochrane review looked at 24 studies comparing active acupuncture with sham acupuncture (using needles at other places in the body not thought to be useful) or other control conditions. They included randomized trials comparing a form of acupuncture with no intervention, sham treatment, or another intervention for smoking cessation. The odds ratio for the short-term effect of quitting was significant at 1.36 (95% CI: 1.07 to 1.72). However, the review was strongly influenced by one individual positive study and concluded that there is no consistent evidence whether the effectiveness of acupuncture, or any of its various techniques, is any different from a placebo effect. Wu *et al.* (2007) arrived at a similar conclusion showing that auricular acupuncture did not have a better efficacy in smoking cessation compared to sham acupuncture.

5.3 **Hypnotherapy**

Hypnotherapy has been a recognized therapeutic tool by professional medical groups in a number of countries for many years. Hypnotherapy is believed to weaken the desire to smoke, strengthen the will to stop, or improve the ability to focus on a treatment programme by increasing concentration by acting on underlying impulses. Various hypnotherapy techniques have been employed in smoking cessation. The most common method attempts to modify patients' perception of smoking by using the potential of hypnotherapy to induce deep concentration. Unfortunately, to date, most of the studies in the scientific literature are either case reports or poor quality uncontrolled trials which show a great variability in quit rates. Interpretation of these studies is difficult due to the very many different hypnotherapy regimens, variation in the number and frequency of treatments, and heterogeneous outcomes. As a result, a Cochrane review of nine studies of hypnotherapy versus 14 control interventions for smoking cessation made no attempt to perform a meta-analysis and could not provide an overall summary estimate of the effectiveness of hypnosis. They concluded that there is not enough good evidence to recommend it (or not) for smoking cessation.

5.4 **Herbal cigarettes**

Asian herbal-tobacco cigarettes claim to reduce harm, but no published literature is available to verify these claims or investigate unidentified toxicities.

5.5 **Aversion therapy**

Aversion therapy pairs the pleasurable stimulus of smoking a cigarette with some unpleasant stimulus/negative sensations to extinguish the urge to smoke. A Cochrane review in 2007 of 25 randomized trials lasting at least 6 months calculated the odds ratio for abstinence following rapid smoking compared to control was 2.01 (95% CI 1.36 to 2.95). However, a funnel plot suggested a relative absence of small studies with negative results and most trials had a number of serious methodological problems likely to lead to spurious positive results. The only trial using biochemical validation of all self-reported cessation gave a non-significant result. Other aversion methods were not shown to be effective, and there was a borderline dose–response to the level of aversive stimulation (OR 1.67, 95% CI 0.99 to 2.81). The meta-analysis concluded there was insufficient evidence to recommend aversive therapies but did call for more rigorous evaluation particularly on rapid smoking.

5.6 **Conclusion**

In summary, there is as yet no convincing scientific evidence to recommend CAM for smoking cessation.

Key reading

Abbot NC, Stead LF, White AR, Barnes J. Hypnotherapy for smoking cessation (update). *Cochrane Database Syst Rev* 1998, (2): Art. No. CD00001008.DOI:10.1002/14651858.CD001008.

Hajek P, Stead LF. Aversive smoking for smoking cessation. *Cochrane Database of Syst Rev* 2001; (3) Art. No. CD000546.DOI:10.1002/1465 1858.CD000546.pub 2.

Holroyd J. Hypnosis treatment for smoking: an evaluative review. *Int J Clin Exp Hypnosis* 1980; **28**: 341–57.

Sood A, Ebbert JO, Sood R, Stevens SR. Complementary treatments for tobacco cessation: a survey. *Nicotine Tob Res* 2006; **8**(6): 767–71.

Spiegel D, Frischolz EJ, Fleiss JL, Spiegel H. Predictors of smoking abstinence following a single-session restructuring intervention with self-hypnosis. *Am J Psychiatr* 1993; **150**: 1090–7.

White AR, Rampes H, Campbell JL. Acupuncture and related interventions for smoking cessation. *Cochrane Database Syst Rev* 2006; (1): Art. No. CD000009.DOI:10.1002/1465 1858.CD000009.pub 2.

Wu TP, Chen FP, Liu JY, Lin MH, Hwang SJ. A randomised controlled trial of auricular acupuncture in smoking cessation. *J Chin Med Assoc* 2007; **70**(8): 331–8.

Chapter 6

Smoking cessation and lung disease and COPD

Carlos A. Jiménez-Ruiz

Key points

- Smoking cessation should be an integral part of lung disease treatment.
- Smokers with lung disorders can have specific smoking characteristics that make it difficult for them to quit: higher nicotine dependence, lower self-efficacy, depression, weight gain problems, fatalistic beliefs, and emotional distress.
- Positive advice delivered opportunistically during routine consultations to respiratory patients who smoke, using 'teachable moments', is effective to help them to quit and so should always be provided.
- NRT is efficacious and safe for helping pulmonary patients who smoke to quit. However, higher doses are often needed, often combining different forms, for prolonged duration. NRT is also used to help smokers with chronic obstructive pulmonary disease (COPD) to reduce the number of cigarettes smoked as a gateway to quitting.
- Bupropion is significantly more effective than placebo in smokers with COPD, at least over 6 months There is no increase in the number or intensity of adverse effects associated with taking bupropion in COPD patients compared to other groups.
- Nortriptyline can be an useful alternative for the treatment of smokers with COPD when first-line medications have failed.
- Results using varenicline in COPD patients are awaited; initial experience suggests it is well-tolerated and useful.

6.1 Introduction

Smoking is the most important cause of pulmonary disorders in the developed world. Smoking directly causes many respiratory diseases and worsens almost all of them. Chronic obstructive pulmonary disease (COPD) and lung cancer are the two pulmonary disorders most directly related to smoking. Nevertheless, smoking can aggravate bronchial asthma as well as reducing the effectiveness of inhaled treatments. Smoking worsens all pulmonary infections, including tuberculosis; also pneumothorax, pulmonary haemorrhage, and pulmonary Langerhans cell histiocytosis. Idiopathic pulmonary fibrosis (IPF) is commoner among heavy smokers, but the effects of smoking cessation on the progression of IPF are unknown. In contrast, sarcoidosis and allergic pneumonitis occur more rarely in smokers than in non-smokers.

COPD is the only one of the top 5 killers that is expected to rise in incidence in the next 10 years. Smoking causes over 80% of COPD but only about 15% to 20% of all smokers will develop COPD during their lifetime. More than 50% of patients with mild or moderate COPD continue smoking after their diagnosis.

Smoking cessation is the *only* intervention that can significantly improve all four-core symptoms of COPD (cough, sputum, breathlessness, wheeze), also slow the deterioration in lung function (to a rate comparable to non-smokers), and simultaneously improve mortality.

Patients with lung disorders may find particular difficulties giving up smoking and health professionals should be aware of these so that they can consider more intensive and innovative solutions to maximize respiratory outcomes.

6.2 Smoking characteristics of pulmonary patients

Certain characteristics appear to differentiate smokers with COPD from other smokers. These include higher nicotine dependence, lower motivation to quit, lower self-efficacy, more depression, weight gain problems, fatalistic beliefs, emotional distress, lower-perceived reduced risk, and low-perceived benefit.

6.2.1 Nicotine dependence

Two population-based studies have found that COPD smokers had a statistically higher level of nicotine dependence than smokers without COPD (as measured by the modified Fagerström Test for Nicotine Dependence (FTND)-questionnaire, $p < 0.001$). Compared to 'healthy' smokers, smokers who develop COPD have often smoked many more cigarettes and possibly inhale a greater volume of smoke more deeply, resulting in greater exposure to the toxins known to cause lung damage. One study certainly found that COPD smokers had higher levels of exhaled carbon monoxide (eCO) than 'healthy' smokers although current levels were not independently associated with COPD in a multivariable model.

6.2.2 Motivation and self-efficacy

Motivation, the number of self-reported quit attempts, and self-efficacy for quitting all appear similar in smokers with COPD to other smokers but beliefs among smokers with other pulmonary disorders have not been well-studied. Like most other groups, studies in smokers with lung disease reveal two very distinct groups of either unmotivated smokers or smokers motivated to quit. The main strategy for those who are unmotivated to quit is discussing the advantages of quitting. For those motivated to quit, the best intervention is to offer a specific and intensive action plan.

6.2.3 Depression

Depression is one of the most important factors associated with continued smoking in patients with COPD. One study found that depression in hospitalized COPD smokers was not only strongly associated with increased mortality and longer hospital stay but also independently asociated with persistent smoking at 6 months (OR, 2.30; 95% CI, 1.17 to 4.52). Another population-based study found that 10% of non-smoking COPD patients were clinically depressed compared to 29% in COPD smokers.

6.2.4 Other barriers

Overweight COPD smokers may suffer from a worsening of their symptoms if they gain weight, leading to relapse. The Lung Health Study suggested that such patients would have to gain about 60 kg to have the same effect on their lung function as continuing to smoke. Doctors should advise COPD smokers that stopping smoking is still the healthiest thing they can do in spite of gaining some weight (average 5 to 8 kg).

6.3 Smoking cessation in asthmatic patients

Active and passive smoking trigger and worsen asthmatic symptoms. Smoking can inactivate some of the inhaled treatments for asthma (is often a cause for so-called 'steroid-resistant asthma'). Yet, the prevalence of smoking among asthmatic patients is similar to that of the general population and the highest smoking rates in asthma are found in those attending for emergency treatment. Tonnesen examined the effect of a smoking cessation programme in asthmatic smokers using nicotine gum or inhaler. The abstainers had improvements in asthma-specific quality-of-life scores, asthma symptoms, and in physiological measures of bronchial hyper-reactivity, reductions in rescue and pre-venter medications. Smoking reduction produced some improvements but the biggest health benefits were obtained with complete cessation.

6.4 Therapeutic interventions in smokers with respiratory disease

Combining behavioural interventions with pharmacological treatment seems to be the most effective option to help smokers with lung disease, so they should ideally be referred to a specialist.

6.4.1 Psychological interventions

Their physician should advise every respiratory patient of quitting smoking, at every consultation, indeed some pulmonologists arrange follow-up only to address smoking cessation. To build on their brief repeated advice, health professionals should use key 'teachable moments', personalizing the health risk of smoking and the benefits of stopping. Box 6.1 shows some 'teachable moments' for pulmonary patients.

As outlined in Chapter 3, brief advice should be more positive, nevertheless the negative effects need to be explained too. Most people with COPD have been told it is an incurable and progressive condition, so anything that alters this course can be seen as an 'unexpected' bonus.

Figure 6.1 is a very famous graph used in respiratory medicine. Based on a longitudinal study following male blue-collar workers over 10 yrs, they confirmed the decline in lung function. This can be used as an effective teaching moment. For example, a patient aged 45 yrs performs spirometry in a general practitioner (GP) surgery, resulting

Box 6.1 'Teachable moments' for pulmonary patients

1. When the smoker attends suffering from respiratory symptoms: particularly coughing, wheezing, chest pain, breathlessness
2. When examining the patient
3. When the smoker attends for chest X-ray results
4. When the smoker is performing spirometry and when discussing the results
5. When prescribing respiratory medications that can be influenced by smoking: bronchodilators, oxygen, etc.
6. When the patient has been hospitalized

in an forced expiratory volume (FEV$_1$) of 60% predicted (Point A). If he continues to smoke, his lung function declines so that he will be in a wheelchair (Point B), aged 68 yrs, and dead (Point C) at 72 yrs. If he stops, he will have an *extra 12 yrs* before becoming wheelchair-bound (Point B to D) and live an *extra 6 yrs at least* (Point C to E). No other intervention has such profound disease-modifying effect in COPD. Taking 2 to 3 min, explaining this after spirometry could be a very effective way of conveying personal risk:benefit ratios.

Studies using specific interventions applicable to pulmonary patients, for example using special words like 'smoker's lung', biofeedback with repeated eCO, or lung function tests, show a trend to even better quit rates over typical advice but this is not statistically significant.

6.4.2 Pharmacological treatments

First- and second-line pharmacological agents have been studied to different degrees in smokers with lung disease and some caveats must be acknowledged (Boxes 6.2 to 6.5).

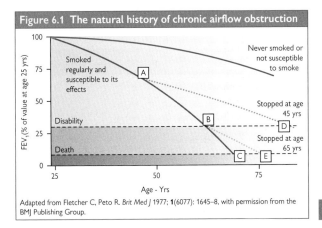

Figure 6.1 The natural history of chronic airflow obstruction

Adapted from Fletcher C, Peto R. *Brit Med J* 1977; **1**(6077): 1645–8, with permission from the BMJ Publishing Group.

Box 6.2 Recommendations for using nicotine replacement therapy (NRT) in smokers with pulmonary disorders

- NRT has shown to be efficacious (odds ratio of quitting ×1.4–2.4) and safe for the treatment of smokers with COPD and other pulmonary diseases. Smokers with pulmonary disorders can suffer from higher nicotine dependence so often need higher doses of NRT. Adequate replacement is usually not obtained with standard NRT doses but patches at high doses significantly increase efficacy
- Combining slow and quick acting forms of NRT and prolonging duration of NRT treatment for up to 6–12 months have led to better quit rates in pulmonary patients
- Using NRT to progressively reduce the number of cigarettes smoked by pulmonary patients (particularly in those who are unmotivated to quit initially), as a gateway to quitting, has been proved in several randomized clinical trials. In an open follow-up study of COPD patients initially unable to quit, Jimenez achieved a 50% quit rate (with 50% halving their smoking) over 18 months, using this approach

Box 6.3 Recommendations for using bupropion in smokers with pulmonary disorders

The efficacy of bupropion over placebo for smokers with COPD has been shown by two clinical trials confirming it to be significantly more effective in achieving continuous abstinence over 6 months with no increase in the number or severity of adverse effects, compared with other smokers

The combination of NRT plus bupropion can help more general smokers to quit and should be specifically tested in pulmonary patients

Box 6.4 Recommendations for using nortriptyline in smokers with pulmonary disorders

One study has shown that nortriptyline is more efficacious than placebo in achiving abstinence over 6 months in smokers with COPD. Nortriptyline can be a useful alternative when first-line medications have failed, possibly because it may help treat the excess depression seen in this group

Box 6.5 Recommendations for using varenicline in smokers with pulmonary disorders

A randomized, placebo-controlled, double-blinded clinical trial is currently assessing the efficacy and safety of varenicline as a pharmacological treatment for COPD smokers. The results are due soon. Most published data regarding varenicline have excluded smokers with known lung disease, but clinical surveys and abstracts within secondary care suggest it is well-tolerated with no increased side-effect profiles in people with COPD

Key reading

Fiore MC, Bailey WC, Cohen SJ et al. Treating Tobacco Use and Dependence. Clinical Practice Guideline. Rockville, MD: US Department of Health and Human Services, Public Health Service; June 2000.

Jiménez Ruiz CA, Masa J, Miravitlles M et al. Smoking characteristics. Differences in attitudes and dependence between healthy smokers and smokers with COPD. Chest 2001; 119: 1365–70.

National Institute for Health and Clinical Excellence (NICE). Final appraisal determination: varenicline for smoking cessation 2007. Available at http//guidance.nice.org.uk/page.aspx?o 431452 (accessed 30 January 2008).

Schnoll RA, Rothman RL, Newman H et al. Characteristics of cancer patients entering a smoking programme and correlates of quit motivation: implications for the development of tobacco control programmes for cancer patients. Psychooncology 2004; 13: 346–58.

Shahab L, Jarvis M, Britton M, West R. Prevalence, diagnosis and relation to tobacco dependence of COPD in a nationally representative population sample. Thorax 2006; 61(12): 1043–7.

Stratelis G, Molstad S, Jakobsson P, Zetterström O. The impact of repeated spirometry and smoking cessation advice on smokers with COPD. Scand J Prim Health Care 2006; 24: 133–9.

Tønnesen P, Carrozzi L, Fagerström KO et al. Task Force Recommendations. Smoking cessation in patients with respiratory diseases: a high priority, integral component of therapy. Eur Respir J 2007; 29: 390–417.

Tonnesen P, Mikkelsen K, Bremann L. Nurse-conducted smoking cessation in patients with COPD using nicotine sublingual tablets and behavioral support. Chest 2006; 130: 314–6.

Wagena EJ, Kant IJ, Huibers MJH et al. Psychological distress and depressed mood in employees with asthma, chronic bronchitis or emphysema. A population-based observational study on prevalence and the relationship with smoking cigarettes. Eur J Epidemiol 2004; 19: 147–53.

Chapter 7

Smoking cessation and heart disease

Clive Weston

Stop . . . Stop now . . . Stop before it's too late
Dr. Mike Norell, Consultant Interventional Cardiologist,
Wolverhampton, UK.

Key points

- Cigarette smoking is an independent risk factor for and roughly doubles the risk of cardiovascular disease (CVD).
- More smokers die of CVD than any other cause.
- Cigarette smoke causes more damage than nicotine.
- Mechanisms include impaired vasodilatation and particularly endovascular inflammation.
- The risk of further CVD events falls quickly after cessation and by up to 40% but can take up to 20 yrs to fall to that of never smokers.
- Smoking cessation treatments are particularly effective in people with established CVD.
- All smoking cessation pharmacotherapies can be given in people with CVD, with certain caveats.

7.1 Introduction

The commonest cause of death in developed countries is cardiovascular disease (CVD). Cigarette smoking is associated with both the development and progression of CVD, presenting as acute coronary syndromes (ACS), sudden cardiac death, peripheral vascular disease, and cerebral infarction. The *relative* risk of death from CVD in smokers is almost double than that in non-smokers and while substantially smaller than the relative risk for developing lung cancer or chronic pulmonary disease, the greater prevalence of diseases of the heart and blood vessels in the developed world mean that smokers in western countries are at greater *absolute* risk of dying of CVD than other causes.

Smoking is an independent risk factor but also interacts with other factors to cause CVD. For instance, in populations with low blood cholesterol levels the effects of cigarette smoking are markedly attenuated. Also, smokers fail to gain the full health benefits of regular physical activity. However, support for a *causal* relationship between smoking and CVD comes from the observation of a dose–response relationship—for example, the odds of myocardial infarction (MI) in smokers compared with non-smokers is 1.63 in those smoking 1 to 9 cigarettes per day but rises to 4.59 with ≥20 cigarettes per day. There is also an increased risk with prolonged exposure (hence the utility of defining 'pack-years') and a reduced CVD risk after smoking cessation.

7.2 **Mechanisms of adverse effect**

Both clinical and experimental investigations of the pathophysiology suggest the effects of the 4,000 compounds in whole smoke are much more deadly when compared to nicotine, which plays a relatively minor part alone. There is uniform agreement that both active and passive smoking have detrimental effects on the cardiovascular system, although a milder (but still clinically important effect) is suggested for the latter. The exact pathophysiological pathways are still being elucidated but are likely to be multiple (see Figure 7.1) and should be considered in terms of impaired vasodilatation (conduit vs resistance arteries and veins), injury to the vascular endothelium, production of superoxide anions, reduced production and bioavailability of nitric oxide (NO), increased production and release of endothelin, endothelial dysfunction, thrombosis, arteriosclerosis, and then heart or brain infarction (and death). These effects are modified by age, gender, other CVD risk factors, and particularly total smoking dosage. For example, a multi-centre study of 2,920 men without obvious CVD examined the associations between cigarette smoking, years since quitting smoking, and inflammatory and haemostatic markers. They adjusted for other cardiovascular risk factors and showed that compared with never smokers, current cigarette smokers had significantly higher levels of C-reactive protein, white cell count, fibrinogen, haematocrit, blood and plasma viscosity, tissue plasminogen activator antigen, and fibrin D-dimers, and lower levels of albumin. Pipe/cigar smokers had levels similar to never smokers and ex-cigarette smokers had intermediate levels of these inflammatory markers. Most inflammatory and haemostatic levels improved within 5 yrs of smoking cessation but took over 20 yrs to revert to levels of never smokers. These authors suggested that activation of inflammation and haemostasis were the main potential mechanisms by which cigarette smoking increases cardiovascular risk.

Stopping smoking should have early beneficial effects by reducing the inflammatory stimuli to plaque rupture and pro-thrombotic tendencies that cause subsequent arterial thrombosis. Later benefits then accrue by reducing *de novo* development of atheroma.

7.3 **Acute coronary events and the smokers' paradox**

Many clinical studies show that smokers are more likely to survive hospitalization with ACS than non-smokers. In one large national registry of MI, in-hospital mortality was 8% for smokers and 16% for non-smokers. This (superficially) counter-intuitive observation has been called '*the smokers' paradox*' and much energy has been expended in attempting to explain it. While there remains a possibility that cigarette smoking may make acute coronary thrombosis both more likely but more survivable, this paradox is largely explained by certain beneficial characteristics found incidentally in smokers. For example, when compared with non-smokers, smokers experiencing ACS tend to be up to 10 yrs younger, are less likely to have hypertension and diabetes (as both increase with age), are less likely to have previous heart disease, are less likely to have extensive (triple-vessel) coronary disease, and are more likely to present with evidence of complete thrombotic coronary occlusion (ST-segment elevation on the presenting electrocardiogram (ECG)). There is no indication that smokers are treated any differently to non-smokers in the early stages of ACS, but younger patients are certainly more likely to be offered aggressive interventional and secondary preventive therapies.

An understanding of the smokers' paradox is important to interpret studies of smoking cessation in patients with confirmed coronary disease. Careful adjustment for age, gender, and co-morbidities is required in order to reliably compare outcomes between those who have never smoked and those who continue to smoke or stop smoking. Additionally, the fact that at presentation with ACS smokers are relatively young and have less extensive coronary disease implies that if smoking cessation is associated with even a modest reduction in re-infarction or death, it may equate to significant benefit in terms of years of life gained.

7.4 **Evidence for benefit of smoking cessation**

The risk of CVD falls rapidly after stopping smoking (halving within about 2 yrs), but most longitudinal cohort studies of currently healthy individuals suggest that CVD risk takes 10 to 20 yrs to fall to that of never smokers.

Figure 7.1 Smoking

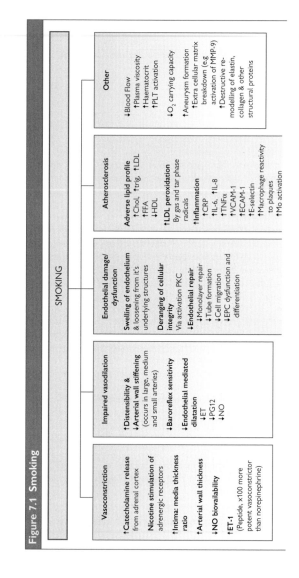

SMOKING

Vasoconstriction

↑Catecholamine release from adrenal cortex

Nicotine stimulation of adrenergic receptors

↑Intima: media thickness ratio

↑Arterial wall thickness

↓NO biovailability

↑ET-1
(Peptide, x100 more potent vasoconstrictor than norepinephrine)

Impaired vasodilation

↑Distensibility & ↓Arterial wall stiffening (occurs in large, medium and small arteries)

↓Baroreflex sensitivity

↓Endothelial mediated dilatation
↑ET
↓PG12
↓NO

Endothelial damage/ dysfunction

Swelling of endothelium & loosening from it's underlying structures

Deranging of cellular integrity
Via activation PKC

↓Endothelial repair
↓Monolayer repair
↓Tube formation
↓Cell migration
↓EPC dysfunction and differentiation

Atherosclerosis

Adverse lipid profile
↑Chol, ↑trig, ↑LDL
↑FFA
↓HDL

↑LDL peroxidation
By gas and tar phase radicals

↑Inflammation
↑CRP
↑IL-6, ↑IL-8
↑TNFα
↑VCAM-1
↑ECAM-1
↑E-selectin
↑Macrophage reactivity to plaques
↑Mo activation

Other

↓Blood Flow
↑Plasma viscosity
↑Haematocrit
↑PLT activation

↓O₂ carrying capacity

↑Aneurysm formation
↑Extra cellular matrix breakdown (e.g activation of MMP-9)
↑Destructive re-modelling of elastin, collagen & other structural proteins

Key:

NO	Nitric oxide	↓ Decrease/attenuated
ET-1	Endothelin-1	↑ Increase/enhanced
PG-12	Prostacyclin	
PKC	Protein kinase C	
EPC	Endothelial progenitor cell	
ROS	Reactive oxygen species	
ENOS	Endothelial nitric oxide synthase	
EDRF	Endothelial derived relaxing factor	
Chol	Cholesterol	
Trig	Triglyceride	
LDL	Low density lipoprotein	
FFA	Free fatty acid	
HDL	High density lipoprotein	
CRP	C reactive protein	
IL-6	Interleukin 6	
IL-8	Interleukin 8	
TNF	Tissue necrosis factor alpha	
VCAM-1	Vascular cell adhesion molecule-1	
ECAM-1	Endothelial cell adhesion molecule-1	
Mo	Monocyte	
PLT	Platelets	
JNK	C-Jun N-terminal Kinase	
TPA	Tissue plasminogen activator	
CGMP	Cyclic guanosine monophosphate	
MMP-9	Metalloproteinase 9	

↓ NO bioavailability
↓ Breakdown from
↓ generation of
superoxide anions/
ROS
↓ Production by eNOS

↓ Antioxidants
↓ Vit C & E

↑ EDRF degradation

↑ **Activated protein C**
(potent anticoagulant)
↑ **Stabilisation thrombin**
deposits at site of
vascular injury

↑ **Immunoreactivity of
thromboplastin**

↑ **Oxidative stress**

↑ **Apoptosis**
Activated PKC
JNK pathway

↓ **tPA release**

↓ **CGMP release**

Secondary prevention in those who already have CVD is still vital. Early studies were powered to show differences in smoking activity rather than clinical outcomes and observational studies had many inherent biases; most importantly, the decision to stop smoking may be associated with other prognostically important factors, such as improvements in dietary behaviour and increased physical activity. Moreover, smoking status in many studies was self-reported and not validated biochemically and particularly repeatedly, over the observation period.

The best estimate of the effect of smoking cessation in patients with coronary heart disease (CHD) comes from systematic review of prospective cohort studies. Using strict inclusion criteria of validating smoking status (at least twice) over at least 2 yrs, controlling for confounding variables and including the main outcome as death from any cause (not just recurrent cardiac events), Critchley analysed 20 studies containing 12,603 smokers with CHD. While, 5,659 subjects stopped, 6,944 continued to smoke. There was a 36% risk reduction in death and 32% in non-fatal MI over 3 to 5 yrs associated with stopping.

There was no obvious relationship between duration of follow-up and size of risk reduction. This 36% risk reduction compares well with other secondary preventive drug therapies in similar patients (e.g. statins 30%, beta-blockers 25%, angiotensin-converting enzyme inhibitors 25%, aspirin 15%). Even when assuming that 10% of those reporting cessation had actually continued to smoke, a similar benefit was obtained. This analysis included those whose index event was ACS or a coronary artery bypass grafting (CABG) operation. Others have reported a 44% increased risk of death following percutaneous coronary intervention, for stable angina, associated with continued smoking, compared to stopping with the estimated *absolute* benefit of stopping smoking increasing year-on-year over at least 10 yrs.

7.5 **Practical aspects**

Based upon this evidence, international guidelines emphasize the importance of encouraging smoking cessation in those with heart disease. Table 7.1 suggests some teachable moments in managing patients with CHD.

It is disappointing that most smokers discharged from hospital with CVD continue to smoke or relapse after stopping. The addictive nature of tobacco, the capacity of smokers to deny an association with CVD, a return to a 'smoking environment', and an oscillation between fatalism ('what will be, will be') and optimism ('it won't happen again') may all contribute. Another obstacle to quitting may be the perceived risk of weight gain following smoking cessation,

Table 7.1 Prompts and teachable moments to emphasise smoking cessation

1. At confirmation of CVD (in patients and relatives)—whether during ECGs, exercise tests, or response to anti-anginal drugs
2. Seeing coronary stenoses during angiography
3. Hospitalization is an opportunity to advocate cessation—access to cigarettes is difficult; pharmacotherapy should be readily available; carers providing a unified message surround the patient. Some (but not all) research suggests that those admitted with CVD are indeed more likely to quit than those admitted with other diagnoses
4. Post-treatment, for example seeing a mid-line sternotomy scar following bypass graft, can provide a powerful reminder of the effects of smoking

especially if counselled on weight gain as CVD risk factor modification. Ex-smokers with CHD can expect about 5% increase in body weight at 12 months.

Lack of explicit advice or continuing support exacerbate the problem. Some clinicians may be embarrassed about promoting smoking cessation for fear of being accused of blaming the patient for their illness. For other cardiologists, the 'stop smoking' message may appear so obvious as to become implicit rather than explicit. Brief advice may have a very small effect but intensive programmes, delivered by specialists, beginning in hospital with continued contact and support for >1 month after discharge, have been shown to increase the odds of quitting by over 80%. Even advice aimed to promote fear of 'a heart attack if smoking continues' can be effective when coupled with further follow-up. Such follow-up has included 'self-help' materials (leaflets, audio-tapes), psychosocial interventions (face-to-face counselling sessions, cognitive/behavioural interventions, or regular telephone interviews) and, where appropriate, drug treatments (notably nicotine replacement therapy (NRT) and bupropion). It has been calculated that if ten smokers with CHD received psychosocial intervention, then at least one of them would be abstinent after 1 yr. This 'number needed to treat' (NNT) of ten compares well with the NNT for many other health interventions.

Patients with MI frequently exhibit moderate depressive symptoms during hospitalization. Such symptoms predict rapid relapse to smoking and perhaps such individuals could be targeted for particularly intensive and prolonged support with early prescription of centrally acting, stop-smoking pharmacotherapy—with careful monitoring for possible worsening of depression.

7.6 Drug therapies

Pharmacological therapy also aids smoking cessation in those with CVD, though prescribers should be aware of potential interactions with cardiac drugs. For example, initiation of bupropion may interfere with metabolism of metoprolol and flecainide; the anti-platelet agent, clopidogrel, may alter conversion of bupropion to its active metabolite. Initial concerns that the acute haemodynamic effects of nicotine may increase cardiac events in patients with CVD during NRT have not been confirmed. NRT is certainly safe in stable CVD. Its use is not encouraged in the early (hospital) stages of ACS only because there are little data on safety in this situation. The current alternatives are inpatients secretly smoking (getting higher and faster nicotine doses) or undergoing acute nicotine withdrawal (including palpitations, sweats, blood pressure surges, and tachycardias). Analyses of primary care databases show no increase in CVD events in the weeks after start of treatment, yet an increase in events in the weeks preceding, implying that clinicians often start treatment soon after acute events with no ill effects.

Information on starting bupropion or varenicline during hospitalization for ACS is also sparse, though randomized trials have been completed. These agents should be prescribed for 1 to 2 weeks before the 'quit date' so they are not useful during an acute (unexpected) presentation. Importantly, many CHD patients who are often 'tablet-naïve' on admission are discharged a few days later on combinations of at least four drugs, so detecting adverse drug effects and identifying the causative agent are difficult. Most smoking cessation drugs should really be prescribed within a programme of behavioural support; simply prescribing a course of treatment in hospital and then passing responsibility to primary care is inadvisable.

Key reading

Barth J, Critchley J, Bengel J. Psychosocial interventions for smoking cessation in patients with coronary heart disease. *Cochrane Database of Syst Rev* 2008; (1).

Critchley J, Capewell S. Smoking cessation for the secondary prevention of coronary heart disease. *Cochrane Database of Syst Rev* 2003; (4).

Gourlay SG, Rundle AC, Barron HV. Smoking and mortality following acute myocardial infarction: results from the National Registry of Myocardial Infarction 2 (NRMI 2). *Nicotine Tob Res* 2002; **4**: 101–7.

Hasdai D, Garratt KN, Grill DE, Lerman A, Holmes DR. Effect of smoking status on the long-term outcome after successful percutaneous coronary revascularization. *N Engl J Med* 1997; **336**: 755–61.

Rahman MM, Laher I. Structural and functional alteration of blood vessels caused by cigarette smoking: an overview of molecular mechanisms. *Curr Vasc Pharmacol* 2007; **5**: 276–92.

Rigotti NA, Munafo MR, Stead LF. Interventions for smoking cessation in hospitalised patients. *Cochrane Database of Syst Rev* 2007; (3).

Rosengren A, Wallentin L, Simoons M et al. Cardiovascular risk factors and clinical presentation in acute coronary syndrome. *Heart* 2005; **91**: 1141–7.

Teo KK, Ounpuu S, Hawken S et al. Tobacco use and risk of myocardial infarction in 52 countries in the INTERHEART study: a case–control study. *Lancet* 2006; **368**(9536):647–58.

Thorndike AN, Regan S, McKool K et al. Depressive symptoms and smoking cessation after hospitalisation for cardiovascular disease. *Arch Intern Med* 2008; **168**: 186–91.

Wannamethee SG, Lowe GD, Shaper AG, Rumley A, Lennon L, Whincup PH. Associations between cigarette smoking, pipe/cigar smoking, and smoking cessation, and haemostatic and inflammatory markers for cardiovascular disease. *Eur Heart J* 2005; **26**: 1765–73.

Yanbaeva DG, Dentener MA, Creutzberg EC, Wesseling G, Wouters EFM. Systemic effects of smoking. *Chest* 2007; **131**: 1557–66.

64

Chapter 8

Smoking cessation and surgery

Anthony Gibson

Key points

- Smokers attend for similar surgery 5 to 10 yrs younger than non-smokers.
- Smokers spend more days in hospital and have a higher post-operative mortality than non-smokers.
- Stopping smoking before surgery can reduce anaesthetic risk and post-operative complications, for example reduce wound infections up to sixfold.
- Very few referrals to a specialist stop-smoking service come from surgical specialties.
- Quitting needs to be achieved at least 8 weeks before surgery for maximum benefit.
- Large, randomized, controlled trials addressing clinical outcomes are needed to design the best stop-smoking service for surgical patients.

8.1 Introduction

Smokers present earlier than non-smokers requiring surgery. For example, smokers undergo the same elective orthopaedic procedures on average 5 yrs earlier than non-smokers. Smokers have an increased risk of many post-operative complications compared to those who have never smoked, or those who have recently quit smoking and stay in hospital for, on average, 2 days longer. Despite this, a quarter of all surgical patients continue to smoke up to and after their operation. Hospitalization itself should be an opportunity to stop smoking as patients are aware of their surgical illness; they are in a place where smoking is banned and pharmacotherapy is readily available. Hopefully they are admitted to a hospital with direct access to a specialist stop-smoking service. This chapter reviews the evidence that smoking adversely affects surgical outcomes but also that stopping smoking prior to surgery may have a real beneficial effect on surgical outcomes.

8.2 Continued smoking and surgical outcomes

Cigarette smoking has multiple adverse physiological effects on the pulmonary and cardiovascular systems and on wound healing. When these systems are placed under extra physiological stress during surgery, then additional damage can occur.

8.2.1 Pulmonary effects

In a large but retrospective study, respiratory events were significantly increased among smokers, occurring 3 to 6 times more often than in non-smokers, even though the smoking cohort was younger.

Smokers have increased bronchial mucous production and decreased mucous clearance (from impaired ciliary function). Increased mucous plugging combined with tobacco smoke directly affects host-defence mechanisms (e.g. phagocyte function, dendritic cell activation, neutrophil chemokine induction, etc.) and a higher likelihood of structural lung disease leads to increased risk of post-operative pulmonary infections. Furthermore, in all patients undergoing surgery (especially thoracic and abdominal surgery), lung volume and gas exchange are further reduced due to lung atelectasis and diaphragmatic dysfunction (caused by sedatives, muscle relaxants, pain, and sutures), and smoking compounds these problems. Therefore, patients who smoke at the time of surgery have a higher risk of all types of post-operative pulmonary complications (in one study, one in three smokers had a pulmonary complication after surgery)—including infections, pulmonary embolus, and lung collapse, and surveys consistently demonstrate that they have a higher usage of critical care beds after their surgery.

8.2.2 Cardiovascular effects

Short-term effects on the cardiovascular system are mainly due to serum concentrations of carbon monoxide (CO) and nicotine. The increased CO reduces oxygen availability to the peripheral tissues by around 12%. Carboxy-haemoglobin levels of 6% have been associated with significantly increased risk of ventricular arrhythmia. Nicotine also increases heart rate and blood pressure via activation of nicotinic acetylcholine receptors in the autonomic system, and serum CO confounds these effects on autonomic cardiovascular tone. These effects are combined with the stress response to surgery to create an even worse tissue imbalance of 'oxygen availability vs consumption'. Coronary artery disease, peripheral vascular disease, and cerebrovascular disease are more likely in smoking patients undergoing surgery—further reducing tissue blood supply.

8.2.3 **Wound healing**

The association between smoking and wound healing is well-recognized in clinical practice but controlled studies are limited and the basic pathophysiological mechanisms are still being elucidated. It is postulated that nicotine acting as a potent vasoconstrictor may reduce blood flow to the wound, resulting in tissue ischaemia and impaired healing; nicotine also increases platelet adhesiveness, increasing the risk of thrombotic microvascular occlusion and tissue ischaemia. CO and hydrogen cyanide also contribute to tissue hypoxia and the effects of whole cigarette smoke on endovascular dysfunction and tissue inflammation are described in Chapter 7. Cigarette smoking also reduces new collagen synthesis and activates enzymes that degrade collagen, further impairing wound healing.

Observational studies confirm that wound infection rates are higher in smokers than in non-smokers who have had joint replacements, thoracic surgery, cholecystectomies, bladder surgery, breast reconstruction, and a variety of other plastic surgery procedures. For example, with breast reconstruction, abdominal-wall (donor site) necrosis is seen in 7.9% of current smokers compared with only 1% of non-smokers, and mastectomy-flap necrosis occurred in 7.7% of smokers compared with 1.5% of non-smokers. Smokers were three times more likely to get anastamotic leak following bowel surgery, and across a variety of procedures wound infection rates are generally around 12% for smokers compared to 2% for non- or ex-smokers.

Surgeons would welcome any intervention that could reduce infection rates sixfold.

8.2.4 **Orthopaedic surgery**

There is increasing evidence that smoking has adverse effects on the musculoskeletal system, so smoking cessation is important in orthopaedic surgery. Smoking has been shown to interfere with bone metabolism, revascularization, and bone formation. Vasoconstriction from nicotine inhibits tissue differentiation and the angiogenic response that is vital in the early stages of fracture healing. Nicotine also interferes with osteoblast function and alters skeletal metabolism. Current smoking has been shown to lower bone mineral density, increases the time to union of tibial fractures, delays healing of dental implants, and has been associated with poorer outcomes after treatment for chronic osteomyelitis.

8.2.5 **Cardiac/vascular surgery**

Stopping smoking after coronary artery bypass grafting (CABG) is vital; a 20-yr follow-up study concluded that those patients who continued to smoke had a greater relative risk (RR) of death from all causes (RR 1.68) and cardiac death (RR 1.75) than those who stopped smoking. Those patients continuing to smoke were also more likely to undergo a repeat CABG (RR 1.42) or a percutaneous coronary revascularization (RR 1.56).

Studies have also shown that those who continue to smoke after CABG have a greater risk of myocardial infarction (RR 2.3) compared with quitters and smoking increases the risk of peri-operative strokes after carotid endarterectomy.

A recent meta-analysis found that continued smoking after lower extremity bypass surgery for peripheral vascular disease caused a threefold increase in the risk of graft failure, also with a dose response with patency lower in heavy smokers compared to moderate smokers.

8.2.6 Solid organ transplant

Smoking is associated with an increased risk of death after renal transplantation but the effects of smoking on death appear to dissipate 5 yrs after quitting. Patients who smoke or have smoked until shortly before heart transplantation have a poorer prognosis and a longer recovery unit stay than non-smokers or those who have quit at least a year before surgery.

Smoking is associated with adverse effects in lung transplant patients including progressive lung damage, acceleration of coronary atherosclerosis, and increased risk of myocardial infarction and malignancy before and after transplantation.

8.2.7 Overall surgical mortality

An observational, longitudinal study followed 1000 patients undergoing a variety of surgical procedures for 20 yrs. They reported a 68% increased risk of death in smokers compared to the non-smokers with an increase of especially early post-operative complications as well as a 40% increase in the risk of cardiac symptoms.

The major mechanisms by which smoking can lead to post-operative complications are listed in Box 8.1.

Box 8.1 Mechanisms of damage

- Hypoxia
- Vasoconstriction
- Detachment of endothelial cells
- Blocking of enzymes that prevent cellular repair
- Decreased function of white blood cells
- Increased stickiness of platelets
- Increased blood viscosity
- Produces increased amounts of fibrinogen leading to clot formation

---

8.3 Pre-operative smoking cessation—does it work?

The experience of hospitalization and an acute illness are known to make patients more amenable to health-changing behaviours. Patients awaiting surgery may be more motivated to quit if they believe that their need for surgery was partly caused by their smoking, that their chances of receiving surgery and their recovery could be adversely affected if they continue to smoke. Studies have shown increased motivation to quit in the pre-operative period. Some studies have shown that the perceived severity of the surgical procedure increases the likelihood of quitting, for example one study showed 1-yr quit rates of 55% for (the more severe) CABG compared to 25% for coronary angioplasty.

However, in one survey only 58% of surgeons and 30% of anaesthetists said they advised their patients to stop smoking before surgery and several studies have found that less than 10% of smokers having surgery recalled being advised by any medical professional to quit smoking.

Box 8.2 shows the important 'teachable moments' when interacting with smokers who are being assessed for surgery.

Box 8.2 Teachable moments for smoking patients undergoing surgery

- When presenting with initial symptoms, for example joint pain, abdominal discomfort, or breast lump
- When the diagnosis is made. The impact of continued smoking on the illness progression should be described
- When surgery is first considered
- When referred to the surgical specialist, a co-incidental referral could be made to a smoking cessation service
- When accepted (or not) onto a waiting list
- When seen in pre-operative assessment clinic
- When admitted to hospital
- When seen by the anaesthetist and surgical team just prior to surgery
- Post-operative stay
- Discharge from hospital. A co-incidental referral could be made to a smoking cessation service when writing to the referring practitioner
- Follow-up surgical clinics

Ideally, patients need to quit at least 8 weeks before surgery to gain maximal benefits. Indeed, small observational studies suggest that those quitting <8 weeks before surgery actually have a *increased* risk of post-operative pulmonary complications but those quitting before 8 weeks had the same risk as non- or ex-smokers. This may be because patients are still experiencing adverse physiological changes associated with withdrawal or that bronchial mucous goblet cell function recover to increase sputum production early but after 8 weeks, the mucous debris may have been cleared so sputum production reduces.

8.3.1 Effects of smoking cessation on quit rates in surgical patients

A Cochrane review found that for hospitalized patients (regardless of admitting diagnosis), programmes to stop smoking that begin during a hospital stay and include follow-up support for at least 1 month after discharge are effective. Is this also effective for surgical patients?

Many studies report considerable success of pre-operative smoking cessation programmes on smoking behaviour, particularly short-term quit rates. Unfortunately, these studies are heterogeneous, applying a wide variety of interventions over varying periods.

A Cochrane review of smoking cessation in surgical patients was limited to four randomized controlled trials involving 627 patients. Two of these studies used biochemical validation of abstinence and few offered any long-term support. All the studies showed the intervention achieved a significant increase in the odds of smoking cessation in the peri-operative period. Only two studies reported longer-term quit rates reporting the success was not maintained at 3 or 12 months.

A recent trial using a multi-component intervention demonstrated a biochemically confirmed quit rate of 15% of the intervention group at 1 yr—compared with 8% of the comparison group. What is not clear is which actual component provided the best outcome and how applicable it would be in the real world.

8.3.2 Effects of smoking cessation on clinical outcomes in surgical patients

While there is some published evidence of the clinical benefits of pre-operative smoking cessation, these are all observational studies and there are very few randomized controlled, intervention trials looking at clinical outcomes or particularly mortality.

In terms of respiratory effects, we know that smoking cessation can result in very early improvement in lung function (e.g. maximal expiratory flow rates and closing volumes). However, the changes in mucous production and clearance occur less quickly and most smokers report increased sputum production in the first few weeks after stopping.

For cardiovascular effects, the evidence suggests that CO levels reduce significantly within 12 hrs and are undetectable after 24 hrs. Nicotine levels are reduced after 2 hrs and so there is good reason to expect early benefits from short-term smoking cessation such as improved oxygen delivery to the patient's tissues.

In one of the few randomized studies examining smoking cessation intervention and clinical outcomes before joint replacement surgery, wound infection rates were reduced from 27% in continuing smokers to 0% in those who quit smoking. To put the smoking-related risk in context in orthopaedic surgery, the adverse effect of failing to quit smoking is similar to that of omitting antibiotic prophylaxis.

One study modelled the potential benefit of a hospital-based smoking cessation service across London. Based on published expected quit rates over 30,000 pre-operative patients could be helped to quit per year, saving over 5,000 post-operative complications and 3,600 bed days a year across the city. This would need to be tested.

8.4 **Conclusions**

Smokers undergoing surgery must be advised of the risks of continuing to do so and the potential benefits of quitting. It would help surgical teams to have some basic facts about the relationship of smoking (cessation) to their speciality and so be able to tailor their advice (specific advice is more effective than generic advice). Surgical teams comprising the pre-operative nurses, junior doctors, surgeons, and anaesthetists could all help and should know how to access a specialist smoking cessation service. Patients must be supported to do this and any intervention programme should aim to get smokers to quit at least 8 weeks before their surgery.

Key reading

Bannister G. Prevention of infection in joint replacement. *Curr Orthopaedics* 2002; **16**: 436–3.

Møller A, Villebro N. Interventions for preoperative smoking cessation. *Cochrane Database Syst Rev* 2005; (3). Art. No. CD002294. DOI: 10.1002/14651858. CD002294. Pub2.

Moller AM, Villebro N, Pederson T, Tonnesen H. Effect of preoperative smoking intervention on postoperative complications: a randomised clinical trial. *Lancet* 2002; **359**: 114–7.

Preoperative Smoking Cessation: A Model To Estimate Potential Short Term Health Gain and Reductions in Length of Stay. A Report by London Health Observatory; September 2005. http://www.lho.org.uk/ Download/Public/9776/1/Preop%20smoking%20cessation.doc (accessed 4 September 2008).

Rigotti NA, Munafo MR, Stead LF. Interventions for smoking cessation in hospitalised patients. *Cochrane Database Syst Rev* 2007; (3). Art. No. CD001837. DOI: 10.1002/14651858. CD001837. Pub2.

Shannon-Cain J, Webster S, Cain B. Prevalence of and reasons for preoperative tobacco use. *AANA J* 2002; **70**: 33–40.

Sorensen LT, Karlsmark T, Gottrup F. Abstinence from smoking reduces incisional wound infection: a randomised controlled trial. *Ann Surg* 2003; **238**: 1–5.

Van Domburg RT, Meeter K, van Berkel DF, Veldkamp RF, Van Herwerden LA, Bogers AJ. Smoking cessation reduces mortality after coronary artery bypass surgery: a 20 year follow up study. *J Am Coll Cardiol* 2001; **37**: 2009–10.

Chapter 9

Smoking cessation and pregnancy

Cath Einon and Keir E. Lewis

Key points

- Smoking while pregnant is harmful to both the mother and the foetus.
- The harm for the child extends past birth and is probably life-long.
- Less than half of pregnant smokers seek specialist support.
- 40% of female smokers smoke for part of their pregnancy, 20% will continue throughout.
- Stop-smoking services need to be more engaging to pregnant smokers but specialist services, outside of routine antenatal care, are successful.
- Nicotine replacement therapy is licensed for use in pregnancy.

9.1 Introduction

Smoking among pregnant women in the developed world has declined by 60% to 75% over the last 20 yrs. Nevertheless, prenatal smoking remains a common habit with between 10% and 35% of women continuing to smoke throughout their pregnancy. This has a detrimental impact on mother and baby before, during, and after pregnancy.

Before pregnancy, cigarette smoking reduces the chances of conception by reducing fertility in both men and women, reducing zygote implantation, and reducing success of infertility treatments (see Chapter 11).

During pregnancy, smoking accounts for a significant proportion of foetal morbidity and mortality through both a direct (foetal) and an indirect (placental) effect. The most important smoking-induced placental pathology is placental abruption with reported risk estimates ranging from 1.4 to 4.0. Although the evidence is less compelling, smoking mothers are at an increased risk also for placenta praevia and placenta-praevia-accreta combination. There is no association between maternal smoking and idiopathic uterine bleeding. The relationship between maternal smoking and foetal growth is causal, including significant reduction in growth of head circumference, abdominal circumference, and especially femur length. Prenatal smoking is associated with a 20% to 30% higher likelihood for stillbirth and has been blamed for directly causing 4000 deaths per annum in the USA through miscarriage, stillbirth, and premature birth.

After pregnancy, babies born to smokers weigh on average 200 g (6.5 oz) less than those born to non-smokers; have a 40% increased risk for infant mortality and a doubling of risk of sudden infant death syndrome.

The harm to the child is likely to be lifelong, suffering an increased risk of developing glue-ear, meningitis, chest infections, asthma, breathlessness, and wheezing during childhood. Physical and mental developments have been found to be slower with increasing numbers of studies reporting higher incidence of conduct disorders, behavioural problems, and poorer development in reading and maths skills up to the age of 16 yrs.

9.2 Mechanisms of harmful effect

The underlying physiological mechanisms for these ill effects are not fully understood. Many of the 4000 or more chemicals in cigarette smoke are toxic to living cells with the carboxy-haemoglobin causing further tissue hypoxia, further impairing foetal growth and differentiation. Nicotine from cigarette smoke exerts its effects indirectly by affecting placental vasculature. After smoking, nicotine is passed from the maternal to the foetal circulation within 15 to 30 min with the foetus receiving higher nicotine levels than the mother. Nicotine itself therefore can also cause direct damage by nicotinic acetylcholine receptor binding in foetal membranes causing dysregulation of the nicotinic, muscarinic, catecholaminergic, and serotonergic neurotransmitter systems that are crucial to lung, immune, and neurological development.

9.3 Difficulties in quitting

There is a need to encourage women of child-bearing age to quit, if not before pregnancy then at least as soon as possible after finding out. This is important because research suggests that smoking between months 4 and 9 of pregnancy does most damage and mothers who stop smoking in the first 3 months have virtually identical outcomes to non-smokers.

Women who continue to smoke during pregnancy often feel criticized by society. They may feel guilt and personal conflict at not quitting and many will report to have stopped but actually continue. Where cotinine levels were routinely taken, 80% of pregnant women who previously smoked had urine and blood levels confirming at least passive smoking—suggesting that self-reports of abstinence are even more inaccurate in pregnancy than in usual stop-smoking clinics.

Pregnancy can be an ideal time to stop smoking but quitting can be difficult for several reasons. Physical changes during pregnancy shorten the half-life of nicotine resulting in an increased desire to smoke. Motivation, which is an essential part of changing health behaviours, is often misplaced and extrinsic pressures (such as being told you should quit smoking for your child) have been found to be less influential than intrinsic factors, where there is an expectation of reward or a personal desire to quit for oneself. Indeed research suggests that expectant mothers who continue to smoke report more scepticism that smoking will harm their baby, than those who quit.

Women most likely to continue smoking throughout their pregnancy are generally of lower age, socio-economic status, level of education, and occupational status. They are likely to come from families where smoking is the norm and 80% of those continuing to smoke have a partner who also smokes.

Emphasizing the dangers of smoking alone, without offering specific support, may alienate many addicted young mothers; the lack of many long-term positive outcomes from anti-smoking campaigns may result from ignorance surrounding these socio-economically disadvantaged women's life circumstances. Many current interventions also ignore the specific psychological stressors and the altered physiological processes that occur during pregnancy. Some authors have claimed that health-care professionals have attempted to manipulate women to stop smoking rather than engage in mutually respectful dialogue.

9.4 What can be done?

Smoking cessation interventions can be effective in pregnant women but because less than half of women receive any sort of intervention during their pregnancy, opportunities are missed. Reluctance by the women to utilize available services has been exacerbated by poor referral rates with many midwives admitting a reluctance to bring up the issue of their patient's smoking.

When the subject of a person's smoking is not brought up by health professionals it can easily give the impression that it is not important, leading to some ambivalence regarding quitting on the part of the smoker. Failure to discuss the topic also results in many women remaining unaware of the services available to help them quit. Some medical professionals encourage cutting down but smoking reduction has not been researched in pregnancy.

More recently, National Health Service (NHS) specialist pregnancy advisors have been put in place in many areas to encourage pregnant smokers to seek help. Behavioural support from a properly trained specialist can address these many barriers to quitting. Intensive counselling can address the guilt and perceived disapproval of others whilst working on developing alternative coping strategies. This treatment can be offered in the client's home or via the telephone outside of other antenatal services, providing greater flexibility and accessibility and reducing the stigma attached to their smoking. Additionally, offering incentives and treating smoking partners/family members improve outcomes.

9.5 Pharmacotherapy in pregnancy for smoking cessation

Many prescribers still prefer the woman to try to quit without the use of pharmacotherapy; 'cold-turkey' appears more possible in women from higher educational backgrounds and social class who are lighter smokers, but the majority of tobacco use in pregnancy is concentrated amongst society's poorest women.

There is a very little evidence to support the use of the pharmacotherapies that are effective in non-pregnant populations. Moreover, we know that nicotine itself has adverse effects on the placenta and foetus, and for safety reasons it is doubtful that definitive trials investigating the effectiveness of either bupropion or varenicline will be conducted in pregnant women in the foreseeable future.

The potential risks of pharmacotherapy need to be weighed, on an individual basis, against the risks of continued smoking with its higher and more rapid nicotine exposure, alongside the other 4000 other toxins in a cigarette.

In the short to medium term, information regarding the use of drugs in pregnancy is likely to come from observational studies that are more difficult to interpret than clinical trials. The principle recommendations from these observational pharmacotherapy studies suggest that nicotine replacement therapy (NRT) is safer than smoking in pregnancy. Pregnant women who have unsuccessfully tried to stop without pharmacotherapy or who feel unable to try without pharmacotherapy should consider using NRT first as this has now been licensed for use in pregnancy. NRT products offering episodic nicotine delivery result in reduced infiltration to the foetus. For this reason, inhalator, microtab, lozenge, or gum are recommended but the NRT patch is still the most popular product as it is easy to use, discreet and many pregnant smokers complain the oral products contribute to nausea. Most specialists recommend the 16-h patches to reduce placental/foetal exposure at night.

A Cochrane review of 64 trials (of varying interventions, involving 28,000 women) suggests smoking cessation can be achieved during pregnancy. There was a significant reduction in the 36 trials that validated cessation with a relative risk 0.94 (95% CI 0.92 to 0.95). This translates into an absolute difference of 6 in 100 women continuing to smoke. Two trials of 'rewards plus social support' seemed particularly effective (relative risk of smoking 0.77, 95% CI 0.72 to 0.82). The reduction in smoking translated into significant improvements in mean birth weight and numbers of pre-term births but the trials were not large enough to show significant improvements in perinatal or neonatal mortality.

9.6 Conclusions

It is encouraging that more women are quitting during pregnancy but unfortunate that those women with the greatest need are still not engaging with the service. There is a need to identify all those pregnant women who smoke and all professionals involved in their care should offer brief support in a non-judgemental way, then be able to refer them to specialist services outside of routine antenatal care.

Finally, relapse rates are very high with 80% of successful quitters returning to smoking after their pregnancy. Good relationships forged with a specialist stop-smoking service should also help avoid this.

Key reading

Dempsey DA, Benowitz NL. Risks and benefits of nicotine to aid smoking cessation in pregnancy. *Drug Saf* 2001; **24**: 277–322.

Elbert LM, Fahy K. Why do women continue to smoke in pregnancy? *Women Birth* 2007; **20**: 161–8.

Kmietowicz Z. Smoking is causing impotence. Miscarriage and infertility. *Br Med J* 2004; **328**: 364.

Koran G. Foetal toxicology of environmental tobacco smoke. *Curr Opin Pediatr* 1995; **17**: 128–31.

Lumley J, Oliver SS, Chamberlain C, Oakley L. Interventions for promoting smoking cessation during pregnancy. *Cochrane Database Syst Rev* 2004; (3).

Owen L, McNeill A, Callum C. Trends in smoking during pregnancy in England, 1992–7: quota sampling surveys. *Br Med J* 1998; **317**: 728–30.

US Department of Health and Human Services. The Health Consequences of Smoking for Women: A Report of the Surgeon General. Rockville, MD: US Department of Health and Human Services, Public Health Service, Office on Smoking and Health; 1980.

Chapter 10

Smoking cessation in young people

Elin Roddy

Key points

- Most adult smokers start smoking in adolescence.
- Smoking uptake is determined by many factors, the main ones being peer and family influence.
- Smoking rates in young people in the UK are declining but there are still many young smokers who want to stop smoking.
- Young people can become addicted to nicotine very soon after starting smoking.
- Behavioural support and nicotine replacement therapy should be offered to young people who want to quit smoking but are finding it difficult.
- Reducing smoking rates in young people requires a broad-based approach.

10.1 Introduction

Most adult smokers start smoking in adolescence. The average age of the first cigarette in young smokers in the UK is 12 yrs old and worldwide, a quarter of teenage smokers smoked their first cigarette before the age of 10 yrs. Individuals who start smoking in adolescence are more likely to become dependent, to smoke more heavily and for more years as adults. Conversely if you do not smoke before the age of 20, you are significantly less likely to start as an adult, so there is a strong case for programmes for young people that address both prevention and treatment.

10.2 Smoking uptake

The uptake of smoking is a complex process and is influenced by many factors (see Box 10.1). The most important influences are family and peer smoking. Young people from deprived backgrounds,

Box 10.1 Factors influencing smoking uptake

- Parental smoking/attitudes to smoking
- Peer smoking/attitudes to smoking
- Sibling smoking
- Parental attachment
- Age
- Ethnicity
- Parental socio-economic status
- Educational achievement
- Self-esteem
- Lifestyle
- Attitudes towards smoking

those with low self-esteem, and those who have poor school performance are also much more likely to become regular smokers. Often multiple factors influence a young person's smoking behaviour.

10.3 Preventing uptake

Traditional solutions to prevent uptake have been knowledge-based, using 'shock tactics' but more complex interventions have been recently used.

10.3.1 Point of sale interventions

It is not clear whether efforts to reduce sales of tobacco to young people work, as young people obtain their cigarettes from a variety of sources. In October 2007, the minimum age for purchasing cigarettes in the UK was raised from 16 to 18 yrs. Other legislation prevents cigarettes to be on sale within 200 m of a school with increasing fines for vendors to under-aged smokers.

10.3.2 Mass media campaigns

Mass media interventions do appear to reduce smoking uptake in young people, particularly if they are of long duration and high intensity.

10.3.3 Social influence programmes

These have been shown to have a positive effect on smoking rates in young people; peer support seems particularly effective; here young people (e.g. popular classmates) are trained to support other young people in school or community settings. A recent study in 59 schools in England and Wales showed that students in the group of schools with a peer-support intervention were 25% less likely to take up regular smoking immediately after the programme than those in the control group and were still 23% less likely to start after 1 yr and 15% less likely after 2 yrs.

10.3.4 Reducing adult smoking

Interventions to reduce adult smoking not only reduce uptake in young people but also reduce children's exposure to environmental tobacco smoke. This is currently responsible for 17,000 admissions to hospital per year in children under 5 yrs old. Environmental tobacco smoke also causes respiratory tract infections, asthma, and middle ear infections and predisposes children to developing cancer and airways disease in later life, even if they have never smoked.

10.4 Smoking rates in young people in the UK

The most recent survey of UK school children found that smoking was at its lowest level since the survey began in 1982, with 6% of pupils aged 11 to 15 yrs admitting to smoking regularly in 2007. This percentage still equates to around 200,000 young smokers (Table 10.1).

As in previous years, girls were more likely than boys to be regular smokers.

Table 10.1 Smoking behaviour, by sex 1996–1998			
All pupils, England			
Smoking behaviour	1996	1997	1998
Boys	%	%	%
Regular smoker	9	9	8
Occasional smoker	6	5	5
Used to smoke	11	10	12
Smoked once	23	21	23
Never smoked	51	55	51
Base (=100%)	**1899**	**1908**	**1757**
Girls			
Regular smoker	11	12	11
Occasional smoker	7	7	6
Used to smoke	13	10	10
Smoked once	19	20	19
Never smoked	50	51	54
Base (=100%)	**1758**	**1891**	**1782**
Total			
Regular smoker	10	11	10
Occasional smoker	6	6	6
Used to smoke	12	10	11
Smoked once	21	20	21
Never smoked	51	53	52
Base (=100%)	**3657**	**3799**	**3539**

From Higgins V. *Young teenagers and smoking in 1998.* 1999, London: Office of National Statistics.

Older pupils were more likely to be regular smokers than younger pupils. Around 15% of 15 year-olds smoke, compared to only 1% of 11 year-olds. Those young people, who smoke regularly, smoke on average six cigarettes per day (Figure 10.2).

10.5 Smoking cessation in young people

'Regular' vs 'occasional' or 'potential' smokers can be difficult to define so most public health interventions aimed at a population level, attempt to combine *prevention* and *cessation*. However, clinicians working with young people need to know how can they help individual young people who are already smoking and who want to stop.

10.5.1 Nicotine addiction in young people

Many young smokers do, in fact, want to quit smoking. Over two-thirds have tried, but many find it more difficult than they thought it would be. Studies show that young people can become addicted to nicotine easily and quickly, often within weeks of starting smoking even occasionally. Girls show signs of addiction sooner than boys. Independent risk factors for high levels of nicotine addiction in young people include:

- Exposure to nicotine when in the womb
- Coming from a poorer background
- Family problems
- Feeling depressed
- Being physically or sexually abused
- Having parents who smoke
- Poor relationship with parents
- No participation in organized activities outside school or work.

It is important to remember that many young smokers do not realize or understand that the reason they continue smoking is due to their

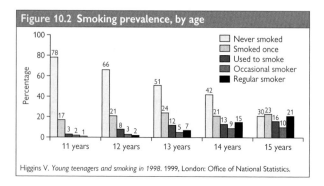

Figure 10.2 Smoking prevalence, by age

Higgins V. *Young teenagers and smoking in 1998.* 1999, London: Office of National Statistics.

addiction to nicotine. Discussing this with them and offering an explanation of nicotine addiction can make their own smoking and quitting behaviour much easier to understand.

10.5.2 Delivering smoking cessation services to young people

It is not clear where the best place to deliver smoking cessation services to young people should be. Studies have based interventions within schools, within the community, and within health-care settings. Many young smokers access the NHS stop-smoking services. These have been developing specific services for young smokers and many now have a Young Peoples Adviser or co-ordinator, often with experience in youth work. Of the 462,690 people setting a quit date with NHS stop-smoking services in the last quarter of 2007, 14,653 (3%) were under 18, but re-attendance was lowest in this age group where quitting intentions can be fluid. Flexibility is crucial in delivering services to young people as many, particularly those from socio-economically deprived backgrounds, will not engage with conventional health services. Interventions may to be opportunistic so health-care professionals need to feel able to raise the subject of smoking at any time.

10.5.3 Behavioural support

A recent Cochrane review identified 15 good quality studies (3605 participants) that researched ways of helping teenagers to quit smoking. Those studies using behavioural interventions, sensitive to the 'Stages of Change' model (See Chapter 3), showed promise, achieving moderate long-term success, with a pooled odds ratio of (biochemically validated) quitting at 1 yr of 1.70 (95% CI, 1.25 to 2.33). Motivational interviewing techniques had no significant benefit.

10.5.4 Nicotine replacement therapy (NRT)

NRT is the only drug treatment for nicotine addiction licensed in the UK for young people aged 12 to 18 yrs, but the very few studies of NRT in young smokers use different definitions of quitting and many are too small to generalize the results. None of the studies showed a definite benefit of NRT over placebo when used as an adjunct to behavioural support. However, none of the studies reported additional problems with toxicity so NRT seems safe in young people, even if its effectiveness has yet to be proven.

National Institute for Health and Clinical Excellence (NICE) states that health professionals should 'use professional judgement to decide whether or not to offer NRT to young people over 12 years, who show clear evidence of nicotine dependence. If NRT is prescribed, offer it as part of a supervised regime.'

There are no data to support any particular NRT preparation. Young people who are at school, where oral products such as gum or inhalators may not be allowed, may prefer patches. Similarly, there are no data available to guide dosing, but unless early morning cravings are a problem it would seem sensible to use the 16-h preparations and to start with a dose of 15 mg/16 hrs transdermal patch. Short acting products such as nicotine gum or inhalators may be suitable in some young people who have not yet established a regular smoking pattern. Short acting preparations can also be useful for young people who forget to remove/replace a daily patch.

10.5.5 **Other pharmacotherapies**

A single study showed no benefit of adding bupropion to NRT in young smokers and there are no studies using varenicline in this group. Neither drug is licensed for use in people under the age of 18 yrs.

10.5.6 **Practical tips for smoking cessation in young people**

The 5 A's framework used for adult smokers (Chapter 3) can be adapted for young smokers (see Table 10.2).

10.6 **Conclusions**

Reducing overall smoking rates in young people requires a broad-based approach involving the smoker, parents, peers, schools, communities, and health-care professionals.

Health-care professionals should raise awareness of the importance of preventing smoking uptake, and of smoking cessation as often as they can to young smokers. They should use their influence to reduce parental smoking and advocate for tobacco control at all levels.

Table 10.2 **The 5 A's framework adapted for young smokers**	
The 5 A's	Example
ASK all young people about smoking	'Do you smoke cigarettes or other drugs such as cannabis?'
ADVISE young people to stop	'Stopping smoking is the best thing you could do for your health and fitness right now. There's no time like the present'.
ASSESS willingness to quit	'Have you ever thought about stopping smoking? Have you ever tried to stop? How do you feel about smoking?'
ASSIST with a quit attempt	'You may find you need some help to stop. I can refer you to someone to talk things through and prescribe some medication to help deal with any cravings you have'.
ARRANGE	'I'm really keen to help you to succeed with this, and I'd like to see you again in a few weeks to see how you're getting on'.

Key reading

Campbell R, Starkey F, Holliday J *et al.* An informal school-based peer-led intervention for smoking prevention in adolescence (ASSIST): a cluster randomised trial. *Lancet* 2008; **371**: 1595–602.

DiFranza JR, Savageau JA, Rigotti NA *et al.* Development of symptoms of tobacco dependence in youths: 30 month follow up date from the DANDY study. *Tobacco Control* 2002; **11**: 223–35.

Drug Use, Smoking and Drinking among Young People in England in 2007. London: The Health and Social Care Information Centre; July 2008. www.ic.nhs.uk

External Evaluation of the NHS/ASH Scotland Young People and Smoking Cessation Pilot Programme, NHS Scotland, Edinburgh; 2006. http://www.healthscotland.com/uploads/documents/2632-RE034Final.pdf

Going smoke-free. The Medical Case for Clean Air in the Home, at Work and in Public Places. A Report on Passive Smoking by the Tobacco Advisory Group of the Royal College of Physicians. London: RCP; 2005.

Grimshaw GM, Stanton A. Tobacco cessation interventions for young people. *Cochrane Database Syst Rev* 2006; (4).

National Institute for Health and Clinical Excellence (NICE). Smoking Cessation Services in Primary Care, Pharmacies, Local Authorities and Workplaces, Particularly for Manual Working Groups, Pregnant Women and Hard to Reach Communities. London (UK): National Institute for Health and Clinical Excellence (NICE); February 2008.

NICE Draft Guidance on Preventing the Uptake of Smoking in Children and Young People. http://www.nice.org.uk/nicemedia/pdf/PreventingSmokingChildrenReviewEffectivenessRevisedFullReportFeb08.pdf

Chapter 11

Smoking cessation in girls/women

Yasir I. Syed

> **Key points**
> - The prevalence of smoking in women is increasing, particularly in developing countries.
> - There are gender-specific consequences of smoking to women.
> - Smoking cessation strategies in women should account for targeted marketing and advertising by tobacco companies and potential problems with body image due to weight gain.

11.1 Introduction

Social norms at the turn of the century limited tobacco use almost exclusively to males, with the exception of some limited snuff 'sniffing' by women. Smoking rates in women have been increasing steadily and the World Health Organization estimates that 12% of women are estimated to smoke globally, compared to 48% of males. Around 106,000 women in Europe and 500,000 women worldwide die prematurely each year as a result of smoking, with the death toll likely to double by 2020.

In the UK ~21% of women smoke (compared with 23% men), but there is an alarming reversal of this trend in teenage smoking in Great Britain with 16% of boys and 24% of girls above 15 yrs admitting to smoking regularly.

11.2 Effects of smoking on women

As in men, smoking is a major risk factor for ill health but there are additional gender-specific effects in women.

11.2.1 Cancers

Smoking is the major cause for lung cancer, which accounts for 11% of all new female cancers diagnosed each year (after breast and bowel cancer). Moreover, lung cancer is the most rapidly increasing cancer diagnosis in women and has overtaken breast cancer as the main cause of cancer deaths in women in developed countries (Figure 11.1).

Smoking is strongly associated with cancers of oropharynx, bladder, liver, and colon. Heavy smokers have an 80% increased risk of developing cancers of the cervix and vulva, and 19% of cervical cancer and 40% of vulval cancer are estimated to be due to smoking. The mechanisms are still being elucidated but are possibly due to antibody response and reduced clearance of human papilloma virus infection, at least in younger women.

11.2.2 Respiratory disease

Cigarette smoking is the major cause for chronic obstructive pulmonary disease (COPD) in women. In the UK, the rate of COPD diagnosis has been increasing nearly three times faster amongst women than men, reflecting the changing demographics of smoking prevalence. For the first time, in 2005, more women than men died with COPD and COPD also now causes more deaths in women than breast cancer.

Smoking by girls may reduce their rate of lung growth and also induce a premature decline of lung function. Exposure to maternal smoking is associated with reduced lung function in infants, while

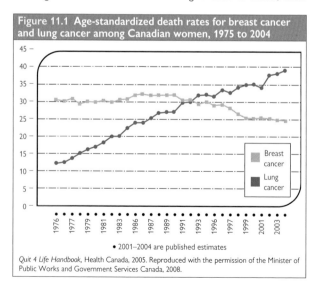

Figure 11.1 Age-standardized death rates for breast cancer and lung cancer among Canadian women, 1975 to 2004

Breast cancer
Lung cancer

• 2001–2004 are published estimates

Quit 4 Life Handbook, Health Canada, 2005. Reproduced with the permission of the Minister of Public Works and Government Services Canada, 2008.

exposure to environmental tobacco smoke during childhood and adolescence may particularly impair lung function in girls. It is possible that the lungs of females are particularly susceptible to smoking-related damage.

11.2.3 Cardiovascular disease

Smoking is a major cause of cardiovascular disease but the risk of heart attack, ischaemic stroke, and peripheral vascular disease is increased in women by approximately ×10-fold if they both smoke and use oral contraceptives but there does not seem to be any additional cardiovascular risk posed by the oral contraceptive pill alone.

11.2.4 Menstrual irregularities and infertility

Smoking increases the risk of dysmenorrhoea, secondary amenorrhea, and menstrual irregularities. It induces early menopause (with secondary ill health effects) and increases the severity of severe premenstrual symptoms. Smoking reduces the ovulatory response, actual fertilization, and zygote implantation causing both primary and secondary infertility. In one study, women who smoked had about 72% of the fertility of non-smokers and were 3.4 times more likely to take more than a year to conceive as non-smokers. Smoking also decreases successful outcomes of *in vitro* fertilization with a pregnancy rate less than half that of non-smokers and those that attained a pregnancy had a markedly elevated risk of miscarriage.

11.2.5 Bone problems

Smoking reduces bone density by reducing the effect of oestrogen. After controlling for other risk factors (including genetics), women who smoke 20 cigarettes a day have reduced their bone marrow density by 5% to 10% by the time they reach menopause, compared to non-smokers and this reduction translates into a real increased risk of hip fractures.

11.2.6 Pregnancy

Smoking is probably one of major modifiable causes of poor pregnancy outcomes. These complications of premature birth, placenta previa, and placental abruption have severe health consequences for the mother.

11.3 Factors influencing tobacco use among women and girls

Multiple factors are responsible for the initiation of smoking in women and teenage girls.

11.3.1 Social and psychological factors

Girls who start smoking are more likely to have smoking parents or friends and tend to have weaker commitments to family, school, and religion with stronger attachments to peers and friends. Girls and women list the desire for weight control and control of negative mood more than men and boys, for reasons to continue smoking.

Like men, women who continue to smoke and fail at attempts to stop smoking tend to have lower education and employment levels than those who manage to quit.

Philip Morris knew this in 1978, when they targeted smoking advertising in romance and fan magazines stating it: *Skews toward younger unemployed, lower income woman.*

Even the trade journal *Tobacco Reporter* in 1982 described women as . . . *a prime target* . . . calling for . . . *a more defined attack on the important market segment represented by female smokers.*

11.3.2 **Body image**

Smoking is associated with a lower body weight on average, and cessation is associated with weight gain. Women are more likely than men to express concern about weight gain and indeed this is cited by many as the reason for relapse. On average, female quitters can gain 5.2 kg while male quitters can gain 4.9 kg in first year after stopping smoking, but ranges are wide.

11.3.3 **Media and marketing influences**

Cigarette smoking by large numbers of women did not become socially acceptable until cigarette advertising began to target women in the late 1920s and early 1930s. As advertising increasingly targeted women during the 1930s and 1940s, cigarette use increased rapidly and compared with men from the same era, initiation occurred largely during adolescence. Through comprehensive social research, the tobacco industry has created and maintained its market in women. Brands like the 'Virginia-Slim' were particularly popular with women and tobacco manufacturers have taken advantage of cultural ideals even running ran overt publicity campaigns emphasizing the role of weight control by smoking (Figure 11.2).

11.4 **Smoking cessation strategies in women and girls**

Biophysical factors such as pregnancy, depression, and fear of weight gain may influence smoking maintenance, cessation and relapse among women. Pregnancy offers a golden opportunity to promote smoking cessation but little research concentrating on pregnant smokers has been published.

Current data do not suggest any consistent gender-specific differences are needed in smoking cessation interventions but more research is needed into the types and dosing of pharmacological therapies

as well as behavioural interventions, specifically designed to address barriers to quitting in women, such as weight gain.

Comprehensive and systematic efforts are required to increase awareness of the health consequences of smoking among women and to counter the tobacco industry's targeting of women. Governmental efforts along with societal pressures are required to prevent uptake of smoking in teenage girls and particularly women in developing countries.

Key reading

Baird D, Wilcox A. Cigarette smoking associated with delayed conception. *JAMA* 1985; **253**: 2979–83.

Baron JA, Byers T, Greenberg ER, Cummings KM, Swanson M. Cigarette smoking in women with cancers of the breast and reproductive organs. *J Natl Cancer Inst* 1986; **77**: 677–80.

Copeland AL, Martin PD, Geiselman PJ, Rash CJ, Kendzor DE. Smoking cessation for weight-concerned women: group vs. individually tailored, dietary, and weight-control follow-up sessions. *Addict Behav* 2006; **31**(1): 115–27.

Downs SH, Brändli O, Zellweger JP, Schindler C, Künzli N, Gerbase MW. Accelerated decline in lung function in smoking women with airway obstruction: SAPALDIA 2 cohort study. *Respiratory Res* 2005; **6**: 45.

Hopper JL, Seeman E. The bone density of female twins discordant for tobacco use. *N Engl J Med* 1994; **330**: 387–92.

Oncken C, Prestwood K, Cooney JL, Unson C, Fall P, Kulldorff M, Raisz LG. Effects of smoking cessation or reduction on hormone profiles and bone turnover in postmenopausal women. *Nicotine Tob Res* 2002; **4**: 451–8.

Pattinson HA, Taylor PJ, Pattinson MH. The effect of cigarette smoking on ovarian function and early pregnancy outcome of in vitro fertilization treatment. *Fertil Steril* 1991; **55**: 780–3.

US Department of Health and Human Services. Surgeon General's Report 2001—Women and Smoking. http://www.cdc.gov/tobacco/data_statistics/sgr/sgr_2001/index

Wetter DW, Kenford SL, Smith SS, Fiore MC, Jorenby DE, Baker TB. Gender differences in smoking cessation. *J Consulting Clin Psychol* 1999; **67**: 555–62.

Wong PK, Christie JJ, Wark JD. The effects of smoking on bone health. *Clin Sci (Lond)* 2007; **113**: 233–41.

World Health Organization. Tobacco Free Initiative. http://www.who.int/tobacco/en/

Chapter 12

Smoking cessation and cancer

Robin Ghosal

Key points

- Smoking is the single biggest cause of cancer worldwide.
- Smoking causes cancer in many parts of the human body.
- Continued smoking after cancer diagnosis worsens survival time, quality of life and leads to more treatment complications compared to stopping smoking.
- Stopping smoking can improve survival for many established cancers to the same degree as many chemotherapy regimes.
- Smoking cessation should be offered to patients with cancer.

12.1 Introduction

Despite early debate fuelled by the tobacco industry, years of research confirm that smoking is the single biggest cause of cancer worldwide. Smoking accounts for 25% of UK cancer deaths being a causal or contributory agent in cancers of the lung, oropharynx, oesophagus, liver, pancreas, kidney, stomach, bladder, cervix, and myeloid leukaemia.

12.2 Why does smoking cause cancer?

Each cigarette contains 60 known carcinogens (tumour initiators or tumour promoters). Particularly 'strong' carcinogens are the tobacco-specific nitrosamines, such as 4-(methylnitrosamino)-1-(3-pyridyl)-1-butanone (NNK) and N'-nitrosonornicotine (NNN). These have induced lung tumours when applied directly to the skin of mice, or when injected into the bladders or swabbed in the oral cavities of rats. Other strong carcinogens include polycyclic aromatic hydrocarbons, such as benzo[a]pyrene and aromatic amines. 'Weak' carcinogens like acetaldehyde are even more abundant.

These different agents act on different biological pathways. For example benzo[a]pyrene directly damages the tumour suppressor gene, p53. Nicotine itself inhibits cell death (apoptosis) through multiple intracellular pathways such as activation of the protein kinase signalling system seen in lung cancer cells.

12.3 Smoking and lung cancer

There are 1.3 million new cases of lung cancer diagnosed worldwide each year and 33,000 new cases in England and Wales in 2006 alone. Eighty per cent of lung cancer is attributable to smoking and so avoidable but it remains by far, the leading cause of cancer deaths in the UK. European 5-yr survival rates are still only 11%.

12.3.1 Smoking and survival in lung cancer

Despite this dismal overall prognosis, increasing evidence suggests that smoking cessation after lung cancer diagnosis has a real beneficial effect. An observational study followed 112 patients with small cell lung cancer who received chemoradiotherapy. Those ($n = 20$) who had already stopped smoking had the best survival followed by those who stopped at the time of diagnosis ($n = 35$). The 57 who continued smoking had significantly worse survival rates with 0% surviving more than 2 yrs compared with 9% to 15% in the other groups surviving, disease-free, for at least 2 to 4 yrs. For those fit enough and with limited disease, current smoking was an independent predictor of reduced survival after surgery for non-small cell lung cancer ($p = 0.001$) suggesting it is beneficial to stop smoking prior to surgery (see Figure 12.1).

Another retrospective study of 237 patients who did not have surgery found a clear survival advantage in less advanced disease (stage I/II) with non-smokers living a median of 27.9 months compared to smokers (otherwise matched at baseline) living a median of 13.7 months ($p = 0.01$). There was no statistical differences in survival with more advanced (stage III) disease.

12.3.2 Smoking and treatment complications in lung cancer

Clinically detectable radiation pneumonitis following curative radiotherapy is significantly increased in those with a significant smoking history. In another study those who continue to smoke needed more treatment breaks in chemoradiotherapy and had poorer survival outcomes (5-yr survival 4% vs 8.9% for former smokers).

12.3.3 Smoking and quality of life in lung cancer

A large study of 1028 patients applied a lung cancer symptom scale in lung cancer survivors. Appetite, fatigue, cough, shortness of breath,

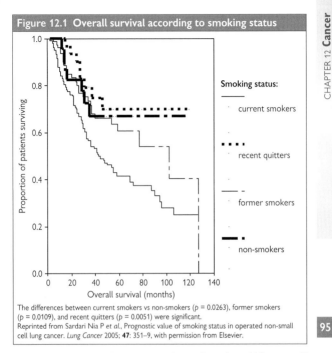

Figure 12.1 Overall survival according to smoking status

The differences between current smokers vs non-smokers ($p = 0.0263$), former smokers ($p = 0.0109$), and recent quitters ($p = 0.0051$) were significant.
Reprinted from Sardari Nia P et al., Prognostic value of smoking status in operated non-small cell lung cancer. Lung Cancer 2005; **47**: 351–9, with permission from Elsevier.

illness affecting normal activities, and overall quality of life were all statistically and clinically worse in the 24% who were current smokers, after adjusting for age, gender, stage, and time of assessment.

12.4 Smoking and other cancers

The effects of continued smoking on other cancers have been less well studied.

Smokers with localized prostate cancer had higher levels of prostate-specific antigen and Gleason grading compared to former or non-smokers ($p = 0.017$). Outcomes and overall mortality following curative external beam radiation therapy were poorer in this 15% who continued to smoke, although there was no difference in prostate cancer-specific mortality.

In those with breast cancer, the frequency of second primary cancers (especially lung cancer) is greater in those who continue to smoke and breast radiation therapy appears to increase these risks further. There was also a significantly higher risk of mastectomy skin flap necrosis, abdominal flap necrosis, and hernia from the donor site in current smokers compared to former or non-smokers.

A case–control study found a sixfold increased risk of lung cancer in patients treated with radiotherapy for Hodgkin's lymphoma if they had a >10 pack year smoking history compared to non-smokers.

12.5 How does continued smoking exert its effects on cancer patients?

Firstly, potential hypotheses are that tobacco carcinogens are 'fuelling' the cancer, hence causing more rapid progression and death.

Secondly, various tobacco chemicals can directly interfere with chemoradiotherapy actions at a cellular level or indirectly via inducing hypoxia and further angiogenesis. There is also potential for nicotine to induce hepatic enzymes, leading to increased clearance of chemo-therapeutic agents. Many trials of new agents can be criticized for not even reporting smoking status.

Finally, continued smoking leads to worse drug toxicity and side effects, via direct damage to lung tissue itself or further impairment of immune function so increasing the incidence of infection (especially if already neutropenic).

12.6 Barriers to smoking cessation

12.6.1 High nicotine dependence

Patients diagnosed with tobacco-related cancers usually have a long history of heavy tobacco use. The fact that even when told they have cancer, a proportion will continue to smoke, shows the addictive nature of nicotine. The stress of being told they may have a terminal illness can even lead former smokers to restart.

The majority of patients will have symptoms at presentation. These symptoms are likely to progress and thus the patients will be reluctant to stop in fear of additional symptoms of withdrawal, such as anxiety, insomnia, restlessness, cravings, and even depression. It is important in these instances to provide pharmacotherapy to address nicotine withdrawal.

12.6.2 Urgency of cessation

Smoking cessation programmes usually have the luxury of time and planning to help patients stop smoking. However, once diagnosed with cancer, many of the patients will embark on treatment almost immediately but do not know that in order to gain the most benefit from these treatments, smoking should be stopped pre-treatment. Sudden change in habitual behaviour can be difficult to sustain. Even arranging extra visits to yet another health professional at such a chaotic time is a barrier to many.

12.6.3 'The damage is done' belief

Once diagnosed with cancer, patients may believe that it is too late to stop smoking. This is generally due to theirs and the doctor's lack of knowledge of the evidence behind quitting.

12.7 How good is the evidence?

Most studies are observational, pointing to associations and usually relying on self-reported smoking status. They are not randomized controlled trials and stopping smoking may be a marker for other health-related behaviours. Randomized trials offering 'no smoking cessation treatment' pose ethical dilemmas, given the proven benefits of cessation to other health. However, prospective observational trials, validating smoking status biochemically, need to be performed.

12.8 Smoking cessation and cancer—the health-care professionals' role

It is an emotional time for patients, families, and health-care professionals when diagnosing and treating cancer. However, it also provides specific opportunities to advise about the continued risks of smoking. Patients will react in two ways:

1. The shock of the diagnosis and the fear of the unknown will lead to stress; smoking is seen as their stress-reliever so they will continue to smoke.
2. The shock of being told they have got cancer and that smoking is more than likely a causative factor will motivate them to stop.

It is the oncologists and health-care professionals' duty to inform those with cancer on the benefits of stopping smoking with respect to their disease, to provide advice to those with cancer who are willing to stop, and then be to refer to a specialist smoking cessation clinic. Box 12.1 provides 'Teachable moments' for cancer patients.

Summary

Health-care professionals try to prevent disease wherever possible including the cancer burden to society. Less known are the benefits of cessation in cancer patients. Traditionally, cancer health-care professionals may not have been active in helping patients with cancer to quit smoking—perhaps believing that the benefits in quality and length of life are not worthwhile. There is considerable and growing evidence against this approach.

> ## Box 12.1 Teachable moments for smoking cessation in cancer patients
>
> 1. When patients are first referred in with symptoms such as cough, haemoptysis, and breathlessness. The symptoms can be directly related to the continued smoking
> 2. When reviewing imaging such as X-rays and CT scans that suggests cancer. Whilst discussing the differential diagnosis, which includes cancer, advising that it is still important to stop
> 3. When reviewing the results of investigations and treatment response. For those without cancer or those cured of cancer, then re-iterating that continued smoking may lead cancer in the future
> 4. On meeting with family members. It could provide a good opportunity for them to stop collectively
> 5. When deciding treatment options with the Oncologist; the potential detrimental effect smoking may have on treatment success and/or toxicity should be discussed prior to starting treatment and be repeated at each treatment session

Key reading

Dresler CM, Gritz ER. Smoking, smoking cessation and the oncologist. *Lung Cancer* 2001; **34**(3): 315–23.

Garces YI, Yang P, Parkinson J et al. The relationship between cigarette smoking and quality of life after lung cancer diagnosis. *Chest* 2004; **126**(6): 1733–41.

Hecht SS. Tobacco carcinogens, their biomarkers and tobacco-induced cancer. *Nat Rev Cancer* 2003; **3**(10): 733–44.

Johnston-Early A, Cohen MH, Minna JD et al. Smoking abstinence and small cell lung cancer survival. An association. *JAMA* 1980; **244**(19): 2175–9.

Key Findings about the Quality of Care for People with Lung Cancer in England and Wales—Report for the Audit Period 2006, in National Lung Cancer Audit 2006; 26.

Pickles T, Liu M, Berthelet E, Kim-Sing C, Kwan W, Tyldesley S. The effect of smoking on outcome following external radiation for localized prostate cancer. *J Urol* 2004; **171**(4): 1543–6.

Prochazka M, Granath F, Ekbom A, Shields PG, Hall P. Lung cancer risks in women with previous breast cancer. *Eur J Cancer* 2002; **38**(11): 1520–5.

Sardari Nia P, Weyler J, Colpaert C, Vermeulen P, Van Marck E, Van Schil P. Prognostic value of smoking status in operated non-small cell lung cancer. *Lung Cancer* 2005; **47**(3): 351–9.

Verdecchia A, Francisci S, Brenner H et al. Recent cancer survival in Europe: a 2000–02 period analysis of EUROCARE-4 data. *Lancet Oncol* 2007; **8**(9): 784–96.

Videtic GM, Stitt LW, Dar AR et al. Continued cigarette smoking by patients receiving concurrent chemoradiotherapy for limited-stage small-cell lung cancer is associated with decreased survival. *J Clin Oncol* 2003; **21**(8): 1544–9.

Chapter 13

Smoking cessation and mental illness

Cath Einon

> ## Key points
> - People with mental health problems are more likely to smoke than the general population.
> - Smokers with mental illness are twice as likely to suffer cardiovascular and respiratory disease as non-smokers.
> - More than half of smokers with mental illness want to quit smoking.
> - Smokers with mental illness may have particular barriers to stopping smoking.
> - Smoking cessation support is not routinely offered to people with mental illness.

13.1 Introduction

Despite smoking prevalence falling in the general population in most Western countries, in recent years it has not reduced in individuals with mental illness who subsequently comprise a larger proportion of the remaining smokers. Smokers with mental illness have been found to have higher levels of nicotine dependence and are less likely to successfully quit. The severe threat to health that smoking poses could account for the difference in life expectancy between the general population and people with mental health problems. It is certainly true that these vulnerable people are more likely to die from (avoidable) smoking-related diseases, than those without mental illness.

13.1.1 What do we mean by mental illness?

Nicotine addiction is now classified as a form of psychiatric disorder in its own right, making it probably the most common, most harmful, and yet most treatable mental illness.

Substance abuse (most commonly smoking) is associated with major psychiatric illnesses. Not only do more people with mental illness smoke (up to 74% of those with schizophrenia) but they also tend to smoke more heavily. Smoking is also far more prevalent in those with post-traumatic stress disorder, anxiety disorder, phobia, obsessive disorder, neurotic disorder, panic disorder, and in those with eating and substance abuse disorders than in the general population.

13.1.2 Why do people with mental illness smoke?

There are many factors contributing to the high prevalence of smoking in people with mental illness.

Smoking could have a positive (at least short-term) effect on the clinical symptoms of depression and schizophrenia. Nicotine facilitates dopaminergic transmission in the mesolimbic and nigrostriatal systems and also increases alertness. These effects could be used to relieve some of the negative symptoms of schizophrenia and depression such as low motivation and poor concentration. Many smokers report that their habit helps them deal with other symptoms of their condition particularly anxiety, stress, and boredom.

Nicotine increases the metabolism of many drugs and so may reduce the side effects of anti-psychotic drugs, if these side effects occur at higher plasma levels than therapeutic beneficial effects. This obviously has implications post quitting and dosage of medication may need to be adjusted once the smoker has quit.

Smoking is indirectly associated with mental illness and both could be markers of something else. Smoking is strongly linked to social deprivation, which in turn is linked to mental illness.

Smoking is more prevalent in individuals living in institutions than in people with similar illnesses living at home. Patients may feel that smoking is something they can control in an otherwise uncontrollable environment or perhaps it serves as a distraction to help combat boredom and stress. Patients also described peer pressure to smoke, whilst in hospital, and staff were reluctant to talk about stopping smoking, seeing it as one of the few pleasures that people with severe mental illness have. Worryingly, there have been reports of a culture of smoking amongst staff whose smoking rates are higher than the national average. Many reporting using cigarettes either to calm or connect with their patients.

13.1.3 Why quit?

The negative effects of smoking far outweigh any perceived benefit. People with schizophrenia die on average 10 yrs younger than the general population (even when deaths from suicide are discounted), this disparity has been attributed to smoking.

13.1.4 Difficulty in treating

Many people with mental health issues recognize their smoking is a problem and up to 50% of smokers living in institutions express a desire to quit.

Despite (or probably because of) the high prevalence of smoking in those with mental illness, this dangerous neurobiological addiction has been seen as a 'bad habit' and often overlooked by psychiatric professionals and caregivers.

Even brief opportunistic advice by a medical professional has been shown to prompt a quit attempt in 40% of smokers, but without the correct support, this attempt is likely to fail and can damage confidence.

Specialist support can address some of the main barriers including motivation, developing alternative stress management skills, difficulties with social contact, full comprehension of harm, interpreting and coping with withdrawal symptoms, and especially providing expert advice on the appropriate doses, side effects, and drug interactions of pharmacotherapy.

Access to stop-smoking specialist help for those with mental illness can be a problem. Uptake by patients with mental illness to the NHS stop-smoking service remains low, as are referrals from their professional carers. There is also a physical lack of stop-smoking specialists offering high-level support to those with mental health problems.

The use of appropriate pharmacotherapy doubles a person's chance of quitting but there has been a reluctance to use it due to perceived risk. Bupropion (Zyban®) is rarely used in the UK but is commonly prescribed in those with mental health issues in the USA. Both nicotine replacement therapy (NRT) and varenicline (Champix®) have been used successfully in patients with mental illness with no evidence of worsening mental state nor increased/different side-effect profiles. Those people prone to mental illness prescribed varenicline should be warned as it can cause mood disturbance and vivid dreams (as per usual prescription).

13.1.5 What works?

As in other groups, the best quit rates are achieved with a combination of pharmacotherapy and behavioural counselling. Early work suggests the following could improve outcomes:

- Offering flexible appointments over longer periods than standard 4 weeks post quitting
- Prescribing higher dose NRT (or combinations) for more than 12 weeks
- Integrating treatment into the individual's overall care plan.

Ideally a quit attempt should involve all caregivers and treatment through a specialist clinic would better prepare the quitter for any withdrawal problems and assist with coping strategies. It is important that any symptoms of withdrawal are identified and not mistaken for medication side effects or worsening of their underlying mental illness.

Stress is often sited as a barrier to quitting with many smokers believing that they need to smoke to cope with life's stresses. Chapter 2 describes how it is nicotine withdrawal that causes symptoms of stress and the relaxed feeling following a cigarette is simply the craving being satisfied albeit temporarily.

Smokers and health professionals need to be challenged by the findings of Cohen *et al.* who found that longer-term improvements in stress were seen in quitters—not in those who continued to smoke.

13.2 **The future**

Positive results have been found using varenicline to help people with mental illness quit smoking but more research needs to be done.

There have been a number of media reports suggesting varenicline use is associated with increased suicides but there is currently no evidence that varenicline causes depression or suicidal thoughts. Stopping smoking can exacerbate existing psychiatric conditions whether medication is used or not. Smokers as a group are also more likely to attempt to take their own life but these facts do highlight the need for intensive counselling to be included in any care plan.

The UK ban on public smoking is now extended to institutions and have an impact on smoking behaviour. Whilst there are concerns that this may actually deter smokers from receiving inpatient treatment for mental illness, if enforced properly, this ban should reduce relapse risk for those hospitalized at a vulnerable time and encourage prescriptions of anti-smoking medication.

It is important that more mental-health professionals learn how to advise their clients regarding smoking and have better access to specialist stop-smoking services who are able to dedicate the time and knowledge to such vulnerable patients. More research is needed on preventing smoking relapse as many people get recurrent mental health problems (see Figure 13.1).

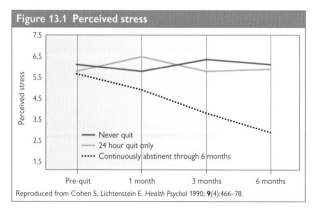

Figure 13.1 Perceived stress

Perceived stress

- Never quit
- 24 hour quit only
- Continuously abstinent through 6 months

Pre-quit   1 month   3 months   6 months

Reproduced from Cohen S, Lichtenstein E. *Health Psychol* 1990; **9**(4):466–78.

Key reading

Adler LE, Hoffer LD, Wiser A, Freedman R. Normalization of auditory physiology by cigarette smoking in schizophrenic patients. *Am J Psychiatry* 1993; **150**:1856–61.

Diwan A, Castine M, Pomerleau CS, Meador-Woodruff JH, Dalack GW. Differential prevalence of cigarette smoking in patients with schizophrenic vs mood disorders. *Schizophrenia Res* 1998; **3**: 113–8.

Gasp Booklet 'Smoking and Mental Health—Helping Smokers to Quit in Mental Health Settings'.

Hughes J. Possible effects of smoke-free inpatients units on psychiatric diagnosis and treatment. *J Clin Psychiatry* 1993; **54**: 109–14.

Jeste DV, Gladsjo JA, Lindamer LA, Lacro JP. Medical co-morbidity in schizophrenia. *Schizophrenia Bull* 1996; **22**: 413–30.

Kessler RC, Berglund PA, Borges G. *et al.*, Smoking and suicidal behaviours in the national comorbidity survey replication. *J. Nerv. Ment. Dis.*, 2007; 195950: 367–77.

Lohr JB, Flynn K. Smoking and schizophrenia. *Schizophrenia Res* 1992; **8**: 93–102.

Quit Guide to Stopping Smoking and Mental Health 'So you want a smoke-free life?'

Raw M, McNeill A, West R. Smoking cessation guidelines for health professionals—a guide to effective smoking cessation. *Thorax* 1998; **53**: 987–99.

Sandyk R. Cigarette smoking: effects on cognitive functions and drug-induced parkinsonism in chronic schizophrenia. *Int J Neurosci* 1993; **70**: 193–7.

Stapleton J, Watson L, Spirling L et al. Varenicline in the routine treatment of tobacco dependence: a pre–post comparison with nicotine replacement therapy and an evaluation in those with mental illness. *Addiction* 2008; **103**: 146–54.

Chapter 14

Smoking cessation and other medical illness

Keir E. Lewis

> **Key points**
>
> - Smoking is associated with a wide variety of dermatological, neurological, gastrointestinal, renal, endocrine, ocular, upper respiratory/middle ear, and musculoskeletal illnesses.
> - There is growing evidence of clinical improvement with stopping smoking in many of these conditions but there are very few randomized interventional trials.

14.1 Introduction

Whilst more commonly associated with cardiovascular and pulmonary diseases and cancers, smoking is associated with illnesses in every system in the body and directly leads to and/or exacerbates a wide variety of medical problems.

14.2 Smoking and skin diseases

It has been long established that smoking has deleterious effects on the skin and its appendages. These include poor wound healing, squamous cell carcinoma, psoriasis, hidradenitis suppurativa, hair loss, oral cancers, and other oral conditions. Smoking has an impact on the skin lesions observed in diabetes, systemic lupus, and the acquired immunodeficiency syndrome (AIDS). The evidence linking smoking and melanoma, eczema, and acne is inconclusive.

Epidemiological studies suggest smoking is an important environmental factor in premature skin aging. For example, in one large study, after accounting for known genetic and other environmental confounders, smoking was one of the main factors involved in facial wrinkling and the larger the tobacco load, the larger the amount of facial wrinkling. *In vitro* studies show tobacco smoke extract impairs collagen production and increases the production of enzymes, which degrade collagen, elastic fibres, and proteoglycans; tobacco smoke extract causes reactive oxygen species also known to cause premature skin aging.

There is no evidence that stopping smoking will reverse the changes of premature ageing.

14.3 **Smoking and neurological diseases**

Smoking is an independent risk factor for ischaemic stroke and so probably vascular dementia (see Chapter 7).

Epidemiological studies suggest that smoking is associated with a lower risk of developing Parkinson's disease (PD). This seems biologically plausible because nicotine causes extra dopamine release (deficient in PD). However, there is no evidence that nicotine replacement therapy (NRT) improves clinical outcome in PD and whilst a review confirmed a negative association of current smoking with PD [risk estimate 0.37 (95% CI 0.33 to 0.41)] there was no dose–response effect. Perhaps the opposite direction of causation is a more probable explanation, that is, PD protects against smoking and that failure to develop strong smoking habits in early adult life might even be a prodromal symptom of PD and could perhaps be its first clinical manifestation?

Nicotine has been related to recovery of memory in humans and animals and some observational studies have suggested a protective effect of nicotine inhalation against Alzheimer's disease. These results are controversial and the balance between nicotine neuroprotection and toxicity depends on dose, developmental stage, and regimen of administration. A Cochrane review, updated in January 2008, found no single appropriate trial to recommend nicotine (or not) as a useful treatment for Alzheimer's disease.

There has been no causal link between smoking and epilepsy but the effects of smoking (and cessation) on the metabolism of drugs used to treat epilepsy should be considered (see Chapter 4).

Epidemiological studies show how exposure to active and even passive smoking is independently associated with increased risk for developing multiple sclerosis (MS) (odds ratio (OR) = 2.9; 1.3 to 6.3), particularly in women. Smoking is also increasingly associated with progression of MS ($p = 0.008$).

After adjustment for known causes in a nationally representative sample of 3081 school children, parental smoking was associated with increased risk of conduct disorder (OR = 3.00; 1.36 to 6.63). Increased postnatal tobacco exposure (estimated by children's serum cotinine levels) was also associated with increased prevalence of conduct disorder symptoms (OR 1.97; 1.15 to 3.40).

14.4 Smoking and gastrointestinal diseases

Smoking increases the risk of peptic ulcer disease and death from it. Smoking delays peptic ulcer healing with or without treatment and increases the risk of ulcer recurrence.

Smoking is an independent risk factor for Barrett's oesophagitis and oesophageal/stomach adenocarcinoma with most population and case control studies showing significant values of 1.7- to 3-fold increased risk compared to never smokers.

Smoking may be a risk factor for gallstones but is a definite causal factor for pancreatic cancer. Smoking does not appear to be a risk factor for cirrhosis of the liver but does complicate treatment in chronic hepatitis.

Numerous epidemiological studies suggest cigarette smoking is an important risk factor for colorectal cancer, with as many as one in five cases attributable to tobacco use. A meta-analysis also associates smoking with both increased adenoma incidence and with more advanced clinico-pathological features. Newer prospective population and in vitro studies point increasingly to a causal role for smoking in colorectal carcinogenesis.

There is growing evidence that cigarette smoking is a risk factor for both developing Crohn's disease and adversely affecting its clinical course—particularly in women. Smoking seems to protect against ulcerative colitis and moreover a Cochrane review confirmed that transdermal nicotine was statistically superior to placebo and equally effective as standard treatments in inducing remission of mild to moderate ulcerative colitis.

After adjustment for confounders, there is a significant increase in risk of appendectomy among current smokers and quitting significantly reduces appendectomy risk.

14.5 Smoking and renal diseases

Smoking is a causal factor for renal cell carcinoma. Increasing evidence suggests it is an independent risk factor for developing chronic kidney disease, especially in males who are heavy smokers but a meta-analysis is not yet possible because of study heterogeneity. Other data indicate that smoking exacerbates renal function deterioration and particularly cardiovascular risk in renal patients with established disease.

14.6 Smoking and endocrine diseases

Smoking has multiple effects on hormone secretion, mediated by nicotine and also by toxins such as thiocyanate. Smoking affects pituitary, thyroid, adrenal, testicular and ovarian function, calcium metabolism, and the action of insulin.

The major clinical consequences include the increased risk and severity of thyroid eye disease (TED), particularly Graves's opthalmoplegia. There is strong evidence for a causal link that included consistent association across studies, a dose–response effect, temporal relationship, and a reduced risk of TED in ex-smokers. Current smokers were also more likely to experience TED progression and poorer outcome following similar treatment to non-smokers.

The effects of smoking on osteoporosis and reduced fertility have been discussed.

The relations among smoking and diabetes are complex. Nicotine increases energy expenditure and reduces appetite acutely, which may explain why smokers tend to have lower body weight than do non-smokers and why smoking cessation is frequently followed by weight gain. In contrast, heavy smokers tend to have greater body weight than do light/non-smokers but this likely reflects a clustering of risky behaviours (e.g. low degree of physical activity, poor diet, and smoking) causing weight gain.

However, we now know that smoking increases insulin resistance and is associated with central fat accumulation. Active smoking is associated with an increased risk of Type 2 diabetes with a meta-analysis of 25 studies (involving over 1.2 million participants) suggesting a pooled adjusted relative risk of 1.44 (1.31 to 1.58). Results were consistent and statistically significant in all subgroups also showing a dose–response effect. Further research will clarify whether these association's are truly casual and also clarify specific mechanisms.

Smoking also directly affects the endocrine system of the foetus and young children. Passive transfer of thiocyanate (a major constituent of cigarette smoke) can cause disturbance of thyroid size and function. Furthermore, maternal smoking indirectly effects the foetus via other hormonal mechanisms, for example, increased catecholamine production contributes to the under-perfusion of the foetal–placental unit.

14.7 Smoking and erectile dysfunction (ED)

A literature review of 18 studies revealed that smokers were 1.5 to 2 times more likely to suffer ED than non-smokers, but many men seem unaware of this. Mechanisms include alterations in testosterone levels, endothelial dysfunction, and indirect effects of smoking via increased rates of diabetes, arteriosclerosis, depression, and so on. The prevalence of ED in former smokers is the same as never-smokers, implying that smoking cessation is likely to reduce the risk of ED.

14.8 Smoking and eye diseases

Many of the 4000 compounds in cigarette smoke are poisonous to ocular tissues causing morphological and functional changes to the lens and retina due to ateriosclerotic and thrombotic effects on the ocular capillaries. Smoking also enhances the generation of free radicals and decreases the levels of antioxidants in the blood circulation, aqueous humour, and ocular tissue.

Smoking has consistently been identified as an independent risk factor for cataract, the leading cause of blindness worldwide. A review of 27 studies suggests that smokers have a threefold increased risk for developing (nuclear) cataracts with other causality criteria such as evidence of dose–response, temporal relationship, and reversibility of effect when quitting. Blindness can be particularly devastating in developing countries and this is where smoking incidence is most rapidly growing.

Smoking is also strongly associated with the other leading cause of worldwide blindness—age-related macular degeneration (OR 1.76; 1.56 to 1.99) and again risk reduces in past smokers.

Other common ocular disorders, such as retinal ischaemia, anterior ischaemic optic neuropathy have been linked independently to smoking (with a dose-dependent effect) despite their multifactorial aetiology. Tobacco smoking is the direct cause of tobacco–alcohol amblyopia, a once common but now rare disease characterized by severe visual loss, from direct toxic optic nerve damage. The babies of smoking mothers are more prone to develop strabismus.

Ophthalmologists have recently called *for adding the increased risk of blindness to the better-known arguments against smoking.*

Although highly irritating to the conjunctivae, very scarce data exist on the effect of environmental tobacco smoke causing actual diseases of the eye.

14.9 Smoking and upper respiratory tract diseases

Smokers have more infections of the upper respiratory tract and there are differences in the amount and types of bacteria found in the nasopharynx in smokers and also after smoking cessation. The last systematic review showed children had significantly higher levels of middle ear disease (OR 1.48), recurrent otitis media/middle ear effusion (OR 1.38) if either parent smoked. Studies were inconsistent with regard to the association of parental smoking and tonsillectomy. There is now sufficient evidence to establish a causal association between cigarette smoking and cancer of the nasal cavities and paranasal sinuses, nasopharynx.

By causing direct inflammation of the upper airway mucosa, cigarette smoking causes acute and chronic laryngitis. It is a causal risk factor for laryngeal carcinoma and continued smoking is associated with poor response to treatment (e.g. poor wound healing after laryngectomy, increased radiotherapy side effects).

Smoking is strongly associated with periodontal disease in a dose-dependent manner and further evidence of a causal relationship is the marked improvement in periodontal disease observed when stopping smoking. Dentists and oral surgeons are becoming increasingly interested in the effects of smoking on gum disease (particularly gum recession), tooth decay/discolouration, chronic mouth infections, mouth ulcers, and oral cancers. The use of smokeless tobacco is also strongly discouraged by most dentists.

14.10 Smoking and other lower respiratory tract diseases

Smoking increases asthma risk and is associated with poorer control and increased risk of respiratory infections. Either parent smoking is associated with increased risk of childhood wheeze, breathlessness, and infections, asthma and asthma admissions in children—but the effect is strongest for maternal smoking.

14.11 Smoking and musculoskeletal diseases

Tobacco smoking modulates the immune system via induction of the inflammatory response, immune suppression, alteration of cytokine balance, induction of apoptosis, and DNA damage that results in the formation of anti-DNA antibodies. It is not surprising then that smoking has been shown to interact with genetic factors to create a significant combined risk of developing systemic lupus erythematosus (SLE) and rheumatoid arthritis (RA). Smoking also affects the course of rheumatic diseases; for example, increasing the risk of dermatological features and nephritis in SLE, rheumatoid nodules, and multiple joint involvement in RA and worsening of digital ischaemia in systemic sclerosis. Smoking also particularly increases the risk of accelerated arteriosclerosis in rheumatic diseases as it does in renal diseases. No sole mechanism, however, has been linked to any of the autoimmune illnesses and it is likely that it affects each differently.

Maternal smoking is an independent risk factor for Legg-Calvé-Perthes Disease in a dose-dependent manner.

Key reading

Allam MF, Campbell MJ, Del Castillo AS, Fernández-Crehuet Navajas R. Parkinson's disease protects against smoking? *Behav Neurol* 2004; **15**: 65–71.

Ashley MJ. Smoking and diseases of the gastrointestinal system: an epidemiological review with special reference to sex differences. *Can J Gastroenterol* 1997; **11**: 345–52.

Bergstrom J. Periodontitis and smoking: an evidence based appraisal. *J Evid Based Dent Pract* 2006; **6**: 33–41.

Botteri E, Iodice S, Raimondi S, Maisonneuve P, Lowenfels AB. Cigarette smoking and adenomatous polyps: a meta-analysis. *Gastroenterology* 2008; **134**: 388–95.

Braun JM, Froehlich TE, Daniels JL et al. Association of Environmental Toxicants and Conduct Disorder in U.S. Children: NHANES 2001–2004. *Environ Health Perspect* 2008; **116**: 956–62.

Cheng AC, Pang CP, Leung AT, Chua JK, Fan DS, Lam DS. The association between cigarette smoking and ocular diseases. *Hong Kong Med J* 2000; **6**: 195–202.

Cong R, Zhou B, Sun Q, Gu H, Tang N, Wang B. Smoking and the risk of age-related macular degeneration: a meta-analysis. *Ann Epidemiol* 2008; **18**: 647–56.

Cook DG, Strachan DP. Health effects of passive smoking. 3. Parental smoking and prevalence of respiratory symptoms and asthma in school age children. *Thorax* 1997; **52**: 1081–94.

Freiman A, Bird G, Metelitsa AI, Barankin B, Lauzon GJ. Cutaneous effects of smoking. *J Cutan Med Surg* 2004; **8**: 415–23.

Giovannucci E. An updated review of the epidemiological evidence that cigarette smoking increases risk of colorectal cancer. *Cancer Epidemiol Biomarkers Prev* 2001; **10**: 725–31.

Harel-Meir M, Sherer Y, Shoenfeld Y. Tobacco smoking and autoimmune rheumatic diseases. *Nat Clin Pract Rheumatol* 2007; **3**: 707–15.

Jones-Burton C, Seliger SL, Scherer RW et al. Cigarette smoking and incident chronic kidney disease: a systematic review. *Am J Nephrol* 2007; **27**: 342–51.

Kapoor D, Jones TH. Smoking and hormones in health and endocrine disorders. *Eur J Endocrinol* 2005; **152**: 491–9.

Kelly SP, Thornton J, Edwards R, Sahu A, Harrison R. Smoking and cataract: review of causal association. *J Cataract Refract Surg* 2005; **12**: 2395–404.

López-Arrieta JLA, Sanz FJ. Nicotine for Alzheimer's disease. *Cochrane Database of Syst Rev* 2001; (2): Art. No. CD001749. DOI: 10.1002/14651858. CD001749.

McGrath J, McDonald JWD, MacDonald JK. Transdermal nicotine for induction of remission in ulcerative colitis. *Cochrane Database of Syst Rev* 2004; (4): Art. No. CD004722. DOI: 10.1002/14651858. CD004722 pub2.

McVary KT, Carrier S, Wessells H. Smoking and erectile dysfunction: evidence based analysis. *J Urol* 2001; **166**: 1624–32.

Morita A. Tobacco smoke causes premature skin aging. *J Dermatol Sci* 2007; **48**: 169–75.

Orth SR, Hallan SI. Smoking: a risk factor for progression of chronic kidney disease and for cardiovascular morbidity and mortality in renal patients—absence of evidence or evidence of absence? *Clin J Am Soc Nephrol* 2008; **3**: 226–36.

Sasco AJ, Secretan MB, Straif K. Tobacco smoking and cancer: a brief review of recent epidemiological evidence. *Lung Cancer* 200; **45**(Suppl 2): S3–9.

Strachan DP, Cook DG. Health effects of passive smoking. 4. Parental smoking, middle ear disease and adenotonsillectomy in children. *Thorax* 1998; **53**: 50–6.

Sundström P, Nyström L. Smoking worsens the prognosis in multiple sclerosis. *Mult Scler* 16 July 2008 [Epub ahead of print].

Sundström P, Nyström L, Hallmans G. Smoke exposure increases the risk for multiple sclerosis. *Eur J Neurol* 2008; **15**: 579–83.

Thornton J, Kelly SP, Harrison RA, Edwards R. Cigarette smoking and thyroid eye disease: a systematic review. *Eye* 2007; **21**: 1135–45.

Vianna EO, Gutierrez MR, Barbieri MA *et al.* Respiratory effects of tobacco smoking among young adults. *Am J Med Sci* 2008; **336**: 44–9.

Willi C, Bodenmann P, Ghali WA, Faris PD, Cornuz J. Active smoking and the risk of type 2 diabetes: a systematic review and meta-analysis. *JAMA* 2007; **298**: 2654–64.

Chapter 15

New treatments and the future

Christina Gratziou

Key points

- New drugs being developed for use in stopping smoking include:
    - Novel ways of delivering nicotine
    - Applying existing non-nicotinic centrally acting drugs
    - Cytochrome P450 (CYP) 2A6 inhibitors
    - Opioid antagonists
    - Gamma-aminobutyric acid-ergic agents
    - Nicotine vaccines.
- The nicotine vaccines and opioid antagonist rimonabant look the most promising and are in Phase II to III trials.

15.1 Introduction

Nicotine replacement therapies (NRT), bupropion and varenicline, are effective in the treatment of tobacco dependence but many smokers cannot stop despite wanting to and whilst using these drugs. Improvements in treating tobacco dependence are likely to rely at least in part on new pharmacotherapy regimes, including novel nicotine delivery systems, new applications of existing drugs, and completely new chemical entities. These are all currently being evaluated to address the present unmet needs of many smokers.

15.2 Novel nicotine delivery systems

Two novel nicotine delivery systems are being evaluated. The oral products, nicotine through a 'straw' and nicotine drops, are absorbed from the intestine allowing the user to take nicotine in a beverage. No efficacy data have been published yet.

Another formulation for nicotine under development is a pulmonary inhaler, delivering nicotine directly to the lung in a similar manner to the cigarette. The pulmonary mode of delivery could reduce background cravings and withdrawal symptoms, given the lung's large surface area and excellent blood supply, should allow for rapid relief of acute cravings. This could allow flexible dosing but may have the potential for abuse.

15.3 **Existing non-nicotinic medications**

These drugs influence the effects of nicotine on the neural pathways that are implicated in nicotine/tobacco dependence (See Chapter 2). This class of medication includes antidepressants (bupropion, nortriptyline), a_2 noradrenergic agonists (clonidine), and the $\alpha_4\beta_2$ nicotine partial agonist (varenicline). They have been described in Chapter 4 but are still being evaluated using different dosing regimes and in different sub-groups of smokers (e.g. those with depression or who have failed with NRT).

15.4 **Novel chemical entities**

15.4.1 **Cytochrome P450 (CYP) 2A6 inhibitors**

Nicotine is converted to cotinine in the liver by the enzyme CYP2A6. Genetic variations in the CYP2A6 allele have been shown to affect nicotine metabolism and subsequent smoking behaviour, leading to the possibility that inhibitors of CYP2A6 may be an interesting category for a new medication to control nicotine addiction.

Animal models suggest these substances increase the plasma half-life of nicotine and do indeed reduce nicotine-seeking behaviour. By reducing the activation of pre-carcinogens to carcinogens, they have the potential to reduce the risks of tobacco-induced cancer.

Inhibition of CYP2A6 could be used as part of a harm reduction strategy to reduce the number of cigarettes consumed. It could also be used in combination with NRT to enhance the levels of plasma nicotine so achieving optimal replacement without the associated damage of other cigarette toxins. Early Phase II and III studies in human volunteers of two strong CYP2A6 inhibitors, methoxsalen and tranylcypromine, given in combination with oral nicotine have significantly increased plasma nicotine concentrations and reduced the desire to smoke. Side effects of these drugs appear tolerable. Selegeline (a monoamine oxidase inhibitor used to treat Parkinson's disease) may also exert some anti-smoking effect by this mechanism. Larger studies are ongoing but no CYP2A6 inhibitors have yet been approved for treatment of tobacco dependence.

15.4.2 **Opioid antagonists**

Medications affecting the opioid system in the brain cause pleasure and may be involved in the reinforcing properties of several drugs of abuse including nicotine.

15.4.2.1 *Rimonabant*

In experimental animals, blockade of the cannabinoid CB1 receptors with rimonabant diminishes feeding behaviour, decreases the self-administration of nicotine and dopamine turnover in the nucleus accumbens after nicotine stimulation. In addition, rimonabant attenuates the reinstatement of nicotine-seeking behaviour, evoked by non-contingent exposure to a conditioned stimulus after extinction of nicotine self-administration, suggesting that the stimulation of CB1 receptors by endocannabinoids within the brain plays an integral role in the development and maintenance of nicotine and tobacco dependence.

The clinical effectiveness of rimonabant for smoking cessation has been tested in two large, multi-centre, Phase III trials. In the first US study, the drug was given for 10 weeks resulting in quit rates at 10 weeks of 28% for rimonabant 20 mg, 16% for rimonabant 5 mg, and 16% for placebo. The difference between the 20-mg dose and placebo was highly significant ($p < 0.005$) but in a European study the 10-week abstinence rates were more modest at 25%, 24%, and 20%, respectively (not statistically significant). The most frequent side effects of rimonabant were nausea, diarrhoea, vomiting, urinary tract infections, anxiety, and upper respiratory tract infections. No cardio-vascular safety concerns were identified.

Interestingly, US smokers who quit in the rimonabant group, gained less weight than the quitters prescribed placebo. At 10 weeks in the European study, abstinent subjects in the 20 and 5 mg and placebo groups had gained 0.7, 2, and 3 kg of weight, respectively, suggesting a dose–response. Weight gain is a common adverse effect of smoking cessation and is often reported to be one of the factors associated with relapse, so any medication that also limits the weight gain associated with cessation could be useful. In 2006, rimonabant was approved for marketing in Europe for weight control, but not for smoking cessation. More clinical trials may support the regulatory approval of rimonabant for smoking cessation treatment in the near future.

15.4.2.2 *Naltrexone*

This is another opioid antagonist approved by the US Food and Drugs Administration for the treatment of alcohol and opioid dependence. It has a higher affinity for opioid kappa receptors and a longer half-life than naloxone but studies using it for nicotine dependence have been disappointing.

15.4.2.3 *Nalmefene*

This has shown higher quit rates than placebo in a small Phase II study using healthy, volunteer smokers, and is being evaluated further.

15.4.3 **Gamma-aminobutyric acid-ergic agents**

In the nucleus accumbens, gamma-aminobutyric acid (GABA) neurones inhibit dopaminergic activity. Current GABAergic medications like anti-epileptics (tiagabine, vigabatrin, gabapentin) and baclofen have been tested for treating tobacco dependency but are limited by their adverse effects. New medications that interact with GABA may be beneficial in the future.

15.4.4 **Nicotine vaccines**

A vaccine against nicotine induces antibodies that bind to nicotine molecules in the plasma, before they pass through the blood–brain barrier and so prevent them reaching their neuronal receptors to produce the effects normally associated with smoking (see Figure 15.1). In theory, reducing or eliminating the nicotine reaching the brain will reduce the reinforcing effects of tobacco smoking so eventually leading to extinction of the behaviour. Theoretical advantages might be guaranteed compliance (non-daily use), minimal side effects on the central nervous system, and the potential to be combined with other therapies.

There are at least three different types of vaccine in clinical development, now undergoing Phase II and III trials in humans (CYT002-NicQb, NicVAX®, and TA-NIC).

A nicotine vaccine could also be useful as a relapse prevention treatment or in the preparation phase for heavy smokers and even be considered for use in adolescents to prevent initiation of smoking. However, the doses, treatment intervals as well as the risks (e.g. long-term immunomodulation), clinical benefits, and ethical issues of such interventions have to be better evaluated.

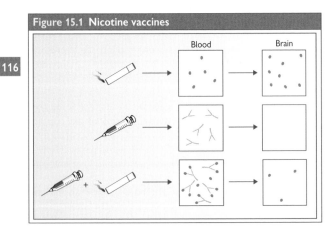

Figure 15.1 Nicotine vaccines

Even if the early trials are successful, regulatory approval will take at least 2 to 3 yrs before these vaccines can be recommended.

15.5 Conclusions

Novel delivery devices, new applications of existing medications, and new compounds for the treatment of tobacco addiction are being researched but are several years away. Varenicline has been the only new class of drug licensed for smoking cessation in the last 15 yrs. Yet more studies are needed on treatments to control smoking addiction when other co-morbidities (depression, schizophrenia, alcoholism, etc.) are present. Finally, advances in pharmacogenetics might assess how genetic polymorphisms not only predict addiction but also the best choice of treatment for every individual smoker.

We have to keep in mind, however, that tobacco addiction is complex. Smokers will never simply be able to 'take a pill' to make them stop smoking. Smokers must want to stop smoking and must be willing to work hard to achieve the goal of smoking abstinence, but at least they now have different pharmacological options.

Key reading

Buchhalter AR, Fant RV, Henningfield JE. Novel pharmacological approaches for treating tobacco dependence and withdrawal. Current status. *Drugs* 2008; **68**: 1067–88.

Celtic Pharma. The Portfolio: TA-NIC [online]. Available from URL: http://www.celticpharma.com/theportfolio/ta-nic.html (accessed 22 April 2008).

Cerny T. Anti-nicotine vaccination: where are we? Recent results. *Cancer Res* 2005; **166**: 167–75.

Cleland JG, Ghosh J, Freemantle N *et al*. Clinical trials update and cumulative meta-analyses from the American College of Cardiology: WATCH, SCD-HeFT, DINAMIT, CASINO, IN- SPIRE, STRATUS-US, RIO-Lipids and cardiac resynchronisation therapy in heart failure. *Eur J Heart Fail* 2004; **6**: 501–8.

Cohen C, Kodas E, Griebel G. CB(1) receptor antagonists for the treatment of nicotine addiction. *Pharmacol Biochem Behav* 2005; **81**: 387–95.

Cousins MS, Stamat HM, De Wit H. Effects of a single dose baclofen on self-reported subjective effects and tobacco smoking. *Nicotine Tob Res* 2001; **3**(2): 123–9.

Covey LS, Glassman AH, Stetner F. Naltrexone effects on short-term and long-term smoking cessation. *J Addict Dis* 1999; **18**: 31–40.

D'Orlando KJ, Fox BS. Tolerability and pharmacokinetics of single and repeated doses of nicotine with The Straw, a novel nicotine replacement product. *Nicotine Tob Res* 2004; **6**: 63–70.

Hatsukami DK, Rennard S, Jorenby D et al. Safety and immunogenicity of a nicotine conjugate vaccine in current smokers. *Clin Pharmacol Ther* 2005; **78**(5): 456–67.

Henningfield JE, Fant RV, Gitchell J et al. Tobacco dependence: global public health potential for new medications development and indications. *Ann N Y Acad Sci* 2000; **909**: 247–56.

Markou A, Paterson NE, Semenova S. Role of gamma-aminobutyric acid (GABA) and metabotropic glutamate receptors in nicotine reinforcement: potential pharmacotherapies for smoking cessation. *Ann N Y Acad Sci* 2004; **1025**: 491–503.

Maurer P, Jennings GT, Willers J et al. A therapeutic vaccine for nicotine dependence: preclinical efficacy, and phase I safety and immunogenicity. *Eur J Immunol* 2005; **35**(7): 2031–40.

Sellers EM, Kaplan HL, Tyndale RF. Inhibition of cytochrome P450 2A6 increases nicotine's oral bioavailability and decreases smoking. *Clin Pharmacol Ther* 2000; **68**: 35–43.

Vaan Gaal LF, Rissanrn AM, Scheen AJ et al. Effects of the cannabinoid-1 receptor blocker rimonabant on weight reduction and cardiovascular risk factors in overweight patients: 1-year experience from the RIO-Europe study. *Lancet* 2005; **365**: 1389–64.

Westman EC, Tomlin KF, Perkins CE et al. Oral nicotine solution for smoking cessation: a pilot tolerability study. *Nicotine Tob Res* 2001; **3**: 391–6.

Appendix 1

Case studies

Case study 1: Male patient

Aged 34, he smokes 40 cigarettes a day and the first cigarette is smoked in bed. He started smoking when he was 16 yrs old. He is a professional person, who after finishing work each day calls into the pub for a few pints before going home.

Current medical problems include sleep apnoea, psoriasis, obesity, and depression. He says he has tried to quit on numerous occasions, has tried everything but nothing works. He does not believe he can stop. He says he does not know why he has come to see you. Everyone has to die sometime.

He lives with his mother. He has a dog. He has no hobbies. Has no self-confidence in his ability to quit. He is very angry with his mother because she is nagging him to stop smoking and lose weight.

Questions to ask yourself:

- Is your patient motivated to stop?
- How would you motivate this patient?
- What pharmacological product (if any) would you suggest appropriate for the patient to use?

Initially one may assume that he does not want to stop smoking but as the first interview progressed it became apparent that he did not believe he was capable of stopping. The fact that he turned up for the interview showed that he was asking for help.

This patient needed a lot of support and motivation and the first interview was used for building his confidence and removing his fear about stopping, the withdrawal symptoms and the fear of failure. It was explained that giving up smoking should be seen as a new beginning and a new lifestyle.

The patient scored a high dependency to nicotine and was prescribed 4 mg nicotine lozenges. (If the patient had wished he could have used 4 mg nicotine gum but he disliked chewing gum.) The nicotine patch would not have been strong enough alone to alleviate the physical withdrawal symptoms and he had psoriasis. He was on antidepressants so bupropion and varenicline were not used as first line.

It was suggested that he alter his habit of going straight to the pub from work and that immediately after dinner, start a new routine to walk his dog. (Normally his mother walked the dog.) We also recommended him joining a leisure centre/club and perhaps swimming. Weight was discussed and a sensible snack diet was suggested between his meals. He was also encouraged to keep appointments with the dietitian.

Result

The patient reduced his pub nights to twice weekly and went home immediately from work. He also started walking the dog and actually enjoyed and looked forward to his evening walk.

He started swimming on weekends and kept a diary about his progress. He gained more confidence and had stopped smoking by his third appointment. This achievement boosted his self-esteem. He also became very conscious of how much money he was saving and started planning a holiday. He also reported that he felt fitter, healthier, and happier.

12-month confirmed success.

Case study 2: Female patient

Aged 70, Mrs. P smokes 5 to 10 cigs a day with her first of the day is about 2 hrs after waking. She started smoking when she was 12 yrs old. Current medical problems include severe COPD and stable ischaemic heart disease. She is only able to go out if her son and daughter-in-law take her in the car.

She lives alone but her son and grandchildren visit twice a week. She has a cat. She thinks that the damage is done and its too late to stop. The patient agreed that the cigarette was like a 'friend' to her and if she felt fed up or lonely she would smoke. She said that the habit of handling the cigarette was important to her. Quite often the cigarette would burn away in her hand or in the ashtray. She had managed to 'cut down' a couple of times when she had a chest infection. When hospitalized, she is able to stop smoking.

She has never tried any nicotine replacement therapy (NRT) product. Her family members (especially her grandchildren) are worried about her smoking. They are all non-smokers.

Questions to ask yourself

- Is your patient motivated to stop?
- How would you motivate this patient?
- What pharmacological product (if any) would you suggest appropriate for the patient to use?

Fortunately the patient's family were very supportive and were concerned about her health but also the risk of a fire in her home. In the first interview, the patient needed to understand that stopping smoking would not undo any damage already done but it would reduce the damage progressing. It was explained in simple language what benefits could occur and that they would occur within hours–days of stopping smoking.

After discussion, she could have used any of the NRT products as she had scored a low dependency to nicotine. She felt that the nicotine inhalator was the most appealing for her as it gave her something to hold. Nicotine gum, lozenges, and microtabs did not appeal to her and the patch was her second choice.

We discussed passive smoking and gave her a leaflet to read in more detail. She was shocked to discover the danger of passive smoke and said she now understood why her family made such a fuss when they visited her home. It was suggested that not only would her family be happier when visiting but also her cat would benefit.

It was suggested that her grandchildren became her 'minders' and checked her daily progress and smoking status and that promising her grandchildren a 100% effort in quitting smoking, might improve her determination and willpower. The patient happily agreed to do this and said her grandchildren would be delighted to help.

She used to enjoy knitting but had not done so for quite awhile so it was suggested that she asked her grandchildren if she could knit something for them when she felt fed up or bored. It was also suggested that she would save the money spent on cigarettes daily in a jar. This also appealed to her.

Result

12-month confirmed success. Patient is still using (an empty) nicotine inhalator.

Consultation forms

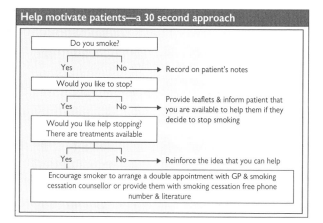

Help motivate patients—a 30 second approach

Do you smoke?

Yes — No ──→ Record on patient's notes

Would you like to stop?

Yes — No ──→ Provide leaflets & inform patient that you are available to help them if they decide to stop smoking

Would you like help stopping? There are treatments available

Yes — No ──→ Reinforce the idea that you can help

Encourage smoker to arrange a double appointment with GP & smoking cessation counsellor or provide them with smoking cessation free phone number & literature

Detailed consultation form, for stop-smoking specialists

Personal details to ask

- How many cigarettes do you smoke per day?
- Do you need a cigarette within 20 min of waking or last thing at night?
- What age did you start smoking?
- Previous attempts—find what worked/didn't before. Did you use any products?
- Do you live with anyone who smokes? (Hardest for people who live alone).
- Find the motivation factors to quit (e.g. health, money, smell, children, etc.).

Risk facts

- Explain what is in a cigarette:
  - Nicotine (reaches the brain in around 4 s)
  - Carbon monoxide (CO) compare to putting your mouth around the exhaust pipe of car
  - Tar: 70% of which deposits on lungs and is not cleared
  - 4,000 chemicals, 60 which are cancer causing
- 120,000 people die each year in the UK from smoking-related diseases.

Benefit facts—why it's never too late

- Within 24 hrs CO is eliminated from body. If you smoke 20 cigarettes a day, you will now have an increase of around 15% oxygen to heart/lungs.
- Within 48 hrs no nicotine is left in body. Blood becomes less sticky.
- If you stop smoking, it significantly reduces the chance of heart attack, stroke, and blood clotting.
- Personal benefits—reiterate motivating factors mentioned earlier.
- If you have emphysema/bronchitis we cannot repair most of the damage done but within 3 months quitting can increase lung capacity, improve oxygen levels, improve all respiratory symptoms, and make you live longer.

Aids to stopping

- Cold turkey—using your own will power and cognitive support (change habits—way think/do things). Advantages: cheap and no exposure to drug side effects. Disadvantages: only 3% to 6% succeed using this method, as cigarettes are so addictive.
- NRT—gum, patch, inhalator, lozenge, microtab, spray.
  - Bupropion (Zyban®)
  - Varenicline (Champix®)

Practical tips on prescribing

Nicotine patch—24 hrs patch useful if you are not sleeping well or need a cigarette within 30 min of waking:

- If you suffer nightmares, take it off before bed and put a fresh one on in the morning
- Move patch around every day using any part of the upper torso (try to avoid hairy areas)
- Remove before bath/shower and reapply to dry/cool skin
- More effective if smoke <30 cigs a day

Nicotine lozenge—you should take 12 to 15 lozenges per day, at least every 3 to 4 hrs.

- Useful if you miss 'hand action' or something going into your mouth after meals and so on
- Each one lasts 20 to 30 min—if you don't like the taste, just spit it out
- Gently suck on it but do not bite or swallow or crunch—it will be too strong
- 4 mg very effective for 40 per day smoker.

Varenicline (Champix®)—start 1 to 2 weeks before target stop date. Start 1 tablet (500 mcg) once daily for 3 days then increased to 500 mcg twice daily for 4 days, then 1 mg twice daily for 11 weeks. Warn the drug can cause nausea and sleep disturbances (including vivid dreams and insomnia). If you feel unwell, try reducing it rather than an abrupt withdrawal.

Action plan

- Give a written list of withdrawal symptoms—ask '*which of these do you fear most and how would you cope with it?*'
- Remind them that a craving only lasts 6 min so do 10 min activity/distraction
- Ask if they want to join programme
- Decide quit date.

Remember to test CO levels and weigh patient before leaving.

Appendix 3

Tips for improving success in high-risk groups

Factor	Practical considerations
Female sex	Address body weight gain concerns; medication use in pregnant smokers; consider effect of menstrual cycle influences on mood and withdrawal symptoms
Age	Early age at initiation suggests stronger addiction and more intensive support is needed
Family	Children of smokers are far more likely to smoke and start earlier. This can be used as an incentive to help parents. Smokers living with another smoker will find it very hard to quit but married smokers often quit at the same time and help motivate each other. Offer support simultaneously to other smokers in the same household
Previous cessation	More previous attempts and particularly longer periods of abstinence predict better long-term success. Build on their motivation and explain that most smokers take several attempts
Depression	Specifically look for symptoms of concomitant depression in the first consultation. Depressed smokers experience intense withdrawal symptoms and need intensive pharmacological and behavioural support over the first 2 to 3 weeks. Consider antidepressants early and/or specialist referral
High level of addiction	Those with a FTND score ≥7 will benefit from higher doses and combinations of pharmacotherapy
Low motivation	Apply motivational interviewing more and physicians can use their regular contacts with such patients to gradually change their beliefs and increase their level of motivation over time—building to a quit attempt
Alcohol misuse	Consider referral to a specialist if high levels of misuse but as alcohol probably increases nicotine cravings and enjoyment these smokers should be warned that it does lower success rates

Nicotine dependence questionnaire

Example (modified) Fagerström Tolerance Scale

1. How soon after you wake do you smoke your first cigarette?
   0. After 30 minutes   1. Within 30 minutes

2. Do you find it difficult to refrain from smoking in places where it is forbidden?
   0. No   1. Yes

3. Which of all the cigarettes you smoke in a day is the most satisfying?
   0. Not the first one   1. The first one in the
      in the morning.   morning.

4. How many cigarettes a day do you smoke?
   0. 1–15   1. 16–25   2. >25

5. Do you smoke more during the morning, than during the rest of the day?
   0. No   1. Yes

6. Do you smoke when you are so ill that you are in bed most of the day?
   0. No   1. Yes

7. Does the brand you smoke have a low, medium, or high nicotine content?
   0. Low   1. Medium   2. High

8. How often do you inhale the smoke from your cigarette?
   0. Never   1. Sometimes   2. Always

Scoring instructions: Add up responses to all the items. Total scores should range from 0 to 11. Where ≥7 suggests physical dependence on nicotine.

Data adapted from: Heatherton *et al.* The Fagerström test for nicotinic dependence. Describing the development and validity of the FTND scale. *Br J Addict* 1991; **86**: 1119–27.

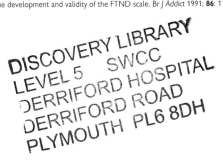

Appendix 5

Timeline of tobacco use and control

- **circa 6000 BC**: The tobacco plant begins growing in the Americas
- **circa 100 BC**: American inhabitants begin using tobacco, including smoking and in enemas
- **12th century**: A Maya pot depicts a man smoking a roll of tobacco leaves tied with a string. The Mayan term for smoking was sik'ar
- **1492**: Columbus discovers smoking
- **1564**: Sir John Hawkins introduces tobacco to England
- **1603**: Physicians are upset that tobacco is used without their prescription and complain to King James I
- **1604**: King James I writes 'A Counterblaste to Tobacco' saying it is 'loathsome to the eye, hateful to the nose, harmful to the brain, dangerous to the lungs'
- **1628**: Shah Sefi punishes two merchants for selling tobacco by pouring hot lead down their throats
- **1633**: Sultan Murad IV of Turkey orders tobacco users executed as infidels
- **1634**: Czar Alexis in Russia creates penalties for smoking: first offence is whipping, a slit nose, and transportation to Siberia. Second offence is execution
- **1638**: Use or distribution of tobacco in China is made a crime punishable by decapitation
- **1650**: Colony of Connecticut General Court orders—'no smoking except with physicians order'
- **1701**: Nicholas Boisregard warns that young people taking too much tobacco have 'trembling, unsteady hands, staggering feet, and suffer a withering of their noble parts'

- **1761**: Dr. John Hill (UK) performs perhaps first clinical study of tobacco effects, warns snuff users they are vulnerable to cancers of the nose
- **1761**: Dr. Percival Pott notes incidence of cancer of the scrotum among chimney sweeps, theorizing a connection between cancer and exposure to soot
- **1795**: Samuel von Soemmering reports on cancers of the lip in pipe smokers

- **1847:** Philip Morris opens his tobacconist shop selling hand-rolled Turkish cigarettes
- **1852:** Matches are introduced, making smoking more convenient
- **1853–1856:** During the Crimean War, British soldiers learn how cheap and convenient the cigarettes ('Papirossi') used by their Turkish allies are, and bring the practice back to England
- **1850s:** Thomas Reynolds' *Anti-Tobaccoism: Three Hundred and Sixty-Five interviews with Smokers, Chewers and Snufftakers* in a Series of Letters to John Lee, one of the vice presidents of the British Anti-Tobacco Society, published some time in the 1850s, with 'prefatory remarks' by Thomas Hodgkin (of Hodgkin's disease), who opined that 'reading' these letters would be more profitable to most persons than reading a fashionable novel . . .'
- **1884:** Duke and Sons (US) buy two Bonsack cigarette roll-in machines and start producing 744 million cigarettes per year. They soon consolidate their rivals into the American Tobacco Company
- **1901:** The largest British tobacco companies unite to combat America's take-over, forming the Imperial Tobacco Group
- **1902:** Imperial and American agree to stay in their own countries, and unite to form the British American Tobacco Company (BAT)
- **1912:** Dr. I. Adler suggests that lung cancer is related to smoking
- **1928:** Lombard and Doering, in the *New England Journal of Medicine* report on 217 cancer deaths. They report that 34 of 35 site-specific (lung, lips, cheek, jaw) cancer sufferers are heavy smokers
- **1939–1945:** By the end of the Second World War, cigarette sales are at an all-time high
- **1941:** Dr. Michael DeBakey notes a correlation between the increased sale of tobacco and the increasing prevalence of lung cancer in the USA
- **1950:** Two important epidemiological studies confirm a link between smoking and lung cancer: *JAMA*, 96.5% of lung cancer patients interviewed were moderate heavy-to-chain smokers and in the September 30 edition of *BMJ*, Richard Doll and Bradford Hill reported heavy smokers were 50 times as likely as non-smokers to contract lung cancer
- **1953:** Wynder finds that painting cigarette tar on the backs of mice creates tumours—the first definitive biological link between smoking and cancer

- **1954:** Tobacco Industry Research Committee placed a two-page ad in 448 newspapers reaching a circulation of 43 million people. It quoted cancer scientists who disregarded environmental factors in causing cancer. It also published a booklet quoting 36 scientists questioning smokings' link to health problems, which was sent to 176,800 doctors
- **1954:** Marlboro Cowboy created for Philip Morris
- **1957:** An internal report by the British tobacco industry refers to cancer by the code name, zephyr: 'as a result of several statistical surveys, the idea has arisen that there is a causal relation between zephyr and tobacco smoking, particularly cigarette smoking'
- **1962:** UK: first report of the British Royal College of Physicians (RCP) of London—Smoking and Health
- **1965:** TV cigarette ads are taken off the air in the UK
- **1966:** Health warnings on cigarette packs begin
- **1967:** US Surgeon General's report concludes that smoking is the principal cause of lung cancer; finds evidence linking smoking to heart disease
- **1971:** Second RCP Report refers to the cigarette death toll as *this present holocaust*
- **1971:** contd. A cigarette smoking and health report by an Interdepartmental Parliament Group concludes, 'all things considered, tobacco use brings in more money than it costs in health and disability'. Report is unknown to the public until the Guardian newspaper publishes an account on May 6, 1980
- **1984:** FDA approves nicotine gum as a 'new drug' and quit-smoking aid
- **1988:** First World No-Tobacco Day, sponsored by World Health Organization
- **1992:** Nicotine patch is introduced
- **1992:** 'Marlboro Man' Wayne McLaren, 51, dies of lung cancer
- **1994:** Seven tobacco company executives begin testimony in Congressional hearings
- **1995:** July 19 issue of *JAMA* is heavily devoted to tobacco papers and finds 'the evidence is unequivocal—the US public has been duped by the tobacco industry. We should all be outraged, and we should force the removal of this scourge from our nation'
- **1995:** The second 'Marlboro Man', David McLean, dies of lung cancer
- **1996:** Benzo(a)pyrene derivative in cigarette tar is shown to damage the p53 tumour suppressor gene (*Science* magazine)

- **2002**: RCP Report, 'Forty Fatal Years'—a review of the 40 yrs since the publication of the 1962 report
- **2004:** New York publishes 1-yr results of its ban quoting unheralded success. Global cigarette production declines 2.3% to the lowest since 1972. China now produces 32% of the global total
- **2004:** UK Wanless Report concluded that cutting smoking rates was *a key determinant of success* in meeting the Government's public health targets and that the National Health Service (NHS) needed to shift its balance of effort towards prevention
- **2006** March: Ban on smoking in enclosed public spaces in Scotland
- **2007:** NHS officially becomes smoke-free. Further bans on smoking in enclosed spaces in Wales, Northern Ireland, and England. Minimum age to buy cigarettes will be raised to 18 yrs.

Appendix 6

Business case for a Stop Smoking Service (SSS) in secondary care

This business case is adapted from a successful business case from 2006, based on 43-hrs specialist time, for a Trust-based Stop Smoking Service (SSS). This is within two district general hospitals serving a population of 200,000 people in a semi-rural setting.

The headings can be used as a template and is a guide only and local data should be inserted where indicated by XX. We suggest two small key patient surveys (see below) will also strengthen the business case.

The formula in section 8.0 was particularly useful in getting our manager's attention.

1.0 Introduction

In 2003 around half the NHS Trusts in the UK had direct access to a smoking cessation service (Lewis, 2003). In 2008 this number had slightly risen but there are marked geographical variations in service provision (McAlpine, 2008). Well-designed stop-smoking treatments are among the most cost-effective disease prevention interventions available (Fiore, 2000). This business case identifies the costs and benefits of funding a hospital-based SSS on a recurring basis.

2.0 Outline of the purpose and nature of the proposal

XX% of all adults in [Insert county area] smoke. It is likely that a bigger proportion of those attending hospital are smokers.

Smoking causes lung and cardiovascular disease, which are the biggest killers in our society. Continued smoking is independently associated with re-admissions for COPD, heart disease, and nearly all surgical complications. The UK Government, in its *White Paper* 1988 reported:

> . . . *smoking is the greatest single cause of preventable illness and premature death in the UK* . . .

The proposed Respiratory Framework documents (as part of the UK Government Strategy, RCP Reports (1962, 1971, 2002) and Chronic

Disease Management by the Welsh Assembly Government) state the importance of stopping smoking for general and respiratory health, in particular for those with chronic disease.

The UK Government, Scottish, Northern Ireland, and Welsh Assemblies have banned smoking in public buildings and enclosed spaces. We need a service to support smokers on hospital premises to achieve this complete ban.

3.0 **National targets**

The decision to fund the continuation of a SSS provides an ideal opportunity for local **[Primary Care Trust/Local Health Board]** and **[Insert name]** Trust Senior Managers to signal both to government and the **[Insert Area]** public, their commitment to health promotion and disease prevention.

This proposal provides a perfect strategic fit with key SAFF targets including:

- 10% reduction in Medical Readmissions—Target No. 18
- 10% reduction in total bed days for Medical Emergency Admissions—Target No. 18
- Reductions in Length of Stay—Modernization and Efficiency— Target 21.

It would also form an integral part of **[Insert Area if applicable]** Chronic Disease Management Strategy.

4.0 **Proposal benefits**

This proposal identifies the proven benefits associated with a smoking cessation service, which, whilst integrated with the community service, is managed and delivered within secondary care.

Those who have stopped smoking in hospital do well with secondary care support with up to 37% to 53% quitting over 4 weeks. However, when advised to contact the community teams <8% did so over the next year (Lewis, 2009). We believe that patients attending the Trust and who are at greatest risk, that is with established smoking-related illnesses are not transferring appropriately to a community-based service. A continued programme within the Trust with whom smokers are already familiar—offers a better alternative and improved attendance.

A pilot survey of XX adults attending our Medical Admissions Unit showed XX% of smokers would like to have been offered pharmacotherapy and XX% would have liked counselling on smoking cessation during their hospital admission. [We recommend these simple surveys be done locally.]

Another internal survey confirms that more than XX% of smokers attending respiratory outpatients would prefer a smoking cessation service to be based wholly or partly in secondary care [We recommend these simple surveys be done locally.]

5.0 Medical benefits

Chronic obstructive pulmonary disease (COPD)

Smoking causes over 80% of COPD (GOLD Guidelines, 2007).

• Lung function and quality of life

Stopping smoking is the only intervention that results in a significantly slower decline in lung function ($p < 0.05$) and improvement in *all 4* of the symptoms of COPD, that is cough, sputum, wheezing, and breathlessness (*Am J Resp Crit Care Med* 2000; *Lancet* 2001; *Am J Med* 1999; and so on).

• Exacerbations

Strategies to reduce exacerbations of COPD are essential. There were XXX COPD admissions to *[insert Trust]* with the average length of stay being X days. The impact of smoking cessation on exacerbation risk has not been exactly calculated but:

- Inpatient costs for COPD exacerbations were on average 12% higher for current smokers vs ex-smokers. Moreover cost was directly correlated with number of pack-years of smoking (Targowska, 2004).
- Smoking and passive smoking are independently and significantly associated with increased risk of re-admission, with smokers 63% more likely to have >3 admissions per year than ex-smokers (Garcia-Aymerich, 2003).

• Coronary heart disease (CHD)

A year after quitting, the risk of a heart attack falls to half that of a current smoker (British Heart Foundation, 2005).

6.0 Surgical benefits

Despite being on average 5 to 7 yrs younger than non-smokers attending for the same surgery (Glassman, 2000; Moller, 2003), smokers have a 68% increased risk of death (all cause mortality) compared with non-smokers (Van Domberg, 2000); specific complications have been related to smoking:

1. High rates of surgical wound breakdown with 40% dehiscence vs 25% in non-smokers (Padubidri, 2001)
2. Three times more likely to get *anastomic leakage* following colorectal surgery than non-smokers (Sorensen, 1999)
3. Higher rates of *wound infection* (12% vs 2%; Sorensen, 2003)

4. Three to five times the rate of *pulmonary complications* (Warner, 1989; Bluman, 1999; Brooks-Brunn, 2001)

5. 75% excess risk of *cardiac deaths* post-operatively (Van Domberg, 2000)

6. Lower rates of *bone-healing*, for example of the spine (Glasman, 2000), dental implants (Bain, 1993)

7. Increased need for *repeat surgery* (e.g. Persistent smokers are 1.4 times more likely to need repeat cardiac procedures (Van Domberg, 2000), repeat orthopaedic procedures are needed in 15% of smokers vs 4% in quitters (Moller *et al.*, 2001).

7.0 **Length of stay after surgery**

Length of stay (LOS): Following elective orthopaedic surgery, smokers had a median LOS 2 days longer than ex-smokers and were more than 18 times more likely to have a LOS in a non-orthopaedic (i.e. medical or rehabilitation ward) than ex-smokers. In most age groups (except 50 to 55 yrs), the average LOS for smokers following cardiac surgery was greater than for ex-smokers (National Adult Cardiac Surgical Database, 2003).

Smoking cessation pre- and post-operatively is particularly effective because patients are motivated. Controlled trials suggest quit rates of up to 60% to 90% with counselling and pharmacotherapy can be achieved over the first 6 months (McHugh, 2001; Moller, 2004; Ratner, 2004). Moreover this quitting will tangible benefits:

1. Quitting for >2 months is associated with a drop in the rate of pulmonary complications from 33% to 14.5%; in fact those patients who had stopped smoking for >6 months had post-operative complication rates similar to those who had never smoked (Warner *et al.* 1989)

2. Of the 1,041 people who underwent coronary bypass in the 1970s to 1980s, smoking cessation after surgery was an important independent predictor of a lower risk of death from coronary vascular events and of fewer coronary interventions during the 20-yr follow-up (van Domberg, 2000).

3. Preliminary results suggest that a part-time service targeting all patients undergoing elective surgery in London could result in saving between 2,200 and 36,000 bed days in London hospitals (www.LHO.org.uk)

4. In a randomized controlled trial, smoking counselling and NRT 6 to 8 weeks prior to surgery resulted in an overall post-operative complication rate of 18% compared with 52% in similar patients receiving no smoking cessation treatment ($p = 0.0003$). The most significant effects of intervention were seen for wound-related complications (5% vs 31%, $p = 0.001$), and cardiovascular complications (0% vs 10%, $p = 0.08$), secondary surgery (4% vs 15%, $p = 0.07$) (Moller, 2002).

8.0 Occupational/staff benefits

All NHS staff have a significant opportunity to act as role models as part of the wider community. Continuing to provide this service to staff would send a very strong message to all **[insert area]** residents over the importance of this initiative and its wider public health benefits.

We already know that smokers have more illness, take more time off work and are less productive (e.g. additional smoke breaks) than non-smoking employees. The Canadian Health Ministry estimates that every member of staff who smokes costs their employer around an extra £1115 per year through decreased productivity, more absenteeism, earlier retirement, increased accidents, and fire-risk/insurance (*Smoking: The Bottom Line*, 1997).

Our Trust employs XXXX people with, whole time equivalent = XXX. Smoking status in hospital staff is no longer recorded on job applications but our staff prevalence probably reflects local population rates (26%). Around 70% of smokers want to stop but assume around half, that is 13% would be willing (and able) to see an in-house stop-smoking specialist.

We estimate a 30% validated quit rate.

We estimate a Trust saving of **XXXX** $\times$ 0.13 $\times$ 0.30 $\times$ £1115 = **£XXXX** potential savings to the Trust per year by reducing staff smokers.

Assuming that 26% smoke, and they all receive counselling—resulting in up to 40% quitting, we could save up to **£XXX,XXX** per year.

9.0 Miscellaneous benefits

Education

Stop-smoking specialists are involved in staff training; this could include study days and health promotion days.

The stop-smoking specialist should allocated a session in the Junior Doctors Training Programme. Smoking cessation training is now mandatory in the General Medical Core Curriculum, for specialist

Respiratory SpR Training and is recently recommended in the Core Curriculum for Surgical Trainees. Currently there is no formal training for doctors on smoking cessation in this Trust.

The Counsellors are also involved in ad hoc training. Data presented to the European Respiratory Society (Lewis, *Eur Resp J*, 2006) showed that only 10 min explanation and teaching at nursing handover improved the confidence and attitudes of nursing staff and junior doctors. A broad base of staff with skills will not only promote smoking cessation but also encourages personal development under Agenda for Change.

Publicity

[Insert name] Trust could offer a direct Stop Smoking Service to inpatients, outpatients and Trust staff. With the recent political changes and public debates, we have this excellent opportunity to set a leading example to other organizations, nationally and internationally.

10.0 National Institute for Clinical Excellence (NICE)

NICE recommend that 'Arrangements should be made to ensure that smoking cessation advice and support is available to patients at both community and hospital locations' (Technical Appraisal No. 38,7.3, 2003).

The proposed service would fully meet the requirements of this guideline, at present **[Insert name]** Trust is in breach.

11.0 Financial appraisal

The initial start up costs, include a dedicated room, computer, and telephone. The recurring costs therefore relate to staffing and prescribing costs.

11.1 Staffing

The cost of delivering a comprehensive cross Trust Smoking Cessation Service based on two part-time staff is as follows:

Counsellors 18 hrs/week Band 5–6   £XX, XXX
Counsellors 25 hrs/week Band 5–6   £XX,XXX

      £XX,XXX pa
       +3% uplift for inflation 2009
      = £XX,XXX

Admin and clerical support
    1 × 5 hrs/week   *£X,XXX*
    Total pay   **£XX,XXX**

11.2 Non-pay

Travel	£1,000
Stationery	£0,500
Pharmaceutical	£7,500*
Total	**£9,000**

Total proposal cost £xx,000

*Based on actual additional NRT costs incurred during the first 6 months of the pilot, pro-rated and a possible increase of 20% in prescribing rates in 2008 to 2009. (Varenecline prescribing is mainly an elective, outpatient drug, and so is financed by Primary Care.)

12.0 Conclusion

This proposal identifies a significant range of benefits that contribute to a wide range of National and Local Health priorities. It also has the support of local physicians **[Insert Names of any interested clinical leads]** and complements perfectly the Trusts and local [PCT/ Health Boards] Health Promotion and Chronic Disease management strategies.

13.0 Recommendations

The PCT/LHB are requested to commission on a recurring basis from April 200**X** a Stop Smoking Service in secondary care.

References

Fiore MC. Treating tobacco use and dependence: an introduction to the US Public Health Service Clinical Practice Guideline. *Respir Care*. 2000; **45** (10): 1196–1199.

Garcia-Aymerich J, Farrero E, Félez MA, *et al.* Estudi del Factors de Risc d'Agudització de la MPOC investigators. [Risk factors of readmission to hospital for a COPD exacerbation: a prospective study.] *Thorax*. 2003; **58** (2):100–5.

Lewis KE, Durgan L, Edwards VM, *et al.* Can smokers pass from a hospital-based to a community-based stop-smoking service? An open-label, randomised trial comparing three referral schemes. *J Nicotine Tob Res*. 2009; 11: 756–64.

Lewis KE, Preston L, Campbell IA, *et al.* Surveys and assessment of secondary care smoking cessation services in the UK, 2001-2003. *Thorax* 2003; **58**: iii–80.

McAlpine L, Lewis KE, Sharrock R, *et al.* Results of the third BTS National Survey of smoking cessation services. *Thorax*. 2008; **63**: A77.

Moller AM, Villebro N, Pederson T, Tonnesen H. Effect of preoperative smoking intervention on postoperative complications: a randomised clinical trial. *Lancet*. 2002; **359**: 114–7.

Padubidri AN, Yetman R, Browne E, *et al.* Complications of postmastectomy breast reconstructions in smokers, ex-smokers, and nonsmokers. *Plast Reconstr Surg.* 2001; **107**(2): 342-9.

Sorensen LT, Karlsmark T, Gottrup F. Abstinence from smoking reduces incisional wound infection: a randomised controlled trial. *Ann Surg.* 2003; **238**: 1–5.

Targowski T, Jahnz-Rózyk K, From S, *et al.* [Active tobacco smoking as determinant of costs of inpatient treatment of COPD exacerbations]. *Przegl Lek.* 2004; **61**(10): 1049–51.

Van Domburg RT, Meeter K, van Berkel DF, *et al.* Smoking cessation reduces mortality after coronary artery bypass surgery: a 20 year follow up study. *J Am Coll Cardiol.* 2001; **37**: 2009–10.

Warner MA, Offord KP, Warner ME, *et al.* Role of preoperative cessation of smoking and other factors in postoperative pulmonary complications: a blinded prospective study of coronary artery bypass patients. *Mayo Clin Proc.* 1989; **64**(6): 609–16.

Appendix 7

Recommended websites

Medical websites

http://www.nice.org.uk
National Institute for Health and Clinical Excellence is an independent organization responsible for providing national guidance on promoting good health and preventing and treating ill health. It helps health professionals implement our guidance by providing tools such as cost templates, audit criteria, and slide sets. Its guidelines on Stop-Smoking strategies and individual drugs can be found at http://www.nice.org.uk/search/guidancesearchresults.jsp?keywords=smoking&searchType=guidance

http://www.rcplondon.ac.uk
The Royal College of Physicians is a professional body, representing over 20,000 doctors, that aims to improve the quality of patient care by continually raising medical standards. Follow the links to their section on smoking, detailing key statistics and statements, as well as a list of reports/publications (some are free to download) http://www.rcplondon.ac.uk/pubs/topic.aspx?e=2

http://dev.ersnet.org/
The European Respiratory Society is a not-for-profit, international medical organization with nearly 9,000 members in over 100 countries. Aims to alleviate suffering from respiratory disease and to promote lung health through research, knowledge sharing, medical and public education. It provides free access to reports on global control efforts, tobacco regulation, passive smoking, and economic effects. It runs a masterclass on smoking cessation and publishes research in the *European Respiratory Journal*.

http://www.brit-thoracic.org.uk
The British Thoracic Society is a registered charity aimed at health professionals. Their objective is to improve the standards of care of people who have respiratory diseases. They have sections on smoking including key facts, useful links, teaching slides, and guidelines for secondary-care services. It publishes research on smoking in the journal *Thorax*.

http://www.brit-thoracic.org.uk/BASSP/AboutBASSP/tabid/238/Default.aspx
British Association of Stop Smoking Practitioners (BASSP) is a new organization affiliated to the British Thoracic Society (BTS),

Membership is open to all those who have a professional interest in smoking cessation and are committed to reducing the prevalence of smoking in the UK. Its aims are to:

- Raise the profile of the profession nationally
- Improve communication between practitioners themselves and other relevant organizations
- Increase support for practitioners
- Provide representation at national and local levels to highlight issues pertinent to practitioners
- Share and encourage evidence-based best practice.

http://www.scsrn.org

The **Smoking Cessation Service Research Network (SCSRN)** is a collaboration of NHS Stop Smoking Services, interested in developing and evaluating good clinical practice. Their website allows member services to record details of their service and the interventions that they provide, including abstinence rates and discuss ideas for research.

Public health and tobacco control websites

http://www.globalink.org/

GLOBALink is managed by the International Union Against Cancer, and is an international tobacco control community serving all those active in tobacco control, and public health. Membership is free (online application needed) and ranges from individuals to organizations (e.g. cancer societies, health educators, project officers). The website provides links to news bulletins, newsletters, tobacco access law news, discussion forums, full-text databases, and other web-links.

http://www.who.int/tobacco/en/

This is the **World Health Organization's** web page regarding international tobacco control. Useful links here include the WHO Report on the World Tobacco epidemic 2008 http://www.who.int/tobacco/mpower/mpower_report_full_2008.pdf and the first international treaty (with updated list of countries signed-up) of the WHO Framework Convention on Tobacco Control. (http://www.who.int/fctc/en/index.html)

http://www.uknscc.org

Provides details of an **annual UK Smoking Cessation Conference,** attended by public health specialists, counsellors, physicians, and anyone interested in smoking cessation services.

Charities

http://www.ash.org.uk
Action on Smoking and Health (ASH) is a campaigning public health charity that works to eliminate the harm caused by tobacco. This website provides their key facts on smoking, useful links, media briefings, and reports.

http://www.rethink.org
Rethink is a national mental health membership charity, supporting people affected by severe mental illness. It has specific sections on addiction, including how to recognize and cope with tobacco addiction.

Miscellaneous

http://www.tobaccopedia.org/
An International Union against Cancer (UICC) project. This website has interesting sections on advertising and sponsorship, history of tobacco use, health effects. It also has sections on litigation and secret documents and the tobacco industry and its supporters.

http://www.gasp.org.uk
Group Against Smoking in Public (GASP) is UK-based, non-smokers' rights group involved in media campaigns, road shows, lobbying, and education. Their website provides leaflets and sells aids to stopping smoking (e.g. DVDs and some nicotine replacement therapies).

http://www.lho.org.uk
The **London Health Observatory** provides information that policymakers and practitioners need to improve health and health care, working in partnership with the NHS, local authorities, researchers, and national agencies. They have reports on the economic costs of smoking and downloadable tools to commission health services.

Index

149